P9-CJQ-249

American Feminist Playwrights: A Critical History

Twayne's Critical History of American Drama

Jordan Y. Miller
General Editor
University of Rhode Island

American Feminist Playwrights: A Critical History

Sally Burke

University of Rhode Island

Twayne Publishers
An Imprint of Simon & Schuster Macmillan
New York

Prentice Hall International
London Mexico City New Delhi Singapore Sydney Toronto

American Feminist Playwrights: A Critical History
Sally Burke

Twayne's Critical History of American Drama Series

Twayne Publishers
An Imprint of Simon & Schuster Macmillan
1633 Broadway
New York, New York 10019

Library of Congress Cataloging-in-Publication Data

[to come]

The paper used in this publication meets the minimum requirements of American National Standard for Information Sciences—Permanence of Paper for Printed Library Materials, ANSI Z39.48–1984. ∞™

10 9 8 7 6 5 4 3 2 1

Printed in the United States of America

contents

prologue

Until the second wave of the women's movement[1] in America gave rise to a generation of feminist scholars and critics, women writing in any genre were given short shrift. This lack of attention was compounded for the playwright by the difficulty, even near impossibility, of getting her drama produced in a theater ruled by men. Of course, feminist playwrights encountered far more opposition than did women writing from a male-dominated ideology. But despite opposition, a line of feminist playwrights, originating with Mercy Otis Warren in colonial America, arose; they have created out of the oppression of women a drama that challenges the dominant cultural ideology.

The chief force behind woman's oppression is patriarchy, "the power of the fathers: a familial-social, ideological, political system in which men—by force, direct pressure, or through ritual, tradition, law, and language, customs, etiquette, education, and the division of labor, determine what part women shall or shall not play, and in which the female is everywhere subsumed under the male."[2] Racial and economic oppression also play their parts in constructing patriarchal power. Feminist drama exposes the sexism and racism that are the scaffolding of our fathers' houses. A feminist playwright, by bringing woman's previously ignored or discounted thoughts, actions, and words onstage, illuminates the workings of power that the patriarchy would keep dark. Depending on her era and philosophy, she may also offer alternative, even Utopian, visions or suggest how such a reformation, even revolution, might occur. Each of these strategies threatens the dominant order.

The playwrights included here profess a variety of feminisms, definitions of which are often as varied as their practitioners. In general, they may be subsumed under one of three headings: liberal, material, and radical, or cultural. Liberal feminists seek admission to what has been seen as the male "universal"; they stress individuality but also illustrate the need to reform the system. Material feminists find the origins of women's oppression in the material conditions governing their existence, such as race, class, and gender. Radical, or cultural, feminists posit a superiority of the female based on qualities linked to her gender, such as the ability to bear children, and on such attributes as intuition and such values as cooperation, which are often seen as essentially female. They seek a radical revision of society and often call for the creation of separate or alternate female systems to replace those of the patriarchy.

Because this book covers 200 years, I have been forced to be selective. The playwrights discussed here are obviously not the only American feminist playwrights, but I find their works both unique and representative of the dominant varieties of feminist thought and dramatic practice. Rather than attempt to analyze any playwright's entire body of work, I have chosen dramas that illustrate her range as well as her connection to her era and to the feminist tradition.

The six chapters cover four eras. The first includes colonial America and the age of early republic during which the prototypical feminist dramatists wrote. The second section begins with the era of the "New Woman" and covers the suffrage drama and the work of the feminists of the first wave of the women's movement. The period from 1930 to 1960, the era "between the waves," is both a post- and a prefeminist era. This generation, dominated by Lillian Hellman, is less overtly feminist but clearly keeps feminist issues alive in its drama. As the era closed, Lorraine Hansberry brought an explicitly feminist drama back to Broadway. The final section covers the second wave, from the 1960s to the mid-1990s, and examines both avant-garde experimentalists and realists. The chapter introductions were designed to provide merely a brief overview of the complex histories of women and feminism in each period. These playwrights and their dramas, in dialogue with each other and with the groundbreaking feminist drama and performance theory being formulated, encourage further exploration of feminist drama in America.

This study would have been impossible without the generous assistance of both my university and many individuals. I was fortunate to receive a course load reduction from the College of Arts and Sciences and a Summer Faculty Fellowship from the Council for Research of the University of Rhode Island. Vernice (Vickie) Burnett and Marie Rudd of the university library's Interlibrary Loan Department, research assistant Linda Hawksley, and research assistant/typist Kelly Burke, and manuscript editor India Koopman provided invaluable support. I am also grateful to former Twayne editor Liz Traynor Fowler for initiating the project, series general editor Jordan Miller for his expert direction, diligence, and kindness, and Twayne editor Anne Davidson for her consideration, professionalism, and flexibility.

I thank the publisher of *Interviews with Contemporary Women Playwrights* by Kathleen Betsko and Rachel Koening for permission to quote extensively from this book. © Kathleen Betsko and Rachel Koening. By permission of William Morrow & Company, Inc.

1

Pioneers and Prototypes: America's First Feminist Playwrights

In her address "To the Public," which precedes her play *The Sack of Rome* (1785), Mercy Otis Warren asserts: "[l]essons of morality and the consequences of deviation, may, perhaps, be as successfully enforced from the stage, as by modes of instruction less censured by the severe." While attitudes toward drama and the theater became less censorious in the late eighteenth century, drama was definitely not considered an appropriate means of education in early colonial America.

Greatly influential among the first settlers of New England were the Puritan divines and political leaders allied with those Puritans in England who closed the theaters from 1642 to 1660. Their action, coupled with concerns about the wastefulness of production and the moral "looseness" of actors, had a profound effect in the colonies, and it would be the midnineteenth century before American theater approached respectability.

Puritan writers were, however, familiar with the classics of Greece and Rome. The freshman curriculum at Harvard in 1676 included the works of Sophocles, Euripides, and Aristophanes; by 1723 the Harvard Library contained Shakespeare's plays as well as others'. Although the

Puritan view of art as utilitarian allowed no place for the symbolic representations that constitute theater, there is no doubt that the Puritans were of a dramatic turn of mind. Their ministers, from Cotton Mather to Jonathan Edwards, knew the value of a dramatically moving sermon. Nevertheless, dramatic enactment was not merely prohibited; it was considered sinful.

In 1750 the Massachusetts General Court encoded its traditional ban on theater, declaring that "public stage-plays, interludes, and other theatrical entertainments . . . not only occasion great and unnecessary expenses, and discourage industry and frugality, but likewise tend generally to increase immorality, impiety, and a contempt for religion." On 20 October 1774, the First Continental Congress pronounced an outright ban on theater and other amusements by declaring: "We will . . . encourage frugality, economy, and industry, and promote agriculture, arts and the manufacture of this country . . . and will discountenance and discourage every species of extra-vagance [*sic*] and dissipation, especially all horse-racing and all kinds of gaming, cock-fighting, exhibitions of shews, plays and other expensive diversions and entertainments."

If theater was proscribed, drama was not. Even in Massachusetts, public readings of dramatic literature performed by one reader were acceptable. Later, both Whigs and Tories created dramas embodying local settings and focusing, even before the Revolution, on immediate political grievances. Published in newspapers and in pamphlet form, the plays employed satire as both a means of persuasion and a call to action. Thus American playwrights began using drama as a weapon. This tradition of dramatic literature employed as propaganda, established in the Revolutionary era, has been utilized by feminist dramatists in such later works as the suffrage plays of the first wave of the women's movement, the street theater of the Ohio Woman's Crusade of 1873–74 in the temperance movement, the social protest dramas of the 1920s and 1930s, and the dramas of the second wave of the women's movement advocating equal rights for women and societal reform.

Women's Status in the Colonial and Revolutionary Eras

The men who controlled American society also controlled women's access to the theater. The "male gaze," a term made current in the 1980s by such feminist theorists as Laura Mulvey, Sue-Ellen Case, Teresa de Lauretis, and Jill Dolan, describes as the controlling perspective of a film or theater performance that of the male spectator, who identifies with the male hero and sees women as passive beings created to support the male or as pretty toys "doll-ed" up to heighten his viewing pleasure. From Mercy Otis Warren on, American feminist playwrights have called attention to the ways in which the male gaze operates in society. Certainly it was active in colonial America both in depicting women onstage and in deciding what was proper for women to see. An essayist in the New York *Gazette* of 7 December 1761 complained that "plays . . . provided scenes of immodesty upon which no lady should look"; and a tradesman writing in the same paper on 1 February 1768 was infuriated because his wife and daughter, after attending the theater, wasted their time talking about, reading, and acting scenes from plays.

The gaze, on the other hand, made the women who acted with the touring British companies figures of glamor, idealized for their supposed beauty. Note the picture of the "fairy" Maria Storer Hallam presented by William B. Wood: "She usually came fully dressed to the theatre in the old family coach; and the fashion of monstrous hoops worn at that day made it necessary for Mr. Henry to slide her out sideways, take her in his arms and carry her like an infant to the stage entrance."[1] This grotesque creature, an otherworldly being transported by the patriarchal conveyance, encumbered by fashion that immobilizes and infantilizes, was the woman men wished to see onstage.

The images of women represented in the limited number of American dramas were often negative. In Thomas Forrest's *The Disappointment* (1767), the women's roles are those of mistresses, wives, and servants; the anonymous *A Dialogue between a Southern Delegate and His Spouse on His Return from the Grand Continental Congress* (1774) centers on the wife's "tirade" against the Congress. She suggests the delegates' wives could have done a better job, but this early feminist sentiment is undercut by her characterization as an intemperate busybody. *The Battle of Brooklyn* (1776), another anonymous Tory propaganda effort, presents two prostitutes who demean their former clients, George Washington and Benjamin Harrison. Surely these examples are exaggerations. What then was the situation of women in early America?

America's earliest settlers brought with them ideas of woman's inferiority inherited from medieval theology, which, in an attempt to justify woman's subjugation, focused on Eve as the temptress and corrupter of man. The concept of woman's intellectual inferiority was also part of the male colonists' ideology. The Newtonian concept of the universe, taking reason as its highest principle and denying that faculty to women, relegated them to the position of "other," the embodiment of emotion and irrationality, which must be ruled by the rational male. When Locke wrote of the "natural rights" of mankind, women were by no means included in what some in later ages would argue was a universal category. The persons who held natural rights were male, property-owning heads of families. Thus was the patriarchy established and reinforced in America.

Although often attributed to the work of pre–Civil War female liberal abolitionists, feminist consciousness in American women has its roots in the contradictory position accorded women from the founding of the earliest settlements. Omitted from consideration under the doctrine of natural rights, viewed through the lens of Enlightenment science as the "other," and later elided as a human presence in the U.S. Constitution, women were, nevertheless, essential to establishing an orderly society and a viable economy. Often categorized as nothing more than the property of the family patriarch, women in the colonial era worked beside men in forming households and securing the farming economy; during the Revolution large numbers of women ran homes and businesses while men were at war. Thus women worked from the beginning in both the "female" sphere of domesticity and the wider, public sphere supposedly reserved for men. While their work was welcome, their voices were not. Women were virtually prohibited from speaking in any cultural arena. The frustrations and tensions arising from such contradictory expectations led to the formation of informal networks within which women educated, consoled, and supported one another.

Yet from the beginnings of colonization through the Revolution and beyond, the patriarchy held sway. Women were, according to colonial law, not human beings so much as they were chattel. While encoded in the Massachusetts Body of Liberties, this manner of perceiving women was not unique to New England. Southern men insisted more strongly than their northern peers on the doctrine of patriarchal authority, an attitude that led easily to physical, emotional, and sexual abuse. Warren mentions the all too present danger of rape in her drama *The Group* (1775).

Such violence was, of course, one means of enforcing patriarchal authority. The participants in the ministry, the town meeting, and colonial assemblies were all male, with a vested interest in preserving the public sphere as their own. Furthermore, the economy depended greatly on the domestic labor of women.

Intellectual labor was, however, suspect. In his "Epistle to the Reader," appended to Anne Bradstreet's *The Tenth Muse* (1650), her brother-in-law John Woodbridge remarks that her writing did not conflict with her "proper" duties because the time devoted to its composition was taken from hours usually reserved for "sleep and other refreshments." With the birth of the Republic, women's roles became even more restricted, a condition clearly illustrated by John Adams's rebuke of Abigail for suggesting that, if neglected in the new Constitution, the "Ladies" would rebel.

Conceived of as comforts to their husbands and producers of sons, women had negligible legal standing. Colonial women were treated as their fathers' and husbands' property, a status codified in Blackstone's *Commentaries on the Laws of England* (1765–69) as the law of "couverture." Once married, women ceased—legally—to exist. With improved economic times came stricter definitions of gender and a concomitant image, among the middle and upper classes, of femininity. By the middle of the eighteenth century, "highly idealized portraits [depicted] American ladies, draped in satin, endowed with ample and amply-displayed bosoms, surrounded by fruits and flowers and other natural symbols."[2] In "A Paraphrase on Part of the Economy as Human Life," a surprisingly revealing poem written in 1759, James Bowdoin presents such an image of womanhood, inviting the young man to: "[v]iew the maid, the love-inspiring maid / With virtue and modesty array'd / *Survey* her matchless form. . . . *Survey* and *Re-survey* from feet to head" (emphasis added), and to linger over her "tempting breasts" (qtd. in Ryan, 88–89). The poet evidently gave little thought to and had even less care for the concern that his prolonged gaze caused the virtuous and modest maid.

Despite patriarchal restriction, several women managed to assert themselves to a notable extent, some to gain fame, others notoriety. In 1636, John Winthrop examined the religious rebel Anne Hutchinson for heresy. Charging Hutchinson with criticizing the ministers, teaching and holding an assembly in her home, and disobeying her surrogate parents, the magistrates, he cut off her response by telling her: "We do not mean to discourse with those of your sex." For her "disobedience," Hutchinson was branded a heretic and evicted from Boston. She had, however, gained a significant following among women, perhaps because her doctrine of "antinomianism [a doctrine that emphasized the inability of the individual to win salvation] extended the feminine experience to both sexes, which in turn paradoxically created the possibility of feminine pride."[3] Such were the conditions and contradictions of woman's life in early America.

Overtly and sometimes somewhat covertly, early America's feminist playwrights dramatized these oppressive conditions. Women's objectification, their status as property, the silencing of their voices, and the psychological and physical abuse to which they were subjected are issues dramatized by Mercy Otis Warren, Susanna Rowson, and Anna Cora Mowatt.

Mercy Otis Warren, America's First Feminist Playwright

Mercy Otis Warren (1728–1814), America's first female playwright, was also America's first feminist playwright. She created dramas that not only urged the colonists' cause in the Revolutionary War but also argued woman's cause in life itself. Allowed to accompany her brother the patriot James Otis to tutoring sessions, Warren read Pope, Dryden, Milton, and Shakespeare. She argued for equality of race and gender, sharing many ideas with her friend Abigail Adams, who informed Warren of her now famous "Remember the Ladies" letter to her husband, adding that she was thinking of asking Warren to join her in a petition to Congress.

Despite her own notable achievements, Warren indicates an ambivalence about woman's place. The various critics of this poet, playwright, pamphleteer, historian, and revolutionary thus place her on a continuum with positions ranging from nonfeminist through pioneer feminist to, finally, distinctly feminist. Those who deny Warren recognition as a feminist are guilty of judging a woman of the past by contemporary standards. Man being the measure of all things in her era, it is not remarkable that she sometimes spoke deprecatingly of her "womanish" fears or dreaded what she perceived as her less desirable quality, the woman in her, getting the upper hand. In this, she is representative of the paradox faced by many colonial women: her fear and her weakness, qualities that marked her as inferior, were also qualities that men valued in women. In view of such cultural conditioning, the extent to which she identified with and championed women is remarkable.

As a liberal feminist, Warren manifests the desire to be recognized as part of the system that excludes her. Committed to the doctrines of natural rights and human equality, she makes clear the result of her being educated about brutality by the events of the Revolutionary War. While her first dramas emphasize the rights of man, in *The Group* a radical feminism presents itself, and in her *History of the Rise, Progress, and Termination of the American Revolution* (1805) she records specific instances of women being raped and murdered.

Since theater was outlawed in Massachusetts, Warren's choice of dramatic form seems at first perplexing, but there remained the distinction drawn between writing and reading dramatic literature, and full theatrical representation. Furthermore, Warren thought of life itself as a drama. She called America "a theater just erected" and referred to God as "the great Director of the Theater of the Universe." Warren's political dramas were influenced by works she had read; Shakespeare, Molière, Dryden, and Addison were her models. Her political satires in blank verse influenced the mood of pre-Revolutionary America. Governor Thomas Hutchinson, for example, was greatly damaged by her dubbing him Rapatio. Viewing Warren's dramas as "the most consistent and influential of them all," Constance Rourke declared that she "opened the way for the marked sequence of political and partisan plays to follow."[4]

As her dramas developed from sketches written first in the service of a propaganda battle, then an actual war, to the historical tragedies written after the Revolution, Warren's feminist philosophy also developed. While feminist themes are readily observable in *The Group*, the playwright of *The Ladies of Castile* (1784) and *The Sack of Rome* is quite different from the playwright who composed *The Adulateur* and *The Defeat* (both 1773), with their all-male casts and emphasis on the patriots' forefathers. While these dramas served well as propaganda pieces, other than illuminating a belief in natural rights, they illustrate nothing of the feminist consciousness which Warren must have been nurturing, and do little to prepare for the feminist issues raised in her third drama.

The Group is peopled solely by Loyalists; the patriots are present only diegetically. In this drama Warren refines her talent as a playwright, makes greater use of set and setting, and develops a colloquial idiom. The drama opens with a procession; the group of the title, men who have sold their birthright of liberty to become George the Third's Mandamus Councillors, file in attended by "a swarm of . . . sycophants . . . harpies, and . . . danglers." Graphically characterizing the Loyalists, this pageantry gives way to a set described as "a little dark parlour [with] guards standing at the door." The gloomy set and the guards' presence ably convey the mood. Several councillors experience qualms over "sell[ing]

. . . friends . . . country . . . and conscience." In act 2, scene 1, the set is furnished with "bowls, bottles, glasses, and cards," amusements that illustrate debauchery, and with books such as Hobbes's *Leviathan* and Mandeville's *Fable of the Bees*, which underscore self-interest. References to "nut brown Kate" as "the jockey's prey" and to "hen peck'd husband[s]" illustrate Warren's fluency with idiom and growing daring in subject matter.

Most significantly, Warren makes apparent her feminist sympathies. No longer content to limn the Loyalists' evil solely through their lust for power and riches, which she focused on earlier, she delineates it primarily through their attitudes toward and treatment of women. In the third speech of the drama, Simple Sapling discloses that he has abandoned his abode of "rural peace." His wife, the aptly named Sylvia, weeps both for his return and for her "beggar[ed] . . babes." This speech, occurring so early in the drama, establishes the group's lack of humanity and prepares for further disclosure of its members' characters through their attitudes toward women. Hateall announces he would not back down to save his wife from hell and speaks with apparent relish of "the weeping maid thrown helpless on the world" and "The sorrowing mother [who] mourns her starving babes." He appears to find women, as much as patriots, enemies to be destroyed. Pitiless in their treatment of women, the men willingly sacrifice priceless relationships to their quest for power.

Simple, immediately after hearing that only "the very dregs of all mankind / The Stains of nature" would offer to quarter troops in their homes, makes just such a proposal. Making obvious the real danger of rape, Sylla, the troops' general, characterizes his men as "dangerous and vile / Devoid of virtue, rectitude or honor." Simple's appalled cohorts ask if he has no wife for whose virtue he should care. His reply indicates his belief that a wife must obey and serve her husband: "Sylvia's good natur'd, and no doubt will yield, / And take the brawny vet'rans to her board / When she's assured 'twill help her husband's fame." An absolute tyrant who treats his wife with contempt and views her as chattel, he adds that any complaint would earn her only a dismissal from his home.

Through Dick's remark that Sylvia "silent mourns the weakness of her lord," Warren demonstrates that married women are legal nonentities who literally have no voice in determining their destinies. Hateall dismisses Dick's reproof with a demeaning remark about the "whinings of that trifling sex." The verbal, emotional, and physical abuse he wreaks upon his wife, Kate, is promoted as a means of ensuring male "superiority"; he offers a "recipe most sure" to all husbands wishing to enforce their "superior will[s]":

> If crabbed words or surly looks won't tame
> The haughty shrew, nor bend the stubborn mind,
> Then the green hick'ry, or the willow twig
> Will prove a cure for each rebellious dame.

Warren's inclusion of two abused women is telling. Had only one man so mistreated his wife, he might have appeared an aberration, but by using two stories, Warren illustrates that such abuse is common.

Most of the group see any deviation from bellicose posturing as unmanly. When Monsieur rues forsaking his dying father's injunction to resist oppression, Scriblerius taunts him about his "baby fears" and the "soft traces in [his] puny heart." These men define manhood as the possession of wealth, abusive power, and swaggering bravado. Here Warren is at her most radical. By detailing the oppression of women and the deficiencies of the group's ideas of manhood, she calls for a new social order, one that would heed woman's voice and insights in setting the world to rights. This call for the liberation of women from male tyranny anticipates by approximately a year Adams's letter asking her husband not to "put such unlimited power into the hands of the Husbands," but rather, since males are "[n]aturally tyrannical," to "put it out of the power of the vicious and the Lawless to use [women] with cruelty and indignity with impunity." Those who fault Warren for failing to respond to Adams's suggestion that they join in a petition to Congress to limit the power of husbands ought, perhaps, to wonder whether Warren's drama inspired Adams's letter.

The Group is superior to Warren's earlier dramas. Its crisper dialogue characterizes the Tories' venality. The pageantry of the opening procession appeals even to a modern audience, while the symbolism of the dark, gloomy set palpably conveys moral decay. A successful political satire, *The Group* skillfully creates dramatic tension in its accurate forecast of the bloodshed to come. The play was the most popular of Warren's political dramas. Published anonymously, it is the only political satire for which she sought credit. Hearing in 1814 that the play was being ascribed to another, she enlisted the aid of John Adams who, despite advanced age, traveled to the Boston Athenaeum to note in its copy of the pamphlet edition: "August 17, 1814. The 'Group' to my certain

Quincy August 17. 1814. The "Group," to my certain Knowledge was
written by Mrs Mercy Warren of Plymouth. So certifies
John Adams.

Authograph note of John Adams, attesting to Mercy Otis Warren's authorship of *The Group. Photograph courtesy of Boston Athenaeum.*

knowledge was written by Mrs. Mercy Warren of Plymouth. So certifies John Adams."

Warren's disinclination to claim her other satires has led to a dispute about the authorship of two: *The Blockheads* (1776) and *The Motley Assembly* (1779). Her reluctance must be considered against what was then the typical reaction to women writers. In 1650, in "The Prologue," Anne Bradstreet expressed an accurate view of her neighbors' reaction to her poetry:

> I am obnoxious to each carping tongue
> Who says my hand a needle better fits,
> A poet's pen all scorn I should thus wrong,
> For such despite they cast on female wits:
> If what I do prove well, it won't advance,
> They'll say it's stol'n, or else it was by chance.

The persistence of such attitudes over the centuries was well illustrated when, in 1807, John Adams, her onetime and subsequent champion, disputed Warren's portrayal of him in her history. He charged that by writing she had "transgress[ed her] proper womanly sphere" and claimed that she had exposed herself to "eternal ridicule" by such an unladylike action.

Warren claimed only *The Group* and those works published in 1790 in *Poems, Dramatic and Miscellaneous*; objections to attributing *The Blockheads* and *The Motley Assembly* to her are made on the grounds of coarse language and subject and of changing style. About *The Blockheads* Jean Fritz insists that "Mercy Warren would not have allowed a character . . . to say that he had 'shit' his 'breeches.' "[5] While the language may seem indecorous, it is appropriate to the characters. Those who object to the scatology and to the references to cuckoldry in *The Blockheads* would do well to remember the reference in *The Group* to Kate as "the jockey's prey." Close reading of both *The Blockheads* and *The Motley Assembly* reveal similarities to the earlier dramas. The very term "blockhead" appears in the prologue to *The Defeat*; Sylla's reference in *The Group* to the "infected town" anticipates the situation of the Loyalists and the troops isolated by the blockade of Boston central to *The Blockheads*; Meagre's reference to the patriots' "Congresses, Covenants and leagues, / With their committees working in each town" in *The Group* is echoed in *The Blockheads* by Lord Dapper's remark about "Their congresses, committees, etc,"; the Loyalists' motives are those ascribed to them in the earlier plays; Surly's comment that his "family are left to feed on the charity of friends if they can find any" recalls Simple's dismissal of Sylvia in *The Group*, and his complaint that "our wives [are] ravaged and our daughters debauch'd" points to the dangers of housing the troops. The patriots' superiority is again praised, and the Unnamed Soldier conveys the sense of life as theater found in the other plays when he describes the condition of the troops' lives by stating, "Burgoyne could not have contriv'd a prettier satire."[6] The shift to prose in *The Blockheads* occurs because the characters are farmers who move to Boston hoping to gain sophistication and position. Their social class makes their coarseness of behavior and language appropriate. Like *The Group*, this play contains radical sentiment for reordering society. Its basic premise condemns the Tories, "who never [question] the validity or the benevolence of a patriarchal government three thousand miles away."[7] The anonymous women who appear at the work's close are, significantly, denied any identity but that derived from their relationships with the soldiers. Depicting them as required by their men to side with the British indicates their lack of control over their own lives. As the women wish America well, Warren presents a vision of a society that could—and might—do better by its female citizens.

The Motley Assembly presents the socially and politically ambitious men and women who conduct the "mix'd assembly" wherein "lured by fashion, opp'site int'rests join." It, too, contains several reminders of the earlier plays. The trimmers of *The Group* appear in the person of Mr. Turncoat; his hypocrisy and that of the others are links to previous characters. The character names Turncoat, Flourish, and Runt, like some used from *The Adulateur* on, recall the comedy of humours. Also reminiscent of *The Group* are the references to the characters indulging in "cards and wine" and the noun "stain" used as a pejorative for a person. New is Warren's presentation of women as creatures of the male gaze. In the drama's second speech, Mrs. Flourish notes the male preference for female beauty over female intelligence. Later, Runt cuts off Captain Aid's defense of General Washington by reminding him that "[T]here are more fit subjects for a young gentleman's contemplation in this room," thus presenting women as things to be looked at, not as human beings.

The Blockheads and *The Motley Assembly* are essentially plotless, slice-of-life prose works; sharply satiric, they dramatize the differences between British and American values. While *The Blockheads* is best described as low comedy, deriving its thrust from the bickering between Simple and his social-climber wife, Jemima, and *The Motley Assembly* is a comedy of manners centered on the contestation between the Tory-sympathizing civilians and the Whig officers, both plays are marred by didactic, gratuitous epilogues.

Following the Revolution, Warren wrote two plays in the manner of classical tragedy, *The Ladies of Castile* and *the Sack of Rome*. Both are complexly plotted five-act structures in which women now appear as fully realized characters. *The Ladies of Castile* dramatizes for the first time the constructed nature of womanhood. Don Juan de Padilla leads an unsuccessful revolt against tyranny. When he needs funds, his wife, Maria, organizes her women to loot the church and tells her brother that "Necessity must sanctify the deed." To his claim that her soul is wasted "[B]eneath the weakness of a female form," she replies:

> Men rail at weaknesses themselves create,
> And boldly stigmatize the female mind,
> As though kind nature's just impartial hand
> Had form'd its features in a baser mold.

Her words expose female weakness as a myth created by the patriarchy to justify its oppression of women. Usually thought of as a warning about the need for vigilance in retaining political freedom, the drama clearly speaks to the plight of women and seeks an end to the domination of women and children by men.

In *The Sack of Rome,* Warren focuses particular attention on the brutal crime of rape. Aetius, commander of the Roman troops, and Leo, bishop of Rome, use the phrase "shameful fall" in discussing a rape, indicating a patriarchal mentality that blames the victim, not the assailant; they perpetuate the male myth that a virtuous woman cannot be violated. The rapist, when ruing his action, focuses on the victim's husband, commenting that "[a] man thus injur'd never can forgive." The violent victimization of a woman becomes an offense against the man who *owns* her and who must "surely . . . meditate some great revenge." Warren finds ways to instruct both the vicious and the benighted. When the barbarian prince Traulista offers to "vindicate in blood [the victim's] wounded fame," her husband responds that her name needs no clearing.

Modeled to a great extent on Dryden's Restoration tragedies but utilizing Shakespeare's blank-verse form, Warren's tragedies are her most finely plotted plays and feature the most fully dramatized of her female characters. Although somewhat less incisive than the propaganda plays, these later works are multifaceted, presenting worlds of complicated guilt, sophisticatedly portrayed through interwoven plots and subplots. The themes, language, and blank verse of these dramas may strike a contemporary audience as off-putting and artificial, yet they are as worthy of being read as much of Dryden. At the least, Warren's historical dramas certainly rank far above the bombast offered by most of her American male contemporaries.

Warren holds threefold significance as a playwright. Helping to form the drama in America, creating works modeled on European types and her own American originals, such as *The Group* and *The Blockheads,* she also made drama her weapon, as she became a "gadfly of the war, harassing the enemy with bitter satire and poignant observations on liberty and patriotism."[8] Most important, she initiated the feminist tradition in American drama, revealing in her plays the hidden lives of women. Her dramatizations of woman's inferior position in society expose sexist attitudes still—unfortunately—extant.

Warren is the first American playwright to remark the manner in which the patriarchy constructs the female, then uses that construct to demean and denigrate women and their assigned roles. She demonstrates in her dramas the manner in which, as Maria points out in *The Ladies of Castile*, "[m]en rail at weaknesses themselves create."

By spotlighting women's abilities, Warren's plays legitimize their aspirations; by underscoring the evils of man's neglect, of his emotional, psychological, and physical abuse of women, of his disregard for children and family responsibility in favor of power, money, and fame, the works present the rationale behind Warren's radical sentiments for reordering society. Warren articulated with courage and clarity the injustice of the patriarchal system both abroad and at home. These issues are, for feminists, the most important aspects of her dramas and paramount in consideration of the plays' present value.

Drama, Theater, and the Image of Women in the Early Republic

Once the treaty ending the war was signed in 1783, political and economic objections to the theater began to abate; moral objections were stronger and would take longer to overcome. Defenders of the theater based their stance on both moral and social grounds. In 1790, Warren spoke of the theater as a means of inculcating virtue in the audience. Four years later, Susanna Rowson wrote in the preface to *Slaves in Algiers*: "It has been my endeavor to place social virtues in the fairest point of view, and hold up, to merited contempt, their opposite vices." As Helen Chinoy puts it: "Women dramatists and [actors] spoke of themselves as 'reformers' who would grace the theatre with 'their own pure and blameless lives' or . . . with the 'benign influence of a noble womanly spirit.'"[9]

In a culture that held its ideas about woman's proper place as increasingly sacred, the theater provided one of the few areas wherein a woman strong enough to challenge society's perception of its immorality might exercise her talents and earn a living equal to a man's. Susanna Rowson and Anna Cora Mowatt succeeded as actors and playwrights.

Audiences, however, preferred works from male playwrights. Judith E. Barlow summarizes the attitude prevailing just prior to the debut of Mowatt's *Fashion* (1845) in her citation of a newspaper editor who wrote: "We have little confidence in female dramatic productions, of the present time"; despite *Fashion*'s success, Barlow adds, "the notion that women were incapable of dramatic production lingered."[10] Mowatt's friend Epes Sargent satirized this stance in his prologue to *Fashion*: "It takes a man / To write comedy—no woman can"; he concluded by asking the audience to concede that "Art's fair fabric [may] rise from woman's toil." "Art's fair fabric" might also be inspired in others by woman's toil. Such is also the opinion of those who find the seeds of Royall Tyler's *The Contrast* (1787) in Warren's works.[11]

Negative dramatic images of women continued to predominate. The protagonist of Barnabus Bidwell's *The Mercenary Match* (1784) is a woman whose dissatisfaction with her life causes her husband's murder, her death, and her accomplice's execution. In David Humphreys's *The Widow of Malabar* (1790), the title character is called on to resign herself to the funeral pyre, graphically representing the patriarchy's ownership of women.

While male playwrights painted women in negative hues, the audience and the critics were concerned more with the female actor than with her role. That this was true in American drama from the outset is demonstrated in Montrose Moses's comment on the Maryland *Gazette*'s first drama critic:

> This Y. Z. of colonial days . . . showed himself . . . to be very much of a human [read "man"]. He saw Miss Hallam and she conquered; he was charmed, ravished by her delicacy of manner. "How true and thorough her knowledge of the art she presented!" he warbles, trying to hide his emotion beneath some semblance of judgment—for the beauty of Miss Hallam was a narcotic to most men of the colonies—"Her whole form and dimensions how happily convertible to the variety of her part." Which gives us a great deal of the flavor of the woman in the eyes of the man. *Cherchez la critique.*[12]

The voyeurism continued, as Eric Wollencourt Barnes illustrates in his comments on the premiere of *Fashion*: The collegians and the stockbrokers, he writes, "must have derived satisfaction from the performance of the lissome Miss Ellis, who managed to give plausibility to the role of the virtuous Gertrude without wholly obscuring her own personal charms."[13] The male gaze would not allow a character's virtue to mask an actor's beauty, nor it would concede that virtue and beauty might coexist in either or both.

Susanna Rowson: A Voice for Feminism

In Susanna Rowson, American women were offered someone who would not only speak for them in her dramas but who in her academy would also literally teach them to speak. Born in England, Rowson (1762–1824) was brought to America at the age of five by her father, a captain in the Royal Navy. She first lived in Nantasket, Massachusetts, then was interned during the Revolution with her family in both Hingham and Arlington. In 1778, after a stay in Halifax, the Haswells were returned to London as part of a prisoner exchange. While there Rowson attended the theater and, influenced by the plays of Hannah Cowley, Elizabeth Inchbald, and Harriet Lee, began to consider writing drama herself. In 1787 she married William Rowson; when his business failed in 1791, they both began acting careers. In 1792, on their return to the United States, the couple was recruited by Thomas Wignell to join the company of his "New Theatre" in Philadelphia.

In this era, theater in both England and America extended its reach to a middle-class audience, and the acting profession began to gain some small measure of respectability. The male narrator of Rowson's novel *The Inquisitor; or, Invisible Rambler* (1788) contends that it is "illiberal" to suppose that a female actor cannot be virtuous. Still, women were not so readily accepted as were male actors, and Rowson was anxious for a position of respectability and a more secure economic standing. Therefore, after 11 years onstage, playing 129 roles in 126 productions, she left the stage to open her academy for young women in Boston. Her reputation for exemplary behavior was such that despite having been actor and playwright she was able to persuade the leading families of the area to send her their daughters.

During her stay in Nantasket, Rowson established a connection with James Otis, brother of Mercy Otis Warren, who tutored her in literature. She may have known Warren's plays, and she certainly shared many of her views. But while Warren published most of her early work anonymously, Rowson was of a different mind. Although she observed the tradition of apologizing in the preface of a work for its artistic quality, she did so on the basis of the second-class education women received because of their gender, and within her novels she described the prejudice facing the woman writer. Mrs. Greenham in *The Inquisitor*, who claims that women should occupy their hands mending clothes, not holding pens, is a direct descendant of the officious neighbors Anne Bradstreet described in "The Prologue."

Rowson's primary subject is women. She studied them, promoted them, commented on their neglected presence in history, employed them as subjects in her writing, and educated them. For the most part, Rowson was a radical feminist who challenged the Enlightenment tenet of male superiority. She was also a materialist feminist who in her poem "Choice" (1804) mentioned the importance to the individual's development of a "healthy economic base," the very thing lacking in the lives of the majority of women made dependent by that lack. She envisioned bringing about radical social change and effecting material security for women through education. Among the courses offered in her academy was public speaking, the teaching of which was a decidedly subversive activity during an era when women were still virtually prohibited from speaking in any public forum.

In her only extant drama, *Slaves in Algiers; or, A Struggle for Freedom: A Play Interspersed with Songs* (1794), she combined the appeals of the political immediacy of current events, patriotism, and the popular ballad-opera form. Working in the tradition established by Warren and other pamphlet playwrights, she seized on the political battle of the United States with the Barbary Coast pirates as background for her drama. Thus she managed to combine the freshness of the day's news with an appeal to America's burgeoning sense of patriotism.

Rowson declared in her preface her intent to uphold "the social virtues." She also apologized for her errors and limitations. Yet even before she began the play proper, her feminism surfaced as she stated that the deficiency was due not to her sex but to the advantages awarded men. She marked them as a privileged sex-class "who have been instructed in the Classics and have reaped both pleasure and improvement by studying the Ancients in their original purity."

Technically, her play is an amalgam of farce, sentiment, and melodrama. The plot is contrived, shot through with coincidences, and encumbered by an especially melodramatic recognition scene. Among the drama's assets are Rowson's boldness in the treatment of female sexuality, the examination of woman's position in society undertaken through the title's metaphor, and the abolitionist statement made in the dialogue. The plot concerns the four members of the Constant family, all by various means prisoners in Algiers. Two young fellow American captives, Frederic and Henry, plot with Fetnah, the daughter of Ben Hassan, a Jew masquerading as a Moslem, to set all the captives free. When complications ensue, Olivia Constant promises to marry the Dey in exchange for the others' freedom. An uprising occurs, and Olivia is freed with the rest.

Rowson announces her major theme, political and sexual liberty for both genders in the play's first speech, as Fetnah comments that, despite the beauty of the palace, she doesn't wish to be confined. Before being sold to the Dey, Fetnah learned the value of freedom from Rebecca, her father's prisoner. Now Fetnah "wish[es] for liberty," for its worth surpasses that of wealth or the Dey's love. As she proclaims that the Dey's "grave and stately" demeanor takes the pleasure from lovemaking, she also admits fear of his "huge scymitar." Rowson indicates that a woman should be free to exercise her sexuality, not enslaved by the phallic principle that restricts her through fear. The point is reinforced when Fetnah fantasizes being free of the "goggle-ey'd" eunuches who serve as spies for the patriarchy and as guardians of its sexual "property." In song, Fetnah praises the wondrous abilities of woman in her natural state of liberty, while noting that when enslaved, the glorious creature "sinks oppress'd and drooping dies."

Later, Hassan tells Rebecca that he can make her his wife even though he is already married because "our law gives us great many vives [*sic*],—our law gives liberty in love" and adds, "You are an American and you must love liberty." Rebecca's angry injunction that he "prostitute not the sacred word by applying it to licentiousness" highlights both the freedom of Americans in general and the paradoxical position of American women. Although not one among many, the American wife suffered under a political system that refused to recognize her rights but claimed her labor and her allegiance. Thus amid the elegies to freedom lies the irony of Rowson's presentation of women as chattel. The drama's title refers not only to the physical captivity of the Americans in Algiers; it also serves as a metaphor for the situation of wives and daughters at home in America.

Upon Henry's discovery that his fiancée, Olivia, is a captive, Frederic suggests they free her so that Henry can then "turn over [Zoriana] the fair Moriscan [*sic*] to [him]." As do the men in Warren's *The Ladies of Castile* and *The Sack of Rome,* these male celebrants of liberty perceive women as commodities to be exchanged and are unaware of the incongruity of their attitude. The Algerian men behave similarly. The Dey, says Olivia, has "purchased . . . a number of beautiful slaves," and the Alcaide's female "possessions" are recounted by Sebastian: "Twelve wives, thirty concubines, and two pretty daughters." These instances counterpoint the theme of liberty.

Pointing up the incongruity of the male and female conditions whether both are captive or free, Rowson speaks for equality. The males claim superiority in words, while the females, by their deeds, demonstrate their intelligence and bravery. The high-spirited Fetnah, instructed in the love of freedom by Rebecca, the surrogate mother who nourished her mind, dares to tell the Dey she does not love him and is quick-witted enough to deflect his anger. When the men seek to protect her by leaving her out of Mr. Constant's rescue, she explodes:

FETNAH: What, shut me up!—Do you take me for a coward?

HENRY: We respect you as a woman and would shield you from danger.

FETNAH: A woman!—Why so I am; but in the cause of love or friendship, a woman can face danger with as much spirit, and as little fear, as the bravest man amongst you.

Her speech recalls Maria's words in *The Ladies of Castile*: "Men rail at weaknesses themselves create."

Rebecca also speaks as a feminist; she teaches Fetnah that "woman was never formed to be the abject slave of man. Nature made [woman] equal with [man], and gave [women] the power to render [themselves] superior." When the Dey demands that the Constants turn Olivia over to him, Rebecca—not her husband—utters the defiant words: "[n]ever shall Olivia, a daughter of Columbia and a Christian tarnish her name by apostasy or live the slave of a despotic tyrant!"

Can male assertion of prerogative tempered by female example of courage, competence, and leadership result in gender equality? "Perhaps" is Rowson's answer, perhaps when America truly is the Utopia that exists now only in Fetnah's mind as "the country where women do just as they please [in] the regions of Peace and Liberty." Until then, males like Sebastian will see Fetnah's speech about women's abilities as proof that "she's a devil of spirit," one of the "spirited ladies [who] require taming . . . [the] dear, sweet, angry creatures." To him, she is a woman who must be "domesticated" to do the patriarchy's bidding.

Until the Sebastians disappear, woman will hide herself as Fetnah does in playing the "poor little girl" before the Dey, or unsex herself as she does when she dons his son's clothing. Here Rowson uses disguise to indicate the arbitrariness of gender roles. Fetnah poses as a boy to gain freedom, while Hassan disguises himself as a woman to escape the wrath of the Dey.

Sent to rescue Rebecca, Sebastian believes the disguised Hassan to be she, as Rowson satirizes the proclivity of the male gaze to create the woman it wishes to perceive. While Hassan remains veiled, Sebastian calls him/her "beautiful . . . adorable" and says: "Women were never made, with all their prettiness and softness, and bewitching ways, to be hid from us men, who came into the world for no other purpose than to *see* [emphasis added], admire, love, and protect them." Begging to be allowed to "peep" under Hassan's veil, Sebastian describes the "dear little sparkling eyes . . . lovely blooming cheeks . . . and cherry lips" he expects to find. When he tries to kiss her/him, the veil falls. Looking at the bearded Hassan, Sebastian still perceives him as a woman, albeit now, "by the length of [her] beard," an old one. While this scene might titillate an audience, the feminist subtext makes clear man's insistence on seeing woman as he wishes to see her.

Toward the end of the play, slavery, which has been used primarily as a metaphor for women's lives, is spoken against as it affects all human beings. When Sebastian seeks to put the "pretty bracelets" of the slaves' chains on the Dey, Frederic reminds him that, "We are free men, and while we assert the rights of men, we dare not infringe the privileges of a fellow creature." When Sebastian persists, claiming the right of retaliation, Rebecca instructs him in a higher law, saying: "By the Christian law, no man should be a slave; it is a word so abject that, but to speak it dyes the cheek with crimson. Let us affect our own prerogative, be free for ourselves, but let us not throw on another's neck, the chains we scorn to wear." Her speech must have reminded the audience that Algiers was not the only locale in which one found slaves in chains; surely there were those in the audience who blushed for America's shame.

In the drama's famous epilogue Rowson returns to the theme of women and equality. She addresses her female audience, asking them to judge the play. Acting as the women's collective voice, she says:

> "The creature has some sense," methinks you say:
> "And in good truth, we're all of her opinion.
> "Women were born for universal sway,
> "Men to adore, be silent, and obey."

Thus she educes not only the truth of what they have witnessed in the actions of the drama's women but also the truth about the position in society that men expect women to occupy without demurring.

Slaves in Algiers is in many ways a germinative work. Through Rebecca's tutoring of Fetnah, Rowson suggests the manner in which women, by disregarding barriers of age, ethnicity, and class, may become the progenitors of liberty. The expression of abolitionist thought in the play is also most unusual for its era. And, of course, the assertiveness and outspokenness of Fetnah as she refuses to be left out of Constant's rescue and of Rebecca as she defies the Dey are qualities rarely portrayed in women on the early American stage. With its primary themes of freedom and human rights, women as its major characters, and the added asset of song, the play is, despite its artificial language and melodramatic scenes, worthy of study. The drama spawned a number of dramatic imitations, including John Howard Payne's *The Fall of Algiers* (1825), Mordecai Noah's *The Siege of Tripoli* (1820), and James Ellison's *The American Captive* (1811). It is, however, her clear feminist stance that most significantly marks Rowson a pioneer in American drama.

Anna Cora Mowatt: The Woman of Fashion

A child of wealth, Anna Cora Mowatt (1819–70) counted among her ancestors a great-grandfather who signed the Declaration of Independence. At 15 she married James Mowatt, a wealthy lawyer, and in the early days of her marriage wrote, produced, and acted in amateur theatricals staged at her Flatbush estate. When her husband lost his fortune, she began, at the age of 21, supporting him, first through public readings, then as magazine writer, novelist, and eventually professional playwright and celebrated actor.

Like Rowson, Mowatt knew what being a woman who worked outside the home entailed. Although *Fashion* brought her acclaim as a playwright, she ultimately chose acting because it paid better. Her *Autobiography of an Actress* (1854) is an important source of theater history. Her feminism is apparent in *Fashion* and in her remark in her autobiography that *Ingomar the Barbarian* (1842) by Frederick Hahn, a play she often chose to perform for her benefit nights, was "almost a woman's rights drama."

Fashion combines farce, caricature, and melodrama in a satire of the nouveau riche in midnineteenth-century New York. Imitative of Richard Brinsley Sheridan's *The School for Scandal* (1777), *Fashion* is also a child of Warren's *The Blockheads* and *The Motley Assembly* in its satirizing of those who prefer foreign over American manners. Despite its sentimentality and clichéd characters and situations, *Fashion* contains enough wit and sparkle to keep its place among those works frequently revived by college theaters and amateur players. The plot, farcical miscues, and melodramatic gestures of the drama are well known, and modern audiences delight in its mannered style.

Like Rowson, Mowatt utilized popular themes, including the contrasts of city and country life and European and American manners, and the idealization of the common man. In addition, stereotypes, racism, the philosophy of separate spheres, woman as chattel, woman's employment as well as her objectification, and the double standard are all present. Because Mowatt is, at base, pragmatic in her picture of society, Gertrude, the would-be hero, must yield to the patriarchy at the drama's end.

Absent from most critical considerations of *Fashion* is the feminist thought perceptible once the skin of its conventional comedy is pared. Perhaps Mowatt's fall from wealth and privilege awakened the feminist consciousness with which she examines such stereotypical ideas as women running men into debt, being horrified of aging, and overcome by jealousy. Should Mr. Tiffany's claim that his wife ran him into debt be accepted at face value? Mrs. Tiffany's belief that "A woman of fashion *never* grows old! Age is always out of fashion," viewed through the lens Mowatt focuses on fashion itself, becomes as foolish as the poseur poets and jaded pretenders who visit the Tiffany home. Count Jolimaitre's claim, made while watching what he thinks is a struggle of two women over him, that "jealousy makes the dear creatures so spiteful," is laughable. While Millenette, Mrs. Tiffany's maid, is still in love with this barber-cook-valet who stole her money and abandoned her, Gertrude wishes to expose Jolimaitre/Treadmill for the imposter he is.

Though not so direct in dealing with America's racism as Rowson, Mowatt illuminates that racism through the black servant Zeke. Mrs. Tiffany laments his blackness while remarking the near impossibility of

Will Geer and Enid Markey in a scene from Anna Cora Mowatt's *Fashion*, produced at the Little Opera House in Boston, 1959. *Photograph courtesy of Harvard Theatre Collection, The Houghton Library.*

obtaining "a white American for a domestic," adding ironically: "They call this a free country!" Zeke is not a slave, but his position in the underclass and its relation to his race are made clear. Mowatt amplifies this theme as Mrs. Tiffany renames Zeke, telling him: "Your name, I hear, is *Ezekiel*—I consider it too plebeian an appellation to be uttered in my presence. In future you are called A-dolph. Don't reply,—never interrupt me when I'm speaking." In thus silencing him, she denies him both his identity and the voice to protest. Revealing the country's racial schizophrenia, Adam Trueman, Gertrude's grandfather, repeatedly uses the word "nigger" but objects to Zeke's wearing livery because it is the "badge of servitude" and out of place "in a free land." Trueman, secure in his patriarchal privilege, is deaf to his own ignorance and racism.

Assigning men and women to separate roles merely because of gender must have been especially amusing to Mowatt, who took on the support of her household at 21. This separation, announced by the maid—"Monsieur is man of business,—Madame is lady of fashion. Monsieur make de money,—Madame spend it," is repeated in act 3, when the Tiffanys appear together for the first time. Mrs. Tiffany tells her husband to reserve his vulgar remarks for *his* counting house and not to bring them into *her* drawing room. Woman's status as chattel, a concomitant to the philosophy of separate spheres, is also protested. To keep his clerk Snobson from exposing his forgery, Tiffany promises his daughter Seraphina to Snobson in marriage; he describes her not as a human being but as his "sole curb upon that villain." Trueman complains that the money he never wanted made his daughter Ruth "an object of speculation" among fortune hunters. While he appears to spurn the idea of women as items of exchange, in this same speech he also states that the adventurer whom Ruth did marry "robbed [him] of the only treasure [he] ever cherished." Later he berates Tiffany, calling his plea to Seraphina to save him by marrying Snobson selling her and saying, "Shame on you, Anthony! Put a price on your own flesh and blood! Shame on such foul traffic!" This outburst occurs shortly after Trueman has given his granddaughter to Colonel Howard with the words: "Gertrude's yours!" Apparently one may traffic in women as property so long as no money changes hands.

If not the possession of man, what may woman be in this world of fashion? The conventional occupations of maid, milliner, and music teacher are the career opportunities offered; society's opinion makes all of them undesirable. Marriage then becomes woman's way to improve her material condition, as did Mrs. Tiffany in "rising" from milliner. While the surface of *Fashion* may deal with Mrs. Tiffany's attempt to become one of society's elite, the feminist subtext evident in woman's limited choice of employment denotes Mowatt's sympathy. She knew what it meant to work for a living—and at a career considered by most scarcely superior to milliner or governess.

Trueman refers to Mrs. Tiffany as a "damaged bale of goods," indicating his tendency to objectify women. He lumps women together when he tells Colonel Howard: "You don't know these women as well as I do,—they're always ready to pardon; it's their nature, and they can't help it." Not only does this patriarch make the error of generalizing, he also makes the act of forgiving seem shameful. Not so ready to pardon is the patriarchy. When it appears that Gertrude is involved with the Count, Colonel Howard labels her supposed behavior "beyond all endurance" and Trueman snaps: "How dare you have the face, girl, to talk of rights? You had more rights than you thought for, but you have forfeited them all! All right to love, respect, protection, and to not a little else you don't dream of. Go, go!" While all scorn the woman who has, presumably, fallen, the fraudulent Count is free to lead Mrs. Tiffany into the ballroom. The double standard operates fully here, and Mrs. Tiffany is later delighted when she learns, mistakenly, that Seraphina has married the Count.

Mowatt presents Gertrude as something of a hero, but only within the bounds of social plausibility. When his daughter, Ruth, died in childbirth, Trueman gave Gertrude to relatives to raise, hoping she would avoid the fortune hunters who pursued her mother. Not knowing she is his granddaughter and so an heir to wealth, she becomes a music teacher. Her love of independence leads her to leave the women who reared her. As she explains to Colonel Howard: "I had abilities, and desired to use them. I came here at my own request; for here I am no longer *dependent!*" She rejoices in being able to work, even in the demeaning situation that is hers in the Tiffany household.

Clever enough to penetrate the Count's disguise, Gertrude devises a plan to unmask him. Experiencing some misgivings, she cheers herself by remembering that "to lack courage in a difficulty, or ingenuity in a dilemma, are not woman's failings!" and joins Warren's Maria and Rowson's Fetnah in asserting woman's fortitude. Yet when her plan fails because of the meddling of another, Gertrude blames herself for imprudence. She writes a letter explaining all to her former patrons as Mowatt makes clear how illusory is woman's independence. When Trueman happens by, she shows him the letter.

Then enters the world as it is. Warren's Kate and Sylvia could not speak out against their husbands, and Mowatt's Gertrude needs the protection of the patriarchy. Adam, that first of men, True-man, a true man in the contradictions of his being and a representative of the patriarchy's power, reveals himself as her grandfather and takes control. In true patriarchal fashion, he rewards what he judges as virtue and punishes what he deems vice. Rewarding Colonel Howard for not being a fortune hunter by giving him Gertrude, Trueman also declares that Tiffany, the representative of the white male upper class, has suffered enough and may continue in business. Snobson, the blackmailer, is threatened with jail as an accomplice if he informs the law about Tiffany's forgery, then allowed to leave. Trueman offers to set up the false Count in a restaurant if only he will dress in his cook's attire and call upon those "fashionable acquaintances" he has gulled.

The criminal males are pardoned; the merely foolish women Trueman chooses to punish. Mrs. Tiffany and Seraphina must be deprived of the "house and all these gee gaws" and moved to the country, where they will learn "economy, true independence and home virtues." Symbolically imprisoning the women, the patriarchy reestablishes its desired order.

Fashion was an immediate success. One reviewer enthused: "Mrs. Mowatt may lay claim to having produced the best American comedy in existence," while another crowed over a newfound cultural landmark: "The production of a new play, written in our own city, by one of our own citizens, with our own society, hotels, houses, customs, virtues, vices, foibles, and follies as the subject matter, is an event looked forward to as a thing resting somewhere on the outer verge of possibility, but far beyond the known limits of the probable. The presentation . . . of *Fashion* was a realization of the practicality of this hoped for undertaking" (Barnes, 110).

By creating the most successful native comedy to appear on the American stage in the nineteenth century—made-in-America social satire—Mowatt established for herself an important chapter in theatrical history. While her not so gentle satire incorporates the characters and situations typical of farcical exaggeration, and while her debt to Sheridan is obvious, Mowatt, with an insider's knowledge of the upper classes and an artist's eye, truly Americanized the comedy of manners. Furthermore, by integrating within *Fashion* several ideas about women's roles and a feminist perspective on human rights, she became a major contributor to feminist drama in America.

The Contributions of America's First Feminist Playwrights

Rediscovering and reclaiming the work of these pioneer feminist playwrights is crucial to an understanding of the histories of the American stage and of American feminism. The ambiguous position of Mercy Otis Warren in her society—as she was first sought out by John Adams, among others, for her counsel and pressed to put her dramatic talent in the service of the Revolution, then reprimanded by Adams for acting in a manner unbecoming to a "lady"—is reflected in the reluctance of some late-twentieth-century women to proclaim their politics for fear of incurring the wrath of the patriarchy. Like Sylvia and Kate of *The Group*, these women feel that absent the protection of a male they have nowhere to go. Yet, as Warren is remarkable for the manner in which she, as one of the most important and relatively independent women of her time, made common cause with her less fortunate sisters, she may serve as exemplar to women over the centuries. The sorriest lesson observable in her plays is that issues such as domestic abuse, the silencing of women, and the neglect of children, which she vivified in American drama for the first time, are still largely to be resolved. Also, she countered the portrayals of women as hags, harpies, and harridans in the work of her male contemporaries.

All three playwrights, although hampered by limited access to education and lack of the civil and human rights guaranteed by their country's constitution only to those certain males who were endowed with "unalienable rights," and although treated as the possessions of their fathers and husbands, performed extraordinary service in laying the foundations of American drama and in speaking out against the injustices of male-dominated society. Despite their varied lives and backgrounds, they perceived clearly and encoded pertinently the life situations of women in colonial and federal America.

In political propaganda, historical tragedies, ballad opera, and drawing-room comedies, America's first feminist playwrights not only prepared the ground for a robust theater, they also dared confront their audiences and readers with uncomfortable truths. As society increasingly turned its eyes to these truths, the playwrights became posers of the complex questions soon to be subsumed under and become prominent as "The Woman Question"—a topic to be treated onstage by both the suffragists and the chroniclers of the New Woman who compose the second generation of feminist playwrights.

2

The Woman Question Onstage

The Woman Question was an umbrella phrase coined during the nineteenth century to cover a multitude of questions. For some, it signaled a desire for honest debate; for others, it functioned as a code phrase whose purpose was to answer the "Question" by proving woman's inferiority. The Woman Question carried ramifications in politics, the arts, religion, philosophy, economics, science, and the broader area of social relationships. Many and varied questions were raised. For instance, is woman man's property? Is she entitled to property in her own right? To higher education? May she control her sexuality through contraception? What effect does her employment have on the capitalist system and on the family? And of increasing importance, should women vote? How great a fear of women actually exercising power through the ballot does resistance to women suffrage illustrate?

Formal statements of the Question took shape in the second quarter of the nineteenth century. Margaret Fuller's *Woman in the Nineteenth Century* (1845) envisions a future of limitless potential for women, looking forward to the emergence of a "female Newton," for example; Fuller decries the sexual double standard and calls for economic "self-dependence" for women. To those who doubt woman's ability to take part in the affairs of government, she offers the actress and the Quaker preacher as examples of females versed in public expression.

Taking a different position were the patriarchy and its supporters, who had a vested interest in terms of economics, authority, and even comfort in woman remaining subservient and who called on the construct of female inferiority to preserve the status quo, attempting to use the quality of her "womanliness" itself, however vaguely defined, to limit a woman's activity. Proponents of this philosophy ranked African Americans, women, and children as inferior to the white male; both skull and brain size were measured to "prove" quantitatively woman's lesser mental capability. Also argued was woman's functional inferiority, a tenet that led to the trumpeting of woman's presumed inability to deal with scientific and abstract data. Furthermore, even physicians raised alarms about the effects that the rigors of higher education would have on her reproductive system.

Questions of woman's role and nature continued to influence the view of women in an evolving American society; in the June 1914 issue of *Forum*, playwright and critic Florence Kiper stated: "Every play produced on the American stage, with perhaps a few negligible exceptions, has its say on the feminist question." Feminist playwrights confronted political, personal, and social issues both through and beyond the domestic sphere as they interrogated societal values and illuminated age-old conflicts in dramas dealing with suffrage, women's rights, and the New Woman.

From Seneca Falls to Suffrage

In the aftermath of the Revolution, as the public arena open to men expanded while woman's work became increasingly confining and as male enfranchisement broadened, women in ever greater numbers perceived their exclusion from suffrage as untenable. Later, as they organized, gathered signatures on antislavery petitions, and risked wrath and ridicule for speaking in public against slavery, these white, mostly middle-class women began to sense an analogy between parts of the slaves' plight and their own. They, too, were possessions. They were deprived of wage and property rights and even of the guardianship of their children; they were forbidden to vote. That even among male abolitionists they were not always welcome was strikingly apparent when the American women delegates to the 1840 World Anti-Slavery Convention in London were forced to sit in the balcony merely because of their gender. There delegate Lucretia Mott met Elizabeth Cady Stanton. As the women discussed the meaning of their exclusion, seeds were sown that grew into the Seneca Falls Women's Rights Convention of 1848.

The convention itself, now a landmark in the history of women's rights, was called by Stanton in her hometown and attended by 250 women and men. Here was adopted a document variously known as the Declaration of Principles, the Declaration of Rights, and the Declaration of Sentiments. This last title speaks volumes about the socialization of women. Written by Stanton, the declaration was modeled on the Declaration of Independence and held that "the history of mankind is a history of repeated injuries and usurpations on the part of man toward woman, having in direct object the establishment of an absolute tyranny over her." But the title Declaration of Sentiments reveals how completely women had accepted the male view of them as creatures of feeling. The instrument itself, however, insisted on woman's "immediate admission to all the rights and privileges which belong to them as citizens of the United States." The accompanying resolutions included one calling for woman suffrage; more than 70 years were to pass before women would be enfranchised. On 26 August 1920, the Nineteenth Amendment became law. Today the Women's Rights National Historical Park stands on the convention site. A memorial in the form of a water wall, 9 feet tall and 120 feet long, engraved with the text of the Declaration of Sentiments, was completed in 1993.

The Suffrage Dramas; or, Parlor Plays in Peoria

Mercy Warren used drama to urge a revolution against a foreign tyranny; her spiritual daughters employed it to expose domestic tyranny. Warren also cast a searching eye on the dominion men held over women; the suffragist playwrights focused on the injustice done a citizenry deprived of its natural rights because of gender.

Many of the earliest dramas dealing with suffrage, such as *The Spirit of '76*, were against it. Of those plays supporting the cause, quite a few originated as "parlor" dramas, brief, amateurish works utilizing small casts and the props readily found in the average middle-class house-

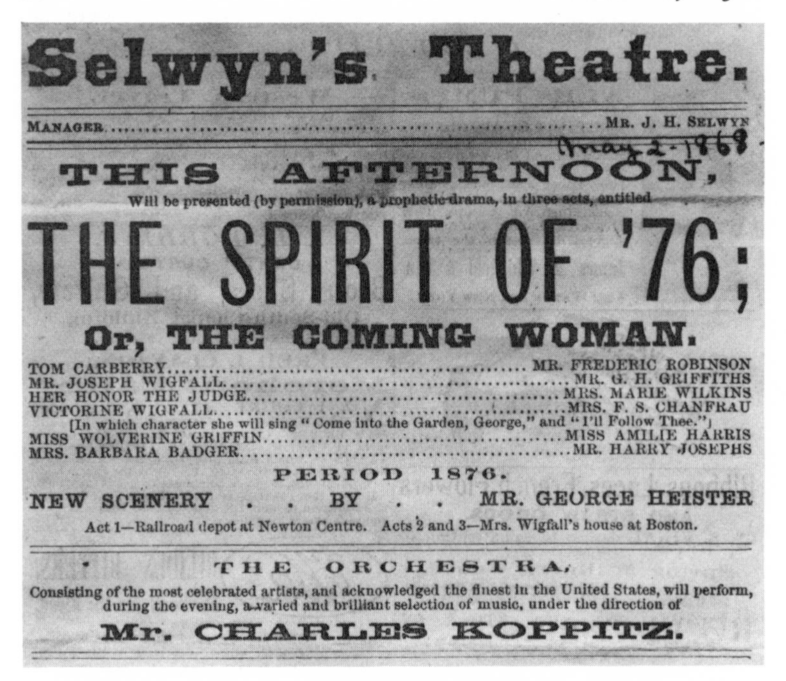

The earliest dramas dealing with suffrage opposed the cause. *The Spirit of '76* (playbill shown) was antisuffrage. *Photograph courtesy of Boston Athenaeum.*

hold; others were closet dramas intended for a reading audience only. The popularity of the parlor play represents a compromise between America's Puritan conscience, still uneasy about theater, and its historical love of the dramatic. Like the young Anna Cora Mowatt, who entertained family and friends with private performances, large numbers of middle-class Americans staged parlor plays. Collections of such plays were published, and popular women's magazines sometimes included plays among their articles.[1] Suffragists used circuses, pageants, picketing, and parades as street theater to win support for their cause. The suffrage parlor plays themselves, first performed in private homes or published in feminist journals, and later performed at suffragist meetings, became such popular vehicles for propaganda and fund-raising that in the later days of the struggle for the vote their venues became rented commercial theaters and fashionable hotels. Students at the women's colleges also presented the plays on their campuses. The male gaze is obvious in the work of a *New York Times* journalist reporting on the 16 December 1910 presentation of *How They Won the Vote* at Barnard. While his only remark on the play was that it had a cast of 10 characters, he did not neglect to notice that "There were no pretty girls selling tickets at the door, as there usually are at Barnard plays."

Suffragists writing for this noncommercial theater argued many different positions. In fact, there are suffragist plays situated in liberal, material, and radical/cultural positions, and several combinations thereof. The liberals argued from an Enlightenment natural rights philosophy; cultural suffragists, on the other hand, contended that the government needed women because of their very difference from men.

The ancestors of these playwrights had, of course, perceived some of the same problems. Warren and Rowson, though predating Mowatt, are the more feminist, Warren through her inference in *The Group* that society could benefit from the patriarchy listening to the women it preferred to silence, and Rowson through both the Utopian vision of Fetnah and the outspokenness of Rebecca. When suffragists began writing and producing plays, they, like Warren and Rowson, offered a feminist solution to inequity, proposing that the ballot would bring justice.

A cultural feminist position is evident in *Something to Vote For* (1911) by Charlotte Perkins Gilman, a social theorist, novelist, short-story writer, and journalist. Oriented toward a materialist position in such works as her famous *Women and Economics* (1898), *The Home: Its Work and Influence* (1903), *Human Work* (1904), and *Man Made World: Our Androcentric Culture* (1911), Gilman takes a different stance in her drama. Addressing women who feel they are well represented at the polls by their influence on the men in their lives, Gilman asks them to examine their womanly concerns and realize that they, more sensitive to human needs than are men, do indeed have reason to vote.

In *Something to Vote For* the antisuffrage members of the wealthy widow Carroll's women's club are set against the suffragist Dr. Strong, the symbolically named female physician who is to speak at the meeting. The closed minds of the club women are illustrated in their bylaws, which preclude discussion of woman suffrage. In this restriction, Gilman mirrors the constitutions of many actual clubs whose members felt that such discussion would be divisive. When Dr. Strong presents the Pure Milk Bill as an issue that appeals to the "motherheart and housekeeping sense of every woman" and that is "sure to make every woman want to vote," the women respond with cries of "No" and hisses.

Dr. Strong is to test milk from the plant of Mr. Billings, head of the Milk Trust and lobbyist against the bill. Before the meeting, she speaks with a milk inspector about the role bad milk plays in the high infant mortality rate. Saying, "I really believe that if mothers ran the milk business they would not be willing to poison other women's babies to make money for their own," she plots to switch the good milk Billings has brought to the meeting for the contaminated product he sells in poor neighborhoods. The doctor and the inspector expose the impure milk and Billings's greed. Shocked by the dirt in the milk, Mrs. Carroll proclaims: "Now we see what our 'influence' amounts to! Rich or poor, we are all helpless together unless we wake up to the danger and protect ourselves. That's what the ballot is for, ladies—to protect our homes! To protect our children! To protect the children of the poor! I'm willing to vote now! I'm glad to vote now! I've got something to vote for! Friends, sisters, all who are in favor of women suffrage and pure milk say Aye!" The play ends with a chorus of "Aye! Aye!"

While suffrage dramas may not have actually played in Peoria, Catherine Waugh McCulloch's *Bridget's Sisters, or, The Legal Status of Illinois Women* (1911) is set in Illinois. Setting her drama in 1868 to show the relevance of past and present abuse, lawyer McCulloch examines women's lack of legal status through Bridget O'Flannigan, a washerwoman who not only must hide her wages from her abusive, alcoholic husband but who has those wages attached to pay his bar bill. Bridget symbolizes all working married women subject to economic and personal exploitation. The courtroom scene highlights patriarchal arrogance. Not only does Patrick O'Flannigan assert that the bar owner "will find I am the only one who owns Bridget and her wages," but the owner admits he ignored Bridget's pleas not to sell liquor to her husband because Pat "is the head of the family and is the best judge whether he wants to drink." With the women who employ Bridget gathered in the courtroom, the play becomes something of a lecture. The laws of coverture, separate estate, and curtsey are discussed as a prelude to the judge's decision that "a wife's wages absolutely belong to her husband." Asking rhetorically why women have not risen to right such "wrongs," he suggests as reasons for female docility the facts that each woman thinks she's alone, that male domination has broken the spirit of most women, and that many women do not care about "sister women's sufferings." A debate among the women follows; woman's lack of human, moral, and civil rights is explained, culminating in a citation of the dismissal of rape charges because the rapist's orphaned 10-year-old victim was, incredible as this may seem to modern sensibilities, past the age of consent under then-current Illinois law. Brought to unity, the women decide to form an Equal Suffrage Association.

As dramas, these and others of the subgenre tend to be simplistic and didactic. Many roles are caricatures. Several make deprecating use of Irish and black servants, reminding us of the many suffragists who were greatly incensed that immigrant and black men were granted the franchise before native-born white women. Several, in their attempts to overcome the cliché of the feminist as a mannishly clad, cigar-smoking harridan, offer the old chestnuts of love and marriage as rewards to the right-thinking suffragist. As propaganda, however, the plays were successful as these feminist suffragist playwrights, working in the tradition of Warren and Rowson and imagining solutions to the Woman Question, seized the power of the pen and the stage and the passion of the current moment to dramatize their political points.

Drama and Society at the Turn of the Century and Beyond

With no little irony, the authors of the 1848 Declaration of Sentiments had resolved "[that] the objection of indelicacy which is so often brought against woman when she addresses a public audience, comes with a very ill-grace from those who encourage, by their attendance, her appearance on the stage, in the concert, or in feats of the circus." By the last decade of the nineteenth century, the coalition of feminists and suffragist playwrights, of dowagers, matrons, and debutantes appearing onstage, had done much to augment the aura of respectability brought to the theater by actors and playwrights such as Rowson and Mowatt.

In 1917, the inclusion of drama as a Pulitzer Prize category marked another milestone in its approach to respectability; the award went to Jesse Lynch Williams's *Why Marry?* Four years later, in 1921, the prize was awarded to a woman for the first time, going to Zona Gale for the dramatization of her novel *Miss Lulu Bett*. Women also were prime movers in the little theater movement, a burgeoning of smaller theaters that grew out of the exploitation of actors and playwrights by the Broadway syndicates. Called variously amateur, nonprofit, and civic, little theaters arose in many major cities in the United States. Philanthropists Alice and Irene Lewisohn presided over the metamorphosis of the Henry Street Settlement House theater into the Neighborhood Playhouse in 1915. That same year, Susan Glaspell helped found the Provincetown Players.

The rise of realism also influenced the stage; dramatists such as William Dean Howells and James A. Herne brought realism in staging, character, plot, and theme to the theater. In 1913 Alice Gerstenberg dramatized the conflict of the id and ego in *Overtones* by splitting her two female characters into projections of each psychological state. Each character was portrayed by two actors, one presenting the social self, the other her alter ego, who voiced the thoughts the social self dared not. Gerstenberg became the first American to present the dramatization of the subconscious mind onstage; by introducing expressionistic devices to the American stage she added the exploration of psychological realism to the dramatist's arsenal. Furthermore, male and female playwrights both began to focus on social issues.

Despite strides made by women in life and in the theater, negative images of them in both areas appeared regularly onstage. Eugene Walter's *The Easiest Way* (1908) combined both, presenting the theater as the site of vice and the central character, a female actor, as corrupt. Fear of the New Woman appears in several works. William Vaughn Moody's *The Faith Healer* (1910) and Clyde Fitch's *The City* (1909) present images of women ostensibly harmed by the new freedoms gained through the women's movement.

The oddest of all the images of women onstage was strange primarily because of its medium, not its message. Geraldine Maschio notes that female impersonators first appeared in American minstrel shows in the 1840s and reached the height of their popularity at the turn of the century. "Created and enacted by men, female impersonation attempted to prescribe and control the behavior of women by offering a three-dimensional image of the feminine ideal. That this image was created by a man meant that, as with other prescriptions, it carried the weight of authority."[2] What better image of the male gaze come to life than a male-created, male-enacted portrayal of the ideal female, the true object of desire? The impersonators were praised for being "more womanly in . . . by-play and mannerisms than the most charming female imaginable, [and] creat[ing] . . . an ideal to which all obedient women aspired"; the belief in supremacy of the white male as creator is reflected in a reviewer's comment that "just as a white man makes the best stage Negro, so a man gives a more photographic interpretation of femininity than the average woman" (Maschio, 45, 46).

The New Woman

Contrary to these images was the New Woman herself. Like the varied questions that led society to try to apprehend her, she was not one but several. She was the social reformer in the settlement house, the factory worker, the telephone operator, the flapper, the stenographer. She was all those women learning to openly question authority that neither included nor heeded her. She was the woman ridiculed for trying to achieve anything on her own in an era that called on middle-class white women merely to exist, to be rather than to do. Knowing also the unequal treatment she was liable to under the law, she joined the National Woman's Party to urge enactment in 1923 of an equal rights amendment, which stated that "men and women shall have equal rights throughout the United States and every place subject to its jurisdiction." She enjoyed the freedom of new courtship patterns made possible by the automobile and the telephone; she feared being left an old maid. She was, in short, all the women celebrated and feared, castigated and feted under the title New Woman—and she was the woman whose unfair treatment, predicated on her sex, lay at the heart of many of the plays in which American feminist playwrights confronted the Woman Question.

From Broadway to Provincetown: Rachel Crothers and Susan Glaspell

Rachel Crothers and Susan Glaspell brought the New Woman to the American stage. Crothers was one of the most successful Broadway dramatists of the first quarter of the twentieth century. Glaspell cofounded the Provincetown Players, a company devoted to innovation in American drama, and wrote many of the company's most successful plays. From the Great White Way of Broadway to the fishing shacks and dunes of Cape Cod, these two playwrights played major roles in the advancement of American dramatic art.

Rachel Crothers: The Trouble With Gender

Rachel Crothers (1870[3]–1958) was a force to be reckoned with in theater for more than three decades. Herself the daughter of a New Woman—

her mother began her medical studies after the age of 40—Crothers brought to the stage more New Women than any dramatist of her era. Among these women are muckraking activist/author Frank Ware of *A Man's World* (1909); journalist Ruth Creel and sculptor Ann Herford of *He and She* (1911); and novelist Mary Howard of *When Ladies Meet* (1932).

In 1891 she studied at the New England School of Dramatic Instruction. On graduating in 1892 she returned to Illinois, but her desire to be part of the theater was unquenched. In 1896 she enrolled at the Stanhope-Wheatcroft School of Acting in New York, where she spent one term as a student and four years as an instructor. The opportunities to write plays for her students, to direct these plays, and to design the costumes, sets, and props were, as she noted "of inestimable value because the doors of the theater are very tightly closed to women in the work of directing and staging plays" (Gottlieb, 18).

Although he begins by stating that "there are not many finer records in the American theatre than that achieved by Rachel Crothers," Burns Mantle calls her "America's first *lady* [emphasis added] dramatist" in his 1938 *Contemporary American Playwrights*, illustrating that the same double standards Crothers resisted in her dramas were alive in theater. This pigeonholing by sex was undoubtedly influenced by the virulent prejudice against women other than as actors at the turn of century. As Doris Abramson remarks: "[I]nterviews with and articles about 'lady playwrights' were often placed on the society page."[4] Critic George Jean Nathan frequently referred to women playwrights as "girls." Walter Pritchard Eaton, while somewhat less sexist, still made man the measure. In his 1910 review of *A Man's World*, he finds the play "just misses the masculinity of structure and the inevitableness of episode necessary to make it dramatic literature" (Abramson, 57).

Crothers represents and celebrates the New Woman. Beginning with her earliest plays, she exposes the fictions about women created by the patriarchy to reinforce its paradigms of womanhood,[5] as she illustrates the arbitrariness of socialization by gender and the concomitant cost for women and society in the unfulfilled human potential for work, love, or both. Aware of the difficulty of resisting such socialization, Crothers portrays many women who are unable or unwilling to pay that price, choosing instead to submit themselves to the "rules" of a patriarchal society. Some critics feel that in the middle years of her career Crothers herself may have bowed to her audience's inability to overcome its patriarchal prejudices and that her dramas from this period somehow impugn her feminist credentials. Yet Crothers was as "woman conscious" in her drama as she was in her life. She told Djuana Barnes during an interview for the May 1931 issue of *Theater Guild* magazine that "For a woman, it is best to look to women for help; women are more daring, they are glad to take the most extraordinary chances." She added: "I think I should have been longer about my destiny if I had to battle with men alone."

In 1931 Crothers told Henry Albert Phillips: "With few exceptions every one of my plays has been a social attitude toward women at the moment I wrote it . . . I [do not] go out stalking the footsteps of women's progress. It is something that comes to me subconsciously. I may say that I sense the trend even before I have hearsay or direct knowledge of it."[6] Whether her perceptions were subconscious or not, Crothers dramatized such human—not exclusively women's—issues as the need for meaningful work and the ensuing conflicts for some women between marriage (and sometimes motherhood) and career; the problems inherent in assuming that double standards were "natural"; the resistance and resentment encountered by assertive, successful women; and the loneliness that might impel a single woman into an unsatisfying marriage. In a 13 February 1912 interview with the *Boston Evening Transcript*, Crothers said that she chose women as her central characters because "women are in themselves more dramatic than men, more changing and a more significant note of the hour in which they live. If you want to see the signs of the times, watch women. Their evolution is the most important thing in modern life."

The tension between woman's increasing awareness of herself as a human being and man's desire to maintain the status quo is illustrated in her plays. In several the male lead refers to his counterpart as "little girl," evincing a desire to keep her dependent on him. From *The Three of Us* (1906) through *When Ladies Meet* (1932), the males in more than a dozen of Crothers's major dramas, including *A Man's World* and *He and She*, express the desire to "take care of" the females, even as Crothers makes it apparent through the accomplishments of these women that they need no caretakers. Many are over 30—Crothers prided herself on creating plays wherein the protagonist was not a 17-year-old ingenue. The male desire to protect actually masks the patriarchal privilege within middle-class marriage whereby a woman traded her youth, beauty, and sexuality for economic dependence on a man. Many of Crothers's plays question the assumptions about male and female grounded in generalizations about gender that inevitably work to secure the comfort and reinforce the power of the patriarchy. Crothers's feminism is visible in her plays, and, despite claims to the contrary by some late-twentieth-century critics, with no subversion of the texts, for most of those texts themselves subvert the patriarchal social order.[7]

Crothers's earliest works were brief one-act dramas written for her students. In two, *Criss-Cross* (1899) and *The Rector* (1902), New Women protagonists confront society's unfairness to women. Crothers's protagonist may have either career or marriage; she evidences artistic or personal competence only at the price of losing the man she loves.

With *The Three of Us* (1906), her first Broadway drama, Crother began to probe the societal conventions that impede women's self-determination. Concepts such as the basis of woman's honor and the double standard are closely questioned, yet Crothers's critics fault her for her protagonist's choosing to "adopt" the patriarchal code rather than abandon her brother. As Judith L. Stephens explains, Progressive Era politics, the dramatic conventions of the time, and "the prevailing belief in women's moral superiority exert[ed] a strong influence in determining the bounds within which the meaning of gender was constructed and negotiated in Progressive era drama."[8] Thus, "Progressive era plays reinforced such gender ideology by their moralistic nature and conventional structure even as they incorporated ideas intended to effect 'progress for women'" (Stephens, 292). While Crothers did not always openly transgress these principles of drama and sexual politics, she managed to subvert several tenets of male-female relationships deemed "natural" in her era.

Rhy MacChesney, the nonconformist protagonist of *The Three of Us*, "is forceful and fearless as a young Amazon, with the courage of belief in herself—the audacity and innocence of youth which has never known anything but freedom—the lovableness of a big nature and sunniness of an undying sense of humor. What she wears is very far from the fashion, but has charm and individuality and leaves her as free and unconscious of her strength and beauty as an animal." Just as her unconventional dress announces freedom from slavery to fashion, her search through an old trunk for "a dress of mother's" to wear to a party and her catching the keys to that trunk "like a boy" signal Crothers's refusal to valorize traditional signs of gender.

Believing herself free to do as she wishes, Rhy resists the idea that she has seriously compromised herself by coming to a man's home alone at night and that she has no alternative but to become his mistress. Shocked at the extent to which she is a prisoner of gender, she angrily responds: "It's true, then—all women must be afraid. I haven't believed it. I've thought we could do anything that was *right* in *itself*. I *still* think it! A good woman hasn't anything to be afraid of. Nothing can make a thing wrong that really is right. I'm not afraid of the *world*—it's *you*—*you* who can't understand. That this *could* have happened to me—to me!" Her belief that only Berresford, a villain, would presume to judge on appearances is dispelled when Townley, her sweetheart, enters, assumes she *has* dishonored herself, and tells her: "You shan't leave here till you say you'll marry this man. Don't you care anything for your honor and your good name?" As the men joust over who'll defend her tarnished honor, Rhy breaks in: "Don't you dare speak to me of my honor and my good name! Don't you dare to say you'll 'take care of it.' My honor! Do you think it's in your hands? It's my own and I'll take care of it and of everyone who *belongs* to me. I don't need you—either of you. 'Love—protection—trust!' Why I have to fight you both. Don't talk to me about whom I'm going to marry. That's a very little thing. Something else comes first!"

Rhy realized that her brother Clem had sold information that Berresford used to discredit Townley; Clem is the "something else [that] comes first." Despite her telling him that he sold his self respect quite cheaply for Berresford's $500, Clem remains defiant until she tells him she went alone to Berresford's and was discovered there by Townley. For her brother's benefit, she "sobs unrestrainedly," telling Clem: "I've got *you* to take care of me." After Rhy reclaims Clem, she and Townley are reconciled when she asks him to believe in the power of her love. The curtain falls as Rhy says, "We must make a good man of [Clem]. I have you to help me."

Although the play falls within the scope of the Progressive Era dramas described by Stephens, with Rhy making the self-sacrificing, moral decision and the men recouping positions of power, not everyone was oblivious to the challenges posed to conventional notions of woman and goodness. Mary Carolyn Davis wrote in the 1 June 1918 issue of the *Nation*—some 12 years after the play's premiere—that it "gave the deathblow to the cherished theatrical convention that a woman's honor must be fatally injured because she happens to be alone in a room with a man after sundown."[9] Surely some in the audience also recognized in the final line a comment on the social construction of manhood. Many reviewers, however, did respond within the range described by Stephens. In the 3 June 1907 edition of the *Chicago News*, the writer praises Rhy because she is "not the emancipating trumpeter of noisy deeds for femininity, but the holy woman of the great resplendent life of throbbing motherhood"! It would appear that for this writer the madonna/feminist dichotomy is more threatening than that of the madonna/whore, a division used by the patriarchy from time immemorial to classify women.

Continuing her scrutiny of the unfairness of a male-dominated world, Crothers anatomized the power of the patriarchy through its manifestations in the double standard in *A Man's World* (1909), a social problem drama that concerns the relationship between Frank Ware, feminist and novelist, and Malcolm Gaskell, a reporter, as it is affected by their attitudes toward the double standard. Frank, raised by her writer father "to see—to know—to touch all kinds of life" discerned very early the limitations put on women: "[t]he more I knew—the more I thought women had the worst of it." While living in Paris, Frank and her father take in a young, unmarried, pregnant woman whom Frank sees "suffer the tortures of hell through her disgrace." When the woman dies giving birth, Frank adopts the baby boy, whom she names Kiddie. Years later, after falling in love with Gaskell, she discovers he is Kiddie's father. When Gaskell, who had abandoned Kiddie's mother without knowing of her pregnancy, learns of his paternity, he claims male prerogative and refuses to acknowledge he's done anything wrong; Frank, therefore, rejects him. Crothers, like most feminists of the era, argues not for more sexual freedom for women but for a single standard of abstinence and fidelity for both sexes.

Branching from this issue are such related topics as the power of love, woman's need for economic independence, the value of work, and the pain of loneliness. Frank, an active and engaging character who is described in her initial appearance as "strong, free, unafraid, with the glowing charm of a woman at the height of her development," is also the primary focus of the debates about these concerns. One of Crothers's superior women, Frank is, through her name, announced as forthright. She is a successful novelist who centers her work around social problems concerning women. Frank's economic independence is an expression of Crothers's materialist feminism; Frank is "free" because her privileged background, education, and talent have enabled her to earn her way, and she recognizes that social conditions that are condoned, even sanctioned, by the patriarchy are responsible for the plights of the women of the Lower East Side about whom she writes.

In her novels, Frank exposes the conditions underlying the poverty, prostitution, and social decay of the slums. Because of her subject matter, the strength of her style, and her "male" name, early reviewers assumed Frank was a man: "*The Beaten Path* is the strongest thing that Frank Ware has ever done. Her first work attracted wide attention when we thought Frank Ware was a man, but now that we know she is a woman we are more than ever impressed by the strength and scope of her work. . . . Her great cry is for women—to make them better by making them freer." Such a "cry" flies in the face of the patriarchal system that seeks to make women virtuous by making them prisoners of the code that so dismayed Rhy. Frank's "friends," no less skeptical of woman's talent, wonder where and how she gets her material and think that a man must be helping her. During one conversation, her male friends also speculate about whether Kiddie is Frank's biological child and wonder why, if he is not, she refuses to divulge his parentage.

Zeroing in on the sexual double standard, Crothers effects a stunning reversal of the situation presented in *The Three of Us*. Rather than dramatizing the plight of a woman who is convicted of immorality on the basis of mere appearances, she presents a man who absolves himself from responsibility for his actions because of his gender. Gaskell, whom Frank agrees to marry while blinded by love for her idealized vision of him, is actually an arrogant, unpleasant character. Crothers makes the true Gaskell very unattractive as she illustrates both his callousness and his conviction of male superiority. Of Frank's book, he says: "You haven't got at the social evil in the real sense. You couldn't tackle that. It's too big for you. . . . You don't get *at* the thing. You keep banging away about woman—woman and what she could do for herself if she would. Why—this is a man's world. Women'll never change anything." Turning then to her activities with the girls' club she sponsors, he declares that she is wasting her time with these lower-class girls whom he sees as promiscuous. In this, Gaskell represents the patriarchal view that once a girl is "ruined" there's no redeeming her. (The "ruiner" is, of course, free from any censure.) This attitude also underlies his urgent desire to know about Kiddie's background; he arrogantly informs Frank: "I'm a man. You're a woman. I love you. I have the right to know your life."

Gaskell's assumption of privilege—like that of all the men, fictional or real, who have subscribed to this view of woman—has a long history. The sexual double standard has been in force for thousands of years. Men often assigned a lower level of sexual desire to women, and then went to great lengths legally and socially to ensure that their myth, necessary to what they saw as the orderly functioning of society, was maintained. Crothers has Gaskell, albeit unknowingly, admit as much when in a marvel of circular logic he proclaims: "Man sets the standard for woman. He knows that she's better than he is and he demands that she be—and if she isn't she got to suffer for it. That's the whole business in a nutshell—and you know it." Not only does he claim to speak for all men, Gaskell is also quite open about his view of woman's role in life. He avers: " Women are only meant to be loved—and men have got to take care of them. That's the whole business."

When revealed as Kiddie's father, he is unrepentant. He insists that nothing has changed and that the separation Frank now perceives between them is based only on her ideas, which are, of course, inconsequential: "[S]ince the beginning of time one thing has been accepted for a man and another for a woman. Why on earth do you beat your head against a stone wall? Why do you try to put up your ideals against the facts?" When Frank will not accept the "facts," he enlists the patriarchy's version of the natural order: "You're a woman. I'm a man. We don't live under the same laws. It was never meant to be. Nature, nature made men different."

Despite Frank's rejection of his argument about the essence of male and female and his recourse to nature, Gaskell insists she not "hold [him] to account by a standard that does not exist." Frank learns that he is not the man she imagined him to be, not the "fine and honest man" her culture encouraged her to lean on. He is not even a man who, to save their relationship, would do the minimum she asks and admit he'd been wrong. Thus, in the only ending possible, Frank remains true to her feminist values and the lovers part.

The play's characters are varied and vivid, the dialogue crisp and convincing, and the tension satisfying. This is not a preachy polemic but a logical working out of the incompatibility of Frank's liberal feminism and Gaskell's inflexible belief in women's inferiority as encoded in the double standard. In the June 1914 issue of *Forum*, Florence Kiper called the play "honest [and] well built drama, interesting to feminists not only because of its exposition of a modern sex-problem, but also because it is written by a woman—one who does not attempt to imitate the masculine viewpoint, but who sees the feminine experience through the feminine temperament." Eaton, in the review previously cited, could not resist sneering as he reported that Frank "has a little theory—women do get such theories tenaciously into their heads nowadays—that she does not care to have to forgive the man she loves for any unsavory episodes connected with 'the living of a man's life!' " Not only is the sneer inappropriate; Eaton is clearly wrong. Frank was ready to forgive Gaskell's past if he would only admit he had been wrong.

A Man's World provoked such a stir that Augustus Thomas responded to it with his dramatic defense of the double standard, *As a*

Man Thinks (1911). Here Dr. Seelig, countering the argument in which his wife makes a direct reference to Crothers—"And that woman dramatist with her play was right. It is a man's world"—proclaims, "There is a double standard of morality because upon the golden basis of women's virtue rests the welfare of the world." The sophistry behind Thomas's argument is worthy of a Malcolm Gaskell.

The secondary theme of *A Man's World,* woman's talent and her right to employ it, becomes the focus in *He and She.* Taken on tour in hopes of securing a Broadway run, the play premiered in Poughkeepsie, New York; rechristened *The Herfords,* it opened in Boston in 1912, but did not make it to Broadway until 1920, at which time the original title was restored and Crothers played the lead. In 1980, playwright Emily Mann directed a revival.

The play concerns the apparently egalitarian marriage of Ann and Tom Herford, two successful sculptors. Tom is completing his entry in a design competition for a building frieze. Ann, having second thoughts about Tom's design, develops one that she wishes him to submit instead. When he refuses, she enters the competition. Ann wins the commission, and the egalitarian spirit of the marriage begins—on Tom's part—to erode. As various family members and friends debate woman's role as mother, worker, and artist, the situation seems to defy resolution until the Herfords' daughter Millicent presents herself as needing her mother's attention. Ann decides that Millicent needs her more than she herself needs her art and asks Tom to execute her design.

The issue of women and work is raised almost with the curtain. Keith, Tom's assistant, asks him: "Have you ever been sorry that Mrs. Herford is a sculptor—instead of just your wife?" Keith's word choice is interesting; the "just" implies that Ann would be something less than she is were she "just" Tom's wife, while the "sorry" infers that there is something less than desirable about a wife who is "more" than just a wife. Keith is engaged to journalist Ruth Creel, who will marry him if he lets her keep working. He wonders how she can keep doing all that has made her so successful and tend a house too. He protests that Ruth, unlike Ann, who works in her studio at home, is "tied down to office hours and it's slavery." He never questions the fact that his ideal of having "a girl by my own fireside to live for me alone" would make her both a slave and a house prisoner. Keith claims to be quite liberal: "I'm strong for women doing anything they want to do—in general—But when it's the girl you love and want to marry it's different."

Tom, mildly amused, tells him that his attitude about working women in the abstract should not differ from his attitude about a particular working woman, but Keith cannot see beyond the fact that "[t]he world [read men] has got to have homes to live in and who's going to make 'em if the women don't do it?" When Tom mentions the excellence of Ruth's mind, Keith responds: "Oh, mind be damned. I want a wife." Later he asks Tom's sister Daisy, who is secretly in love with him, whether she sees anything wrong in "wanting a girl to give up hard, slavish work and let him take care of her." The difficulty of many household tasks is elided in Keith's question; for him it is simply invisible. The audience may realize who is really being taken care of; Keith never will. The basis of Keith's argument is his detestation of the fact that women who work do not need men to survive. As he sees it: "The minute a woman makes enough to buy the clothes on her back, she thinks she and God Almighty are running the earth and men are just little insects crawling around." Keith protests the fact that woman's economic independence saps his power to decree what she will do; Crothers introduces these issues as part of the subplot because this seeming caricature is voicing emotions that Tom will experience.

When Ann wins the competition, Tom shows himself caught in the patriarchal mind-set; although act 1 ends with an egalitarian handshake as Tom welcomes Ann to the competition, in act 2 Crothers shows him to be brother to Keith. They first learn that Tom has come in second; Ann consoles him. Shortly, they learn that Ann has won. Tom seems to handle the news well. Yet minutes later he is asking her what *she* will do with their 16-year-old daughter that summer and telling her that he will not touch any of her commission money. He accuses her of letting her ambition run amok, then, sounding like Malcolm Gaskell, tells her: "You're a woman and I'm a man. You're not free in the same way. If you won't stop because I ask it—I say you *must* . . . I demand it. I say you've *got* to."

Tom is no different from Keith. He feels his manhood threatened by Ann's ability to earn the $100,000 commission and fears her economic success will lessen her interest in her roles as wife, mother, and mistress of the house. At bottom, he too wants "a girl by [his] own fireside to live for [him] alone." Ann and Ruth, on the other hand, speak of the need for economic independence, and Ann tells her father that a woman's ability to make a living can mitigate any blow.

Keith and Tom are figurative sons of Ann's father, the quintessential patriarch Dr. Remington. He is, in Ann's word, "mid-Victorian" in his attitude at best and medieval at worst. A doctor, as representative of the patriarchy, is a frequent character in the drama of this era. In James Herne's *Margaret Fleming* (1890), Dr. Larkin validates Margaret's decision to raise her husband's illegitimate child and to allow Philip back into their home by saying, "[T]his world needs just such women as you"; in *As a Man Thinks*, Dr. Seelig valorizes both the double standard and woman's supposedly superior moral nature. Dr. Remington literally is the patriarch; he issues commands to both the women and the younger men. One of his comments—"And here's that pretty little Ruth thing—knowing so much it makes my head ache"—dehumanizes Ruth and demeans her intelligence, and his words to Tom—"[I]f you don't look out you'll be so mixed up you'll be upstairs keeping house and Ann will be downstairs keeping shop"—clearly indicate his position on woman's place. He assumes that human rights are man's to dispense and explains that women must not exercise their rights: "the more women make good—the more they come into the vital machinery of running the world, the more they complicate their own lives and the more tragedies they lay up for themselves." Claiming recourse to "natural" law, he adds, "The development of women hasn't changed the laws of creation . . . [for] no matter how far she goes she doesn't change the fundamental laws of her own— . . . mechanism." She must choose between the "two sides of her own nature." His biological determinism is debunked by Ruth's and Ann's love for their work, by their success, and by the fact that the men are those who decree that women must choose.

Selecting motherhood as possibly the strongest weapon in his arsenal, he claims that sitting "by her own fireside with children on her knee . . . [is] the only thing in the game that's worth a cent—anyway." Besides ignoring the millions of women who are not of his sociocultural milieu, his argument fails to account for Ruth, who is uninterested in rearing children. The argument falls short in his daughter's case also. Her only child, a selfish daughter who literally pulls Ann away from her work, is at 16 well beyond sitting on her mother's knee.

That Remington, despite his pose of egalitarian benevolence, finds women inferior becomes obvious when he chastises Ann for humiliating Tom. He tells her that Tom has suffered "a blow tonight that no man on earth could stand," that is, being beaten by a *woman*. Later, perhaps advising him to trade a physical blow for a metaphoric one, when Tom says he doesn't give orders to Ann, Remington responds: "The devil you don't. She'd like it. A woman—a dog and a walnut tree—the more you beat 'em the better they be."

Crothers exposes the fear, jealousy, and selfishness underlying the patriarchal order as Ann challenges her father with these words: "You've *never* thought I had any right to work—never believed in my ability, now that I've proved I have some—Why can't you acknowledge it?" In fact, both Ann's husband and her father acknowledge her ability, but not to her. Before he knows the outcome of the contest, Tom tells Keith: "The men judging this *know*. I'd trust them with anything. The fellows who lose will have no kick coming on that score." Remington reminds Tom about Ann's having offered her design to him: "[S]he laid her genius at your feet once and she'd do it again." Even recognizing her genius, he is willing to see it subjugated to her gender; her success bothers him so much that he says he'd rather see her happy as a woman than as an artist, once again refusing to see that, for Ann, the two are inextricably bound, and once again concealing the fact that the choice he would have her make is dictated by his preference, not by woman's "dual" nature.

Because the patriarchy as embodied by the three men will brook no alternative to its ownership of women and children—even though all the men try to veil this ownership by romanticizing, rationalizing, and spiritualizing it—the three adult women must respond to its dictates. Daisy subscribes to the philosophy that a couple cannot be happy unless the man dominates. Although she labels Daisy's emotional restatement of the law of coverture something from the dark ages, Ruth literally disappears from the drama after Remington declares the primacy of motherhood. Ann is left, many critics claim, to effect a compromise with Tom. But Crothers did not write of a compromise; she detailed a sacrifice. Learning that Millicent has become engaged to the chauffeur at her boarding school,[10] Ann succumbs to the pressure to take care of her child and asks Tom to execute her design. Giving up her art, Ann reverts to the gender role prescribed by her father, her era, and her class. What has Tom given? He says he will not let her sacrifice herself for their daughter and warns her that surrendering the commission will cause anguish to the artist in her, but he speaks only after Ann has made her decision. She has sacrificed her art, the work that brought her personal fulfillment and a way of illustrating the talents and capabilities of women. Her last line: "Put out the light," signifies the extinguishing of her inner light of inspiration for the sake of a selfish child who will soon leave home.

Because its conclusion highlights this sacrifice, *He and She* is decidedly more feminist than is usually recognized. Ann bows to the patriarchal vision of what makes woman valuable and lovable: her ability to serve, to submit, to sacrifice. The ending illuminates the wastefulness of her action, for by concluding her drama in darkness Crothers shows that the opposite of Ann's healthy self-interest (branded selfishness by the men) is a bleak self-*less*-ness.

That Ann's sacrifice was most likely undertaken in vain was not lost on the contemporary audience. Alexander Woollcott saw clearly that Crothers was roiling the waters, not calming them. In the *New York Times* of 13 February 1920, he deemed the play a tragedy: "for something fine and strong dies in the last act. It is the hope, the ambition and all the future work of a genius—deliberately slain in order that the 'she' of *He And She* may be able to play more attentively and more wholeheartedly what she is *driven* [emphasis added] to regard as her more important role—that of wife and mother." In the 25 May 1980 *New York Times*, Jean Ashton remarked: "*He And She*, like Miss Crothers's other plays, is a descriptive, not a prescriptive work. Far from accepting this or any of her comedies as anti-feminist, Miss Crothers noted simply that the freedom women had achieved in the early years of the 20th century was tenuous and deceptive. Men still made the rules; women who broke them did so at tremendous cost."

While the 1920 version of *He and She* is decidedly feminist, the decade of the 1920s saw the paradox of women who had secured the right of suffrage and gained access to higher education retreating from social activism and returning to the home. This resurgence of domesticity—an effect of backlash against woman's progress that has recurred with disheartening regularity throughout the history of the woman's movement—finds its way into Crothers's drama, but even when she began to create social comedies rather than deal with social problems, gender issues were never absent from her work.

Although *Susan and God* (1937), the last of Crothers's produced plays, was named the most outstanding play of the season by the Theater Club, it is little more than a satire of the Oxford movement, and its protagonist, Susan Trexler, genuinely unlikable. *When Ladies Meet*, coming five years earlier, is the capstone of Crothers's career in dealing with the evolution of the modern woman. Its protagonist, 32-year-old Mary Howard, is a successful novelist who cares what women of her "*own* kind" think of her work; Mary, despite her success, feels incomplete without a man in her life. Her emotions lead her to contemplate an affair with her married publisher, Rogers Woodruff. Her inclination is prefigured in her latest novel, which centers around such an affair. Woodruff, described as having "an irresistible charm for women," is a romanticized idol for Mary; she cannot see, behind his charismatic mask, the clichéd character who tries to persuade her to become his lover with the oldest of lines: "If you [loved me] you wouldn't hesitate one second. . . . If you loved me—like that—you'd take me." Mary agrees to go with him to Bridget Drake's country place, but Jimmie, who himself loves Mary, shows up with Woodruff's wife, Claire, in tow, having first made sure Woodruff is called away on business.

Neither woman knows of the other's relationship to Woodruff. They like each other almost immediately, and they discuss Mary's books. Claire declares Mary's earlier novel *Alice* "astonishingly true, from a girl's standpoint"; Mary thinks that she's preparing "something *new* and *honest*—from a woman's standpoint." When she asks Claire her opinion of the situation in the novel, her prospective lover's wife reminds her that the other woman "ought to know enough not to believe a married man—if he's making love to her"—and that the wife might not be as much of a "dub" as the novel's protagonist believes her to be. Once the three members of this triangle come together, Woodruff tries to keep up the pretense that he and Mary are at Bridget's merely to work.

Seeing Mary's pain at his rejection enables Claire to see her own. Realizing she, too, has been creating a fiction based on the false premises that her husband can't help attracting women and that his infidelities mean little when he returns home to her, she no longer wants him. Admiring each other, the women can no longer pretend that the wife is a dub and the potential mistress a slut; recognizing each other, they see through him. Rejecting a man-centered existence that merely staves off loneliness, these superior women mature, and this is Crothers's point: when ladies meet in an atmosphere of confidence and trust, they become women, women deserving a better partner than Rogers Woodruff.

In this late play as in Crothers's first works, women decide to forgo love with a particular man, but there is a notable difference. In the earlier plays, the superior woman yields her interest in the male to another, perhaps weaker, woman in an action indicative of the "noble" self-sacrifice held up to women as ideal in this particular mythic mode of womanhood. Now, instead of silent suffering and surrender, the women undergo a course of self-discovery that allows them to realize the unworthiness of the man who lies to them both.

Crothers brought the New Woman—strong, talented, and intelligent—onstage; many of her woman-centered dramas focus on the social problems that arise when woman's human rights conflict with the patriarchal order. Considering that she wrote at a time when for the majority of her audience the overriding question of a woman's life drama concerned who, and sometimes whether, she would marry, Crothers's creation of at least one strongly feminist play in each of the last four decades of her career—*The Three of Us* (1906) and *A Man's World* (1909); the reworking of *The Herfords* (1912) as *He and She* (1920), and *When Ladies Meet* (1932)—is remarkable. Even her social comedies respond to issues raised by the Woman Question. She pursued these issues in a manner calculated to challenge the limitations placed on women by the patriarchal system, chronicling, for example, the folly of man's obsessive concern with woman's body as the repository of *his* honor. Crothers allows audiences to see the arguments about woman's place in society from a woman's perspective, both her own and those of her characters, some of whom mature from their romantic dependence on man as the imagined vehicle of fulfillment to achieve both a sense of self and freedom from the male ego's limited perception of her.

Dramatically, her work is important in the history of the development of serious social comedy in America. Crothers's early plays show her rapidly increasing command of structural and stylistic techniques. Her bright, witty, yet realistic dialogue ranks with the best of its era. Her central focus, which is the Woman Question, gives the Crothers canon a unified purpose. Often criticized as a "formula" playwright or a sentimentalist, Crothers instead presented dramas that dealt with real-life questions. The tragedy she illuminated, as Woollcott noted, was that of women "driven" into choices that sap the power and creativity of one-half of humankind.

Susan Glaspell: New Ways of Imaging Women Onstage

Susan Glaspell (1876–1948), who helped transform American drama through her connection with the Provincetown Players and who created new ways of representing women onstage, began writing early, publishing short stories in such magazines as *Youth's Companion*. Upon graduation from Drake University in Davenport, Iowa, she became a reporter for the Des Moines *Daily News*. In 1901 she returned to Davenport to devote full time to her fiction, publishing two or three stories each year; in 1920 she published *Plays*, a collection of her dramas.

In 1913 Glaspell married George Cram Cook. Whatever else marriage brought Glaspell, its most significant aspect for American drama was her becoming, with Cook, a founder of the Provincetown Players. Founded in a fishing shack on a pier in Provincetown, Massachusetts, and devoted to producing only original plays by American playwrights, the theater counted among its contributors Edna St. Vincent Millay, Theodore Dreiser, and Djuna Barnes, but none so important to transforming American theater as Eugene O'Neill and Glaspell herself. When her first play, *Suppressed Desires*, cowritten with Cook, was rejected by the Washington Square Players, she and Cook presented it in their apartment; in the summer of 1915 they again performed it. Although the players were not formally organized until 1916, the season that introduced Glaspell's *Trifles*, the preceding summer may truly be counted as the birth date of this remarkable theater.

Encouraged by the attendance and by favorable reviews given their summer seasons, the group moved to New York in the winter of 1916. They named themselves the Provincetown Players and, as O'Neill suggested, called their playhouse The Playwrights' Theatre, a move that underscored the primacy of the playwright in their enterprise. They also decided "that active members must either write, act, produce, or donate labor."[11] This dictum provided a showcase for the other talents of Glaspell. In addition to providing more plays for the theater than any playwright except O'Neill, she directed some of her own plays and acted in *Suppressed Desires*, *Trifles*, *The People* (1917), *Close the Book* (1917), *Woman's Honor* (1918), *The Outside* (1918), *Bernice* (1919), and *The Inheritors* (1921), for all of which, with the exception of *Suppressed Desires*, she was the sole author. She not only spoofed Freudian analysis in *Suppressed Desires* and satirized the male vision of woman in *Woman's Honor*, she also illustrated the difficulty of truly representing woman onstage in *Trifles*, *Bernice*, and *Alison's House* (1930). In both *The Outside* and *The Verge* (1922), she dealt with woman's struggle with a male-centered language while at the same time she demonstrated her facility as an expressionist. Almost all of the plays deal with the problems women encounter in attempting, against the strong current of patriarchal authority, to forge identities of their own.

In *Trifles*, *Bernice*, and *Alison's House*, Glaspell constructs dramas around women who never appear onstage; paradoxically, the presence of these characters is strongly felt. In this device lies a striking achievement: she brings the absent women onstage diegetically, while at the same time their absence serves as a commentary on the manner in which the patriarchy has deprived women of their substance. That these women appear only through the words of others speaks to the constructed nature of womanhood itself.

Trifles, Glaspell's first play as sole author, was loosely based on a murder trial she covered for the Des Moines *Daily News*.[12] In her reverential biography of Cook, Glaspell explains that he had announced a play of hers for production and refused to accept that she had none:

> So I went out on the wharf . . . and looked a long time at that bare little stage. After a time the stage became a kitchen—a kitchen there all by itself. I saw just where the stove was, the table, and the steps going upstairs. Then the door at the back opened, and people all bundled up came in—two or three men, I wasn't sure which, but sure enough about the two women, who hung back, reluctant to enter that kitchen. . . . Whenever I got stuck, I would run across the street to the old wharf, sit in that leaning little theater under which the sea sounded, until the play was ready to continue.[13]

The social conditions pertaining to the plot of *Trifles* were set forth by Charlotte Perkins Gilman in *The Man-Made World, or Our Androcentric Culture:* Women have no standing; in the "proprietary family" of the patriarchy, their purpose is "first and foremost [as] a means of pleasure to [man]." Furthermore, family relationships are arranged "from the masculine viewpoint. . . . From this same viewpoint . . . comes the requirement that the woman shall serve the man." Accordingly, "[t]he dominant male, holding his woman as property . . . has hedged them in with restrictions of a thousand sorts," which ensure that "she cannot develop humanly, as he has, through social contact, social service, true social life."[14] These attitudes and restrictions cripple the lives of all three women presented in the play.

Ostensibly a murder mystery, the play deals on its surface with the attempt of Sheriff Peters, County Attorney Henderson, and Mr. Hale, a neighbor, to discover evidence relating to the murder of John Wright, whose wife, Minnie, has been jailed for the crime. Mrs. Peters has come to gather some personal belongings for Minnie, and Mrs. Hale to keep Mrs. Peters company. While the men inspect the bedroom in which Mr. Wright was strangled and search the barn for clues, the women uncover—and cover up—both the motive for the crime and the physical evidence thereof.

The play opens on an empty stage; the kitchen, gloomy and

A scene from Susan Glaspell's *Trifles*, with Marjorie Vonnegut, Elinor M. Cox, John King, Arthur E. Hohl, and T. W. Gibson. From *The Theatre*, January 1917. *Photograph courtesy of The Billy Rose Theatre Collection, The New York Public Library for the Performing Arts, Astor, Lenox and Tilden Foundations.*

cluttered, offers the audience its first glimpse into the Wrights' lives. The set is a mute message, later elaborated in the women's dialogue. Shortly, the door opens; as the characters enter Glaspell offers another wordless message, this one concerning hierarchy. First to enter is the middle-aged sheriff, next the young county attorney, then Hale, followed by the women. The sheriff and the county attorney function as the ultimate emblem of the patriarchy: the law. Hale, not privileged by a connection to the law, as a man takes precedence over the women. The men immediately stride to the stove for warmth while the women, fearful and nervous, "stand close together near the door." Their action presages the warmth of sisterly community, which they will shortly discover.

The men's priorities are obvious; Glaspell indicates that the sheriff steps "away from the stove . . . as if to mark the beginning of official business." They allow nothing they deem extraneous to enter even the periphery of their consciousness. The lack of sensitivity among the men becomes apparent early. When they discover that, as Minnie had feared, the cold in the house had broken her jars of preserves, the sheriff is incredulous: "Well, can you beat the women! Held for murder and worrying about her preserves." Stating a central theme, Hale adds: "Well, women are used to worrying about trifles." Their smug scoffing heightens Glaspell's bipolar irony: "trifles" such as food and housekeeping are basic to the preservation of life itself, and it is the males' ignorance of such details that causes them to overlook the key to the crime itself.

Declaring there to be "[n]othing here but kitchen things," the sheriff leads the men upstairs to examine the murder scene, leaving the women—who had "move[d] a little closer together"—free to move about the kitchen. Years of habit lead them to begin cleaning the unkempt room. As they work, they speak of John Wright. Adding to the faded wallpaper, the uncurtained windows, and Hale's comment about his unwillingness to share the cost of a party-line telephone as evidence of Wright's niggardliness, Mrs. Hale declares: "Wright was close. I think maybe that's why she kept so much to herself. She didn't even belong to the Ladies' Aid. I suppose she felt she couldn't do her part, and then you don't enjoy things when you feel shabby." Her husband's miserliness had cut Minnie off from community, both in person and by telephone. Even in her own home she had no voice, for Hale had noted that he "didn't know as what his wife wanted made much difference to John."

The women who eventually become silent champions of Minnie do not identify themselves as her friends. Mrs. Peters had not met her before she was jailed; Mrs. Hale has known her 20 years, but had not visited in more than a year. They do not, therefore, take her part because of personal bias; rather, they come to see themselves and Minnie as Everywoman, imprisoned by patriarchal convention. The literally imprisoned Minnie, absent from the stage and thereby silent, reminds us of Warren's Sylvia, present in *The Group* only through the dialogue of the men who have arrogated to themselves her voice, a character who, "silent, mourns her fate." Minnie's absence also echoes the social position of a woman after marriage: as the law of coverture made clear, and as Crothers's Daisy approvingly reiterates in *He and She*, marriage erases a woman's identity. Significantly, Mrs. Hale refuses to accept this negation and persists in referring to her as Minnie Foster, not as Minnie Wright.

Glaspell's implicit criticism of the philosophy of separate spheres becomes obvious as the men, counting the women unable to recognize clues, leave them behind in the woman's world of the kitchen. Assuming that nothing merits their attention in this "preserve" of trifles, the men move upstairs. As the audience hears their footsteps on the floor above, Glaspell indulges in an aural pun: physically, the men are literally over the heads of the women—a reminder also of man's position as head of the household—while figuratively, the facts of the case go over the men's heads.

The women find the quilt Minnie had been working, one square of which is marked by erratic stitching quite different from the rest. Without stopping to wonder why, Mrs. Hale resews the square. This direct, but as yet unknowing, action echoes her earlier remarks uttered in Minnie's defense; when the county attorney said Minnie wasn't "much of a housekeeper," Mrs. Hale said in a "stiff" reply: "There's a great deal of work to be done on a farm." And when she says that "[m]en's hands aren't always as clean as they might be" and that she "didn't think a place'd be any cheerfuller for John Wright's being in it," she points out men's failings. Now she and Mrs. Peters speculate about the tension underlying the irregular stitching. As she had earlier moved closer to Mrs. Peters, Mrs. Hale now moves closer to Minnie. She wishes she had visited more often, for she knows how difficult it must have been to live isolated and childless with John Wright, "a hard man. . . . Like a raw wind that gets to the bone."

Discovering the bird cage with its door hanging from one hinge, then the bird with its neck wrung, she decides that Wright killed both Minnie's singing spirit and the bird, so moves to conceal this evidence. Mrs. Hale criticizes the investigators for "sneaking" around Minnie's house: "Locking her up in town and trying to get her own house to turn against her!" Mrs. Peters, as the wife of the sheriff, counsels, "[T]he law is the law." Yet remembrance moves her. Seeing the dead bird, she recalls her own enraged response in childhood to the boy who "took a hatchet . . . before my eyes" to her pet kitten, and remembers the eerie stillness that enveloped her homestead when her two-year-old son, then her only child, had died. Still, even then she persists: "The law has got to punish a crime, Mrs. Hale"; Mrs. Hale declares that her own failure to visit "was a crime! Who's going to punish that?" From this perspective it is but a small step to the third crime—John Wright's spiritual and emotional, if not physical, abuse of his wife—and to the guilt the patriarchy must bear for its dirty hands, for its enforcement of the traditions and codes that led to Minnie's despair. Here one finds the three Everywomen, the wife, the wife of the law, and the murderer, all imprisoned in the patriarchal order; here one begins to appreciate Glaspell's further ironies. The symbolically named Minnie, small and insignificant, has risen against this system, but so far has succeeded only in exchanging one prison for another. But Glaspell is not done; the surname *Wright* also brims with irony: that John could be Mr. Right and that Minnie's rights were violated so severely that she thereby had a right to kill her husband.

The women, resisting for once the gender discrimination that imprisons them, tacitly agree to conceal the evidence; they rebel against abstract justice and act through sympathy and empathy. Glaspell suggests, in the manner of the cultural feminists, that a woman's law, which takes into account not just the deed but also the circumstances and context in which the deed is performed, is superior to the law of the patriarchy. The final line of the play reverberates with this principle as Mrs. Hale, who had initially been abashed by the men's laughter at her question about whether Minnie had intended to quilt or knot the squares of her quilt, later lets Mrs. Peters say: "We think she was going to—knot it," then ends the play by standing center stage, her hand over the pocket that conceals the dead bird, and announcing for Mrs. Peters, for Minnie, for herself, for every woman: "We call it—knot it, Mr. Henderson." This splendid line laces together the image of John Wright with the noose knotted elaborately around his neck and the women's refusal, albeit one they cannot voice without endangering themselves, to be coopted yet again by the male system.

Trifles is the most frequently anthologized one-act play by an American woman; it is often praised as a paradigm of play construction. Overtly and inherently dramatic while at the same time subtle, economical, and understated, the play's form replicates its action in both its departure from the male dramatic traditions of through line—with its rising action, climax, and falling action—and linear exposition and in its lack of resolution. Glaspell must have realized it would be dishonest to resolve a conflict that remains, sadly, unresolved.

Alison's House won Glaspell the 1931 Pulitzer Prize, an award that brought the Pulitzer jury the disapproval of most critics and reviewers; the play was equally unpopular with audiences, running only 41 performances. Conventional in style and structure, the play even conforms to the neoclassic unities, taking place in fewer than 24 hours and utilizing two rooms of the same home as its set. It is notable, however, for being the third in Glaspell's trilogy of dramas focusing on a woman who never appears and for challenging a patriarchal system that cares more about preserving appearances and the status quo than about humanity.

Centered on Emily Dickinson surrogate Alison Stanhope, the

play concerns the discovery, 18 years after her death, of poems that chronicle Alison's affair with a married man. As her surviving family prepares to move Agatha, who served as her sister's caretaker, from the old homestead, which is to be sold, they argue over whether the poems should be destroyed or published.

Glaspell resolves the conflict in favor of the new century. The poems will be published, a "letter to the world," which will allow it to perceive the human Alison, not some spirit treading the ether in virginal white. All will know "the story she never told. She has written it, as it never was written before. The love that never died—loneliness that never died—anguish and beauty of her love!" In *He and She*, Ann Herford regrets not executing her frieze because it would have been a gift for women, who could have looked at its strength and beauty and said: "A woman did that." In *Alison's House*, that gift is given; women will have the strength and beauty of Alison's work: "Because Alison said it—for women."

Saying it for women is Glaspell's concern in two of her more experimental dramas, *The Outside* and *The Verge*. In these works, women's attempts to speak for themselves illustrate the pitfalls inherent in allowing oneself to be defined by a male-devised, gender-centered grammar. The fixity of form basic in such a language contrasts with the flux of nature as, in both these plays, the forces of life contend with those of death.

The Outside begins with a scene that functions as envoi and emblem. Into a lifesaving station now converted into a private home, two men carry a drowning victim. Mrs. Patrick enters and demands that they leave: "You have no right here. This isn't the lifesaving station any more. Just because it used to be—I don't see why you should think—This is my house! And—I want my house to myself!" As she speaks, one of the men "put[s] his head through the door. One arm of the [victim] is raised and the hand reaches through the doorway." Thus the prologue shows death invading Mrs. Patrick's house, just as, on the dunes around the house, the sands encroach on and smother the scrub growth vying for survival on a set that marks Glaspell's move from realism to symbolism and expressionism. Mrs. Patrick bought the house with her husband as a summer place. Subsequently, he left her, and she retreated to this buried house. She appears to enjoy watching the sand engulf the scant life forms on the dunes and fears "Spring—coming through the storm to take me—take me to hurt me." She fears being bruised into life again, and this fear underlies her repeated comment: "I must have my house to myself!"

Seeking someone who "doesn't say an unnecessary word," she hired as her housekeeper Allie Mayo, "a bleak woman" with "that peculiar intensity of twisted things which grow in unfavoring places." Once a young woman teased by her husband for her loquaciousness, Allie, struck by the inanity of the remarks her friends offer when her husband disappears while on a whaling trip, retreats into silence. Through Allie, Glaspell introduces the thematic and structural problem of the play: what to do with and about words when, as inadequate as we know them to be, they are yet all that we have. She handles the issue imitatively, by allowing the halting dialogue of the play to illustrate its own meaning.

As Mrs. Patrick leaves the house, angry at the men for having left the corpse behind, Allie calls out: "Wait." Mrs. Patrick is "held," "arrested," by the unaccustomed sound of Allie's voice. Allie goes on "in a slow, labored way—slow monotonous, as if snowed in by silent years." Her voice falls to a whisper; she labors, rocking back and forth, to give birth to words "not spoken but breathed from pain." Because she assumes Mrs. Patrick's husband has died, Allie tells her own story to illustrate that withdrawal is "not the way." Shocked by Mrs. Patrick's revelation and hurt by her reminder that she'd been told Allie did not "say an unnecessary word," Allie insists that her words are vital. In a mutually stumbling syntax, the women debate their positions. As Glaspell makes obvious, their mistakes lie in investing too much of themselves in their marriages; the symbolic burial they have been undergoing in the dunes repeats their earlier act of burying their own identities in those of their husbands. They must strive now to find words to express themselves, for those selves have only an embryonic existence. Clearly, a command of the idiom of self demands the possession of a sense of self; until woman forges that identity she will struggle in a language that identifies her as the other.

Claire Archer, protagonist of *The Verge*, attempts to save her own life by subjugating herself in marriages to two unimaginative men, but each disappoints her. Now three men—her husband, her friend the philosopher, and her lover the artist, the triumvirate of Harry, Tom, and Dick, who among them cannot come close to understanding her—cause her much impatience as she anxiously awaits the flowering of Breath of Life, a new form of plant life she has created.

This most expressionist of Glaspell's dramas opens in Claire's greenhouse, which is more laboratory than nursery. A shaft of light emitted through an open trapdoor in the floor illuminates a strange plant with a "twisted stem"; frosty "patterns" are visible on the greenhouse glass, a violent "wind . . . makes patterns of sound," and "At the back grows a strange vine. It is arresting rather than beautiful. The leaves of this vine are not the form that leaves have been. They are at once repellent and significant." The ominous mood, sight, and sound dissipate as the dialogue begins. Because Claire has diverted the heat from the house into her greenhouse/laboratory, Harry has come to eat his breakfast in comfort; soon Dick follows. The talk is that of a comedy of manners; as Harry mildly berates Claire for being a poor hostess, Claire tries to persuade Harry to try his egg without salt, and Tom, finding himself locked out, fires a revolver to gain the attention of those inside the glass house. Yet beneath the surface move the roots of another drama, which twists around the conventional comedy. To Dick, Harry says that creating something unsettles a woman. Disturbed because Claire has dared to reach beyond the usual, Harry questions her state of mind, but his real unease arises because she is breaking the bonds of womanhood and presuming to arrogate to herself the male roles of creator and scientist. When he tells Dick, "I'd like to have Charlie Emmons see her—he's fixed up a lot of people shot to pieces in the war," Glaspell's allusion to the war between the sexes is obvious. This reference is especially relevant in light of the research of Judith Lewis Herman, who in *Trauma and Recovery* asserts, "There is a war between the sexes. . . . Hysteria is the combat neurosis of the sex war."[15] Here, too, arises the question of whether Claire is "on edge," that is, in a liminal stage, willing to risk going mad so life itself need not be imprisoned. Or is she on the edge of sanity, driven there by pressures to conform to her "womanly" role?

In the name Claire Archer, Glaspell suggests both clarity of vision and the ability to bridge, to create by spanning and mixing various forms. But behind this "flower of New England" lies the history of her ancestors, "the men who made the laws that made New England." Yearning to break out of this mold, just as her plants sometimes go beyond their species and "go mad—that sanity mayn't lock them in," Claire seeks escape from the prison of the patriarchy, seldom better envisaged than it is here, as the set form, the hardened heritage of the "saints" of Puritanism who inflicted such dehumanizing laws and customs on women.

Claire is distracted; as she holds vigil for Breath of Life, her daughter, Elizabeth, who has spent most of her life in boarding schools and school vacations with Claire's sister Adelaide, arrives. As one who wishes to slip the bounds of forms, Claire is a most unlikely mother for

Elizabeth, who at 17 is a mature conformist. While Claire wards off the embrace of this stranger, Elizabeth confides her wish to help her "produce a new and better kind of plant." Claire, haltingly reaching for the right words, tells her: "These plants—(*beginning flounderingly*) Perhaps they are less beautiful—less sound—than the plants from which they diverged. But they have found—otherness." She indicates the strange vine at the back of the greenhouse as one that had "crept a little way into—what wasn't." But the Edge Vine has now reverted to its original form, so Claire asks Dick to destroy it. Elizabeth declares it is wrong of Claire to play God just to change, not to improve, plants. Suddenly, Claire perceives in Elizabeth her Puritan ancestors; she uproots the Edge Vine and but for Harry's wresting it from her would strike Elizabeth with this traitor plant. Claire's estrangement resounds through her words: "To think that object ever moved my belly and sucked my breasts." Terrible as these words are, nothing less would so blatantly demonstrate Claire's commitment to what she calls "outness" and "otherness" and her refusal to be seduced by what she sees as her creations.

Act 2 opens in the late afternoon of the following day. That Claire has not been liberated by rejecting her creations is obvious; she appears alone in "a tower which is thought to be round but that does not complete the circle. The back is curved, then jagged lines break from that, and the front is a queer bulging window-. . . . The whole structure is as if given a twist by some terrific force—like something wrong." This obvious phallic symbol being both erose and under pressure suggests the "terrific force" may be Claire's own struggle to break out of the patriarchal prison, but the stage directions also emphasize her continuing confinement; she is "seen through the huge ominous window as if shut into the tower." The glass of the greenhouse repeats itself in the window, and both, by promoting a sense of distance, comment on the difficulty of representing women within traditional dramatic forms—as does the play's structure, which twice veers from comedy of manners to *drame*. The coercion to conform continues. Personifying conformity and femininity as defined by the male, Adelaide berates Claire, calling her experiments nonsensical. She prescribes a "cure": Claire must be a mother to her daughter and so cease to be unnatural, and she must become a consumer, not a creator: "Go to Paris and get yourself some awfully good-looking clothes."

But Claire is not Ann Herford, who can sublimate her own needs for those of a grown child. She calls out for Tom, her philosopher, and sends the others away. Earlier Claire had difficulty articulating what her work meant; now she searches for the words with which to ask Tom to pursue their relationship beyond the platonic, to express something that's "not shut up in saying." Although Claire suggests they might find "radiance," Tom refuses; she persists and once again the play breaks form as her words become poetry:

> I want to be;
> Do not want to make a rose or make a
>   poem—
> Want to lie upon the earth and know.
> . . . .
> But scratch a little dirt and make a flower;
> Scratch a bit of brain—something like a poem.

The conflicting sentiments here mirror Claire's conflicted state. The patriarchy tells her that as a woman she should "be," not do, yet her own consciousness pushes her "to make a flower / . . . [or] something like a poem." Rejected by Tom, Claire turns to her present lover, Dick. By now overwhelmed, she desires to disappear: "Anything—everything—that will let me be nothing!"

In act 3 the scene is again the greenhouse, where Harry pursues Dick with a revolver as the play careens toward farce. When Harry claims he wishes to show Claire "I've enough of the man in me to—" Claire tells him he is being ridiculous. In a stage direction charged with double meaning, Claire appropriates the phallic weapon—"taking the revolver from the hand she has shocked to limpness"—puts it out of sight, and becomes again the detached seeker of "outness" and "otherness" as she points to the men and says: "One—two—three. You-love-me. But why do you bring [your quarrel] out here?" Her attention belongs now to Breath of Life, which, unlike the Edge Vine, has gone on: "it is—out." Moving again into poetry, she speaks, even in her victory, with disillusionment:

> Out?
> You have been brought in.
> A thousand years from now, when you are but a form too
>   long repeated
> Perhaps the madness that gave you birth will burst again,
> And from the prison that is you will leap pent queerness
> To make a form that hasn't been—

> To make a person new.
> And this we call creation.
> Go away!

Dick and Harry leave, but Tom, perceiving this Nietzschean overreacher to be on the verge of insanity, offers to keep her "from fartherness—from harm—safe." Claire, aghast that the person who might "be a gate" instead "fill[s] the place," places her hands around his throat, choking off his breath. As the others, alerted by the crash of breaking glass, rush in, Glaspell notes that "she has taken a step forward, past them all." The drama ends as Claire the creator sings "Nearer My God to Thee," not in subservience to the supreme patriarch but in acknowledgment of her own godlike potential.

Glaspell is not, of course, sanctioning murder; the act must be read symbolically. Only by daring to break the confines of the patriarchy, confines that may come disguised as the love that wishes to keep one "safe," can women imagine and create new ways of being. The daring with which the playwright approaches her topic matches the boldness with which she employs expressionist techniques to achieve a spectacularly effective enwrapment of style, subject, structure, symbol, image, and theme.

Unfortunately, the success of the Provincetown Theatre, of which Glaspell's plays were so large a part, was, to Cook, the sign of a spiritual failure; in 1922 he deemed the theater a mediocrity. He and Glaspell left for Greece. By the time Glaspell returned to America following Cook's death, the Provincetown had undergone changes in management and philosophy. The conventional comedy *The Comic Artist* (1928), on which she collaborated with her second husband, Norman Matson, was produced in London, the almost equally conventional *Alison's House* at the Civic Repertory Theatre. After these, Glaspell wrote no more plays. Perhaps she was wounded by the critics' outcry against *Alison's House* receiving the Pulitzer, but it is more likely she realized that while she was away she had quite literally lost her stage.

American theater owes a great debt to Susan Glaspell, whose dramatic talents as playwright, actor, and director exploded on the stage of the Provincetown Players along with Minnie Wright's preserves. The aftershocks continue today, for she dared envision and bring to life onstage her own New Women. These women experience their own anagnorsis, challenging and rejecting male-defined norms, including such concepts as woman's honor, abstract justice, and the male's right to dominate and control, while they move toward the formation of female community.

Dramatically, her innovations were challenging. The economy of stagecraft manifested in most of her settings, perhaps initially dictated by the scant resources of the group, became in time a symbolism that resounded throughout each drama. Her use of the absent woman demonstrated how an offstage story can be used onstage.

Finally, she used language itself in a new way—a way that continues to be misunderstood. C. W. E. Bigsby speaks about her "natural reticence,"[16] an evaluation not far removed from Isaac Goldberg's comments, in 1922, about her being "reticent, laconic." Goldberg notes that Glaspell is "largely the playwright of woman's selfhood," and he realizes that "this acute consciousness of self . . . begins with a mere sense of sexual differentiation."[17] Acute as his perception is, he is unable, as apparently is Bigsby, to realize that Glaspell is not imbuing her characters with any "natural reticence" of her own; rather, she works toward verisimilitude. Woman, even the rebellious woman, having been so long denied a voice in determining her own destiny, would initially be able to exercise a newfound voice only haltingly; her stammer arises from sexist oppression, from silencing. While Glaspell did not create a woman's discourse, she demonstrated the inadequacy of man's for her New Woman.

Twentieth-Century Feminist Foremothers

Rachel Crothers and Susan Glaspell were major forces in early-twentieth-century American drama. As a voice for the New Woman, Crothers explored feminist issues in a manner that marks her a worthy successor to Warren and Rowson; in her comedies she is a more than worthy successor to Mowatt. Glaspell, long held in O'Neill's shadow, is beginning, finally, to be recognized as a major force in reshaping the drama that brought American theater into the twentieth century. She, as much as O'Neill, pioneered a symbolic and expressionist drama on the stage. She deserves to be more widely known and to be known as much more than the author of *Trifles*, excellent as that play is.

3

From Boston to Harlem: The Varied Voices

Along with Rachel Crothers and Susan Glaspell, feminist playwrights of the early twentieth century, black and white, raised their voices against the oppression meted out by a patriarchal society that discriminated along lines of race, class, and gender. Discrimination existed within the theater itself; while all women experienced difficulty getting their plays produced in the commercial theater, female playwrights who were black were doubly disadvantaged. Because of their race, they were almost invariably limited to publishing in black magazines such as *Crisis* and *Opportunity* and being produced in churches, community halls, and academic theaters. The gender discrimination that worked against them is evident in the fact that a drama by a black man, Willis Richardson's *The Chip Woman's Fortune*, was presented on Broadway in 1923, while it was not until 36 years later that Lorraine Hansberry's *A Raisin in The Sun* was produced there.

Feminist Voices, White and Black

Josephine Preston Peabody, Zona Gale, Lula Volmer, and Sophie Treadwell all explored the issues of woman's oppression from their shared perspective as white women. Their protagonists range from ladies-in-waiting to Queen Elizabeth to poor, illiterate mountain women. Black playwrights Angelina Weld Grimké, Mary Burrill, Georgia Douglas Johnson, May Miller, and Marita Bonner exhibit a similar scope in the characters of their dramas, characters whom they explore from an African American perspective. But all of these playwrights, black and white, focus on topics such as inequity, injustice, and oppression, topics that unite them as feminists.

Josephine Preston Peabody: Piper of Protest

Through her ancestor Francis Peabody, who came to America from England in 1635, Josephine Preston Peabody (1874–1922) had deep American roots, yet most of her dramas derive their settings from her study of Renaissance England, medieval Italy, and legend. Her family was devoted to the arts; in lieu of reading bedtime stories, her father enacted scenes from dramas. After his death in 1884, the family moved from Brooklyn to Dorchester, Massachusetts. Peabody had several poems published before she was 14. When one of her poems appeared in the *Atlantic Monthly* in 1894, editor Horace Scudder took an interest in her and arranged for her to attend Radcliffe as a special student from 1894 to 1896. There she became a student of William Vaughn Moody and began her verse tragedy *Marlowe*, which was performed in 1905 for the opening of the theater at Agassiz House, with George Pierce Baker, originator of the famous 47 Workshop playwriting course at Harvard, playing the lead. From 1901 to 1903 she lectured in literature at Wellesley.

Her one-act play *Fortune and Men's Eyes* (1900) concerns the love triangle of Shakespeare, William Herbert, and Mary Fytton, maid of honor to the Queen. Mary identifies herself as:

> The foolishest of women:
> A heart that should have been adventurer
> On the high seas; a seeker in new lands,
> To dare all and to lose. But I was made
> A woman.

This lament over limitations placed on women serves as a prologue to Peabody's masterpiece; in life a voice for woman suffrage, in *The Piper* (1907) she protests the ills wrought by patriarchy.

Submitted to the Stratford Prize Committee, the play was selected from 315 entries to be awarded the $1,500 prize and produced to inaugurate the new Shakespeare Memorial Theatre at Stratford-on-Avon, 26 July 1910. This success led Winthrop Ames, who had previously rejected the script, to produce it in New York with Edith Wynne Matthison in the title role that Frank Benson had played in England. This cross-gender casting caused no little debate. Walter Pritchard Eaton reported that "the illusion of the story was robbed for him by the knowledge that a woman was playing the part," but "others . . . saw in Miss Matthison's *Piper* a vital spiritual force that compensated for whatever strength of reality a man's figure might have added to the play."[1] Except for the brief scene in which the mayor's daughter falls in love with the Piper out of gratitude for his rescuing her, the role is sexless, the Piper more spirit than body. Frequently described as a battle between the Piper's desire for revenge and Christ's power of love, the play is better classified as a struggle between the Piper and a patriarchy consumed by greed.

Beginning with a play-within-the-play, *The Piper* immediately focuses on the children who are the audience of a Noah's Ark miracle play staged by strolling players. The playwright's attitude is established when the children plead for more and Ilse, one of their number, directs: "Oh, leave out Noah!" No tiresome patriarch for her! Other than children, the first townspeople on stage are Jacobus, the drunken Burgomeister; Kurt the Syndic, or councillor; and Anselm, the priest. (This graphic statement of the town's power structure is repeated in the entrance to the second act; the hierarchy is evident as first the priest, then the men, and finally the women enter.) This triumvirate, having engaged the Piper to rid Hamelin of its rats, now seeks to credit the town's patron saint with the "miracle" and avoid paying the promised fee. Saying he had Jacobus's word, the Piper asks that payment be made to his fellow players, but Kurt calls them outcasts and seizes on their being external to the patriarchal order as reason to ignore the claim. He avers:

> Wit ye well, he is a stroller,
> A wastrel, and the shadow of a man!
> Ye waste the day and dally with the law.
> Such have no rights; not in their life nor body!
> We are in no wise bound. Nothing is his.

In this scene from the premiere of Josephine Preston Peabody's *The Piper* at Stratford, England, in 1910, the Piper, hiding in a well, observes the clergy. *Photograph courtesy of Harvard Theatre Collection, The Houghton Library.*

> He may not carry arms, nor have redress
> For any harm that men should put on him,
> Saving to Strike a shadow on the wall!
> He is a Nothing, by the statute book.

When Ursula calls, "The Holy Book! Bring that—or he'll bewitch you," the Piper's demurral—"I charm but fools and children"—adumbrates the action. Anselm enters with a "large, illuminated Gospellbook," which he then supports on the head and shoulders of his acolyte. The Piper protests; it is too heavy. Another boy is called forward and the book laid on the children's backs, symbolizing the passing down of the weighty patriarchal precepts of medieval Catholicism. Ironically, the Piper later hides the children in Hollow Hill, which consists of a cavern adjoining the "cellerage of a ruined, burned-down and forgotten old monastery in

In this scene from the premiere of Josephine Preston Peabody's *The Piper* at Stratford, England, in 1910, the Piper entertains the children in their hiding place. *Photograph courtesy of Harvard Theatre Collection, The Houghton Library.*

the hills," establishing a realm of childish joy on the ruins of the fathers' oppressive religion.

Conjoined with Peabody's critique of religion is her statement on the treatment of women and children. Kurt's speech on the legal position of the players applies as well to women and children. Mocking the men, the Piper claims they value children only as possessions, as:

> Some one to work for me, when I am old;
> Some one to follow me unto my grave;
> Some one—for me!

Veronika, Kurt's wife, tells of selling herself in marriage to buy a home for her crippled son, Jan. Jacobus accedes to the people's demand that he give his daughter to the church as a penance for the town's sin. Calling the nunnery a "cage" and a "grave," the Piper vows to save her from this fate, engendered by the "moneybag / That serves the town of Hamelin for an heart."

Peabody's Piper is a playboy piping his "kinderspell" to lead the children away from the *Dies Irae*, from the cages built by their killjoy fathers, into life. He delivers a soliloquy in which he denounces the town's values yet surrenders to the spirit of the Lonely Man, as Jan calls Christ; he returns the children to the town, almost literally resurrecting Veronika, who lies dying of a broken heart, and imploring her:

> Heed not these grave-makers, Veronika.
> Live, live and laugh once more . . .
> Look, how you have to waken all these dead,
> Waken them—change them!

The play offers hope that the woman, the outsider, the outcasts, the disabled, and the children might open the eyes of the burghers to what is truly valuable.

Walter J. Meserve calls Peabody the "most significant of the early twentieth century poetic dramatists" (Meserve, 195), ranking her before Moody, Percy MacKaye, and Edward Arlington Robinson. *The Piper* would not play well today; several of its speeches slow the action, and eloquent poetry is out of fashion, if not dead, dramatically. Perhaps one might say of *The Piper* what Peabody said of *Portrait of Mrs. W* (1922) in her prologue to that play about Mary Wollstonecraft: "Dramatically, it is wilfully [*sic*] built against traditions of stage structure." Both dramas, however, make powerful statements about the structure of a male-dominated society.

Zona Gale: Midwestern Voices

Like Mowatt and Peabody, Zona Gale (1874–1938) had a strong American heritage; among her ancestors were Richard Gale, who emigrated to Massachusetts in 1640, and a great-great-grandfather who fought at Lexington. After graduating from the University of Wisconsin, she became a reporter, in which capacity she conducted interviews with Ellen Terry and Sir Henry Irving, possibly initiating her own interest in the theater. Winning the $2,000 first prize in a short-story contest sponsored by the *Delineator*, a leading women's magazine, prompted her 1911 return to her hometown, Portage, Wisconsin. There she became active in politics and promoted such causes as woman suffrage and the Progressive Party; she joined the Woman's Peace Party and drafted the 1923 Wisconsin Equal Rights Law. She became the Wisconsin Dramatic Society's patron, authorizing use of her name, contributing financially, and writing articles for its journal. Most important, she responded to the group's request for a one-act play with *The Neighbors* (1912). Arising from Gale's Friendship Village series, collections of short stories characterized by sentimentality and written in tribute to what she saw as innate human goodness, *The Neighbors* portrays a community of rural folk rallying to aid a childless widow awaiting the arrival of her dead sister's eight-year-old son. Representative of the folk drama of its era, the play was well received when the Wisconsin Players brought it to the Neighborhood Playhouse in New York in 1917.

When she wrote the novel *Miss Lulu Bett* (1920), Gale moved beyond sentiment to create a scathing criticism of middle-class complacency and hypocrisy; she dramatized the novel into the play that made her the first woman to receive the Pulitzer Prize for drama. A study of spinsterhood and its concomitant status of dependency, *Miss Lulu Bett* is also an initiation story. Lulu, an uneducated, unattractive woman, lives with the family of her married sister, Ina Deacon. Lulu justifies her own and her widowed mother's existence by functioning as an unpaid servant.

Gale designates "The Middle Class" as her setting; Dwight Deacon typifies the midwestern, middle-class patriarch who is capable of enslaving his sister-in-law even as he eulogizes family: "[T]he family bond is the strongest bond in the world. . . . I tell you of all history the most beautiful product is the family tie." Seated at the dining room table, he pontificates: "I tell you people don't know what living is if they don't belong in a little family circle. . . . Look at this room. See this table. Could anything be pleasanter?" Yet his mother-in-law is sulking, one of his daughters is absent, and Lulu is an afterthought, at best. A justice of the peace and a dentist, this "family man" imperiously instructs his wife not to bother him with domestic details and, in response to Lulu's having spent a quarter on a tulip plant, reminds her of her destitute state by remarking: "We give you a home on the supposition that you have no money to spend, even for necessities."

When Ninian, the brother whom Dwight has not seen for 20 years, visits, he tells Lulu that Dwight "makes a slavey of you." Ninian impulsively invites Lulu to accompany him and the others to the theater.

The invitation begins the rebirth of this 34-year-old innocent. She restyles her hair and wears "the waist I always thought they'd use—if I died." Dwight teases her mean-spiritedly about her appearance, suggesting that because it is too early to leave she should dance on the table to amuse them, or, "They'll begin to read the funeral service over us." Ninian asks, "Why not the wedding service?" and begins dramatically, "I, Ninian, take thee, Lulu, to be my wedded wife." Dwight's taunt: "Lulu don't dare say that," goads her into responding, and this mock wedding begun as dramatic entertainment becomes, as Dwight the magistrate points out, a binding civil ceremony. The woman whose superfluity is announced in the play's title becomes "Mrs. Lulu."

Within a month, she is back; Ninian, it seems, was already married. Lulu tells Dwight: "He hasn't seen her for fifteen years and he thinks she's dead. But he isn't sure," so she is once again *Miss* Lulu Bett. Through these circumstances, Gale demonstrates the economic importance of marriage for most women. Without talent or training, Lulu must return to slavery. Her single state imperils her, but her sister's marriage gives her a place in life.

Gale makes allies of the marginal females in the drama. Mrs. Bett, mother of Ina and Lulu, finds that age and her widowed status necessitate a struggle to be recognized as a person. When Diana's boyfriend asks, "Is—is everyone gone?" she marks this erasure of her humanity by inquiring: "Who's this you're talking to?" Instead of being accepted, these females are merely tolerated: Mrs. Bett because she's Ina's mother, Lulu because she does the household work, and the children because they are, in Dwight's distancing phrase, "the progeny." Their status is obviously not equal to Ina's as the married woman occupying the central supporting role decreed by the patriarchy; Ina lords it over Lulu and flatters Dwight by simpering, "Oh, Dwight . . . that I should have a good kind loving husband—be so protected, so loved, when other women. . . ."

When Lulu wishes to tell people why she returned, Dwight instructs her to think "how this will reflect on us." When she protests, he negates her completely: "You! You're completely out of it. You've nothing more to say about it whatever." Laying open her painful existence, Lulu says:

> I've lived here all my life—on your money. I've not been strong enough to work they say—well, but I've been strong enough to

> be a hired girl in your house—and I've been glad to pay for my keep. . . . But there wasn't a thing about it that I liked. . . . Well, then I got a little something, same as other folks. I thought I was married and I went off on the train and he bought me things and I saw different towns. And then it was all a mistake. I didn't have any of it. I came back here and went into your kitchen again—I don't know why I came back. I suppose it's because I'm most thirty-four and new things ain't so easy anymore—but what have I got or what'll I ever have? And now you want to put on to me having folks look at me and think he run off and left me and having them all wonder. I can't stand it.

Ina and Dwight interpret this rebellion as madness. But Lulu exposes Dwight for the pompous patriarch he is, telling him, "You're one of the men who can smother a whole family and not even know you're doing it." Still, the patriarchy prevails; Dwight reminds Lulu that her story would imperil Ninian: "Don't you realize that bigamy is a crime? If you tell this thing he'll go to prison." Out of love for Ninian, she agrees to keep the secret. Once more, in a tradition reaching back to the rape in Warren's *The Sack of Rome*, a feminist playwright shows the patriarchy excusing the act of a criminal male by ignoring both the crime and the woman against whom it was committed.

Lulu, unable to bear the situation, leaves the Dwight home. Delaying giving an answer to another man's proposal, she says: "[F]irst I want to see out of my own eyes. Good-by, all of you. I'm going I don't know where—to work at I don't know what. But I'm going from choice!" This, the play's original ending, obviously echoes Henrik Ibsen's *A Doll House* (1879). But Gale, in a move that upset critics and feminists alike, composed a revised ending for the play in which Ninian returns, offers proof of his first wife's death, and asks Lulu's forgiveness. She answers: "I forgave you in Savannah, Georgia." This ending dismayed Ludwig Lewisohn, who found "the significance and the strength of the dramatic action sacrificed at one blow."[2] Gale contended that "if a play is to present life—it must not always end an episode unhappily, because life does not always do so. It is true that the ironic, the satiric, the tragic, the casual, must close many and many a volume, must constitute many and many a curtain. But not all."[3] Gale seems too willingly self-deceived in her effort to rationalize away the dramatic effectiveness and feminist message of her original ending.

Audiences, however, increased and "[t]he months of solid booking made it a contender for the Pulitzer Prize."[4] When the play won, the controversy was revived. Hamlin Garland, one of the Pulitzer jurists, explained to Frank Fackenthal: "Feeling that it would be a handsome thing to give the prize to a woman, [Richard] Burton will join [William Lyon] Phelps and me in giving the award to *Lulu Bett*" (Sutherland, 334, n. 27). This patronizing attitude also apparently led the jury to waive the requirement that contenders be original American dramas. In a year that saw the production of O'Neill's *The Emperor Jones* and Crothers's *Nice People*, the other finalist was Frank Craven's *The First Year*, a social comedy about married life. Little wonder that Montrose Moses wrote, "[T]he conditions that prompt the Award Committee for that prize are always strange."[5]

Despite restructuring the play's ending, Gale remained an ardent feminist. Speaking of the settings of her dramas and novels, she pointed out that significant occasions in life often occur outside the patriarchal precincts: "The only thing which I am interested in writing about is life as I see people trying to live it. The human experience, the common human problem, has just as vivid a setting in a little Western town as in a fort or a court" (Derleth, 153). In her politics, too, she emphasized her connection with women: "If I were asked to characterize the progressive policies in one sentence I would say that they are politics socialized. Or that they regard human life and its right to grow as more important than property rights. . . . This means that an ethical principle has been made into a political faith. Broadly speaking, these are the principles and the faith of most women, outside politics" (Derleth, 153).

Like Gale's political principles, *Miss Lulu Bett* remains important. Women without education or training are still being trapped into the service of a patriarchal economy that values property rights over human growth. Lulu's courage and her rebellion against such a condition are noteworthy. Furthermore, Gale successfully dramatized the banality of the Dwight Deacons in a play that reminds us that tyranny begins at home.

Lula Vollmer: Folk Drama and Feminism

Lula Vollmer (1898–1955), a native of North Carolina, came to know the subjects of her folk dramas when her family spent summer vacations among the mountaineers. While attending the Normal and Collegiate Institute at Asheville, she also met the mountain women who brought goods there for sale. At 18 she attended her first professionally produced play; inspired by the performance, she began writing one-acts that were staged by her fellow students. After graduation, she wrote for an Atlanta, Georgia, newspaper and, like Gale, found further inspiration in her interviews of actors. She also reviewed drama for the *Atlanta Pilot*. Moving to New York in 1918, she wrote her most successful play, *Sun-Up*, for which she sought a producer for five years. Finally, the drama was staged by the Beechwood Players in Scarborough, New York; brought to New York City by the Provincetown Players in May 1923, it ran for more than a year at various theaters.

Best known as a paradigm of American folk drama, *Sun-Up* is notable as a feminist work. In it, the Widow Cagle moves from a limited antipatriarchal stance—represented by her resistance to the abstract forces of law and government as distant entities she can neither see nor understand—to a more sweeping sentiment, as she renounces the patriarchy she does see and understand as it is represented in her own feud with the U.S. government agent who killed her moonshiner husband. Through its uneducated characters and isolated setting, the play provides a platform for critiquing the assumptions of a male-dominated society; it also contains a potent message about education and literacy and culminates in a powerful antiwar statement.

As the drama begins, Mrs. Cagle converses about the war with her neighbor, Pap Todd; their naivete and isolation become apparent in their idea that the enemy is, once again, the Yankee. (The war at issue is actually World War I.) Voicing Vollmer's materialist feminist philosophy, Mrs. Cagle resists the rumor of war: " 'Tain't so. Thar ain't no reason fer war, unless us poor folks fight the rich uns for[6] the way they air bleedin' us to death with the prices for meat and bread." Parrying Sheriff Weeks's comment about the underutilization of schools, she remarks, "Well, I reckon it wuz because the most of 'em wuz a hungry. Ye kin fill a young un's brain all ye want to, but hit's a goin' to run out if thar's a hole in his stomach."

Unlike those male writers who portray war as occasion for glory and heroism, Vollmer focuses on its tragedy, especially through the death of Rufe, Mrs. Cagle's son. Even before his enlistment, his mother is antiwar; she sees war as the "Guv'ment['s] feud" and an unfair one at that: "This ain't no feud whar ye have a chance. Hit air murder, and the law air back of hit." Mrs. Cagle condemns the government for killing her husband in what she sees as the private war of moonshiner against revenue agent. Her husband was shot in the back by Zeb Turner, a government man, and she feels her son would do better to pursue him than go off to war.

But Rufe, shortly after marrying Emmy Todd, reports for induction. He sees the war as his opportunity to fight, as he tells his mother, "for ye, and the ole wimen like ye." Firmly rooted in the patriarchy, Rufe instructs Emmy's brother Bud to "look out fer my wimen folks" while he goes to defend "my hills, and my home, and my wimen folks." When Emmy reminds Mrs. Cagle of Rufe's reasons for leaving home, the mother deflates these patriarchal notions: "He mought a thought so, but I calculate his hills don't need no pertectin', and I reckon his wimen folks kin pertect themselves."

Later, as she puzzles over a "yellow letter" from Rufe (actually the telegram informing her of his death), which she, being illiterate, cannot read, a young deserter seeks shelter from a blizzard. She gladly protects him from the sheriff, whom she sees as an employee of that law which killed her husband. When Weeks reveals the deserter to be Zeb Turner, Jr., she raises her gun against this son of her husband's murderer, but Rufe, whom she now knows to be dead, speaks to her, she claims, from beyond the grave. Here Vollmer utilizes another feminist argument, for it is not Rufe but Mrs. Cagle's experience as a woman that leads her to realize: "As long as thar air hate—thar will be—feuds. As long as thar air women—thar will be—sons. [Rufe] ain't no more—to [me]—than other mothers' sons—air to them." With "the hate of the feud gone out of [her]," she becomes, like all resisters of patriarchy, a lawbreaker. She gives Turner Jr. her gun and, to deceive the sheriff, dresses him in Bud's coat and cap. She has realized that wars, employed by the patriarchy in the name of women, home, and family, are fueled by hate and undertaken in the quest for power and glory. Able to see there is no difference between a distant government "feud" and the one in her backyard, she speaks to her dead son: "I heared ye, Rufe. I never knowed nothin' about lovin' anything but ye—til ye showed me hit's lovin' them all that counts."

Like Gale, Vollmer acted on her feminist principles. She donated more than $40,000 in royalties to the education of the mountain folk. Perhaps she hoped that literacy would help create a saner world, one in which women would not have to read telegrams from the War Department.

Dramatically, *Sun-Up* does not merit much attention today; it is sentimental and melodramatic, and its noble hill folk have long since devolved into television situation comedy characters such as those once found in *The Beverly Hillbillies* and *The Real McCoys*. But as a portrait of a woman realizing for herself the patriarchy's misuse of power, it remains relevant.

Sophie Treadwell: Life Within the Machine

Sophie Treadwell (1885[7]–1970) lived the full life that was the ideal of the New Woman. Born in Stockton, California, she wrote her first plays while at the University of California. She pursued careers as divergent as school teacher and vaudeville performer before joining the staff of the *San Francisco Bulletin*. The first American woman to become a war correspondent, she covered the Mexican Revolution and was the only reporter, worldwide, to get an interview with Pancho Villa in Mexico. She lived in France while covering World War I. Her career as a dramatist spanned seven decades, beginning with *A Man's Own* (c. 1905), a one-act advocating woman's rights produced while she was in college, and concluding with the comedy *Now He Doesn't Want to Play* (1967).

Stylistically an experimenter who wrote comedy, melodrama, and social criticism, in *Machinal* (1928), Treadwell employs the spirit of the political left as the basis of this drama about the ways in which society's machines destroy the souls and spirits of humankind, especially women. Emma Goldman's "The Traffic in Women" could well serve as the drama's prologue. In this essay Goldman declares: "Woman is reared as a sex commodity [thus one need not] be surprised if she becomes an easy prey to prostitution, or to any other form of a relationship which degrades her to the position of an object for mere sex gratification." Goldman also finds industrial capitalism dehumanizing: "It is the private dominion over things that condemns millions of people to be mere nonentities, living corpses without originality or power of initiative, human machines of flesh and blood, who pile up mountains of wealth for others and pay for it with gray, dull and wretched existences for themselves."[8]

Incorporating the expressionistic techniques brought to the attention of the American theater by Alice Gerstenberg and Susan Glaspell, Treadwell depicts the nightmare existence of her protagonist as Everywoman, variously identified as the Young Woman, Helen, and Helen (Mrs. George H.) Jones. Working with two basic sets, the first of which contains both a door and a window in its back wall and the second of which has only a small barred window, Treadwell conveys the sense of being none too slowly smothered, as expressed in the protagonist's claustrophobia and anxiety attacks. The window is both barred and masked in episodes 5, 7, 8, and 9, illustrating the prison that life has become for the Young Woman; in this second division of the play the window is disclosed only in episode 6 to symbolize the freedom she feels while with her lover.

Treadwell's production notes call for a lighting design that is "concentrated and intense"; to mark the transitions between episodes, she indicates blackouts as bridges. Continuity of sound amplifies this bridging, the mostly cacophonous soundscape diminishing into a single sound that segues into the following scene. The ominous omission of the sound bridge between episode 6, the scene of the lovers' tryst, and episode 7, the protagonist's *quiet* evening at home with her husband, prepares the audience for her murdering him between this episode and the next. As the scene draws to its end, she hears the music that played outside her lover's window, and hears her lover's comment about getting "free" echoed by a chorus of voices and swelling until she "cries out in terror." But the music and the voices continue until the next scene reveals her on trial for her husband's murder.

Nerve-grating, mechanical sounds occur onstage and off. Business equipment provides aural abrasion in the office scene; the ubiquitous radio announces its presence; a jazz band, a hand organ, and an electric piano—all "mechanical sounding"—continue the tension-filled beat, and a steel riveting gun and an airplane engine carry the sounds of capitalism's progress. Even the dialogue's sound must be displeasing; Treadwell calls for the "the rhythm of our common city speech" to sound "brassy."

The play's title, French for "mechanical," provides the central metaphor; life within the machine leads this Everywoman from marriage to motherhood and murder. In addition to the physical machines, Treadwell presents the crushing forces of the abstract machinery of business, marriage, sex, motherhood, religion, the legal system, and the state. *Machinal* opens in Mr. Jones's office. The soundscape, audible before curtainrise, combines with the omnipresent office machines to which the characters are metaphorically linked, and the automaton-like behavior of the workers to present a portrait of the dehumanizing effects of the machine age. All speak in monotones. The clerk recites the alphabet of business, chanting: "Accounts—A. Bonds—B. Contracts—C." Other characters repeat their lines in the manner of a broken record, and speak telegraphically, dropping articles and auxiliary verbs. Treadwell names her characters after their jobs, designating them as Filing Clerk, Stenographer, and Adding Clerk; they become not persons but office procedures.

The Young Woman, a typist, arrives late because she had to leave

Zita Johann in the 1928 production of Sophie Treadwell's *Machinal. Photograph courtesy of The Billy Rose Theatre Collection, The New York Library for the Performing Arts, Astor, Lenox and Tilden Foundations.*

the subway and get out into the air. Stifled by the mechanized world, by the crowded car with "[a]ll those bodies pressing," she says, "I thought I would faint!" Her habitual tic of covering her ears with her hair signifies her response to the assault being made on her hearing. Her boss plans an assault of another sort. Treadwell focuses on sexual harassment as Jones puts his hand on the Young Woman's shoulder; all stare as she shrinks from his touch. The subsequent dialogue indicates the temptation to recognize the economic machinery inherent in marriage and sell herself as the only product she has:

TELEPHONE GIRL:	Why did you flinch, kid?
YOUNG WOMAN:	Flinch?
TELEPHONE GIRL:	Did he pinch?
YOUNG WOMAN:	No!
TELEPHONE GIRL:	Then what?
YOUNG WOMAN:	Nothing—Just his hand.
TELEPHONE GIRL:	Oh—just his hand—[*Shakes her head thoughtfully*] Uhhuh. [*Negative*] Uhhuh. [*Decisively*] No! Tell him no.
STENOGRAPHER:	If she does she'll lose her job.
ADDING CLERK:	Fired.
FILING CLERK:	The sack!
TELEPHONE GIRL:	[*On the defensive*] And if she doesn't?
ADDING CLERK:	She'll come to work in a taxi!
TELEPHONE GIRL:	Work?
FILING CLERK:	No work.
STENOGRAPHER:	No worry.
ADDING CLERK:	Breakfast in bed.
STENOGRAPHER:	[*Sarcastic*] Did Madame ring?
FILING CLERK:	Lunch in bed!

Foreshadowing the bitterness that will ensue, the Telephone Girl interjects: "A double bed!"

The theme of being bought recurs in episode 3: "Honeymoon." Jones, now identified as "Husband" announces: "They know how to soak you in these pleasure resorts. . . . Well—we'll get our money's worth out of it." As she earlier shrank from his touch, here she shrinks from his kisses. As the scene fades into blackout, the harsh sound of a rivet gun, an audible emblem of the forced, brutal sex taking place, bleeds into the next episode: "Maternity." An addition to "the biggest Maternity Hospital in the world," under construction outside the window of the Young Woman's room, serves as a phallic representation of the visual symbol of the patriarchy's power. The Young Woman has fulfilled her end of the bargain; she, too, has produced—a baby girl. Except to voice her revulsion at hospital odors, she now communicates only by sign with the nurse, her husband, and the doctors, signaling "No" to their every remark, thus indicating her unwillingness to serve this system. Like Glaspell's Allie, Mrs. Patrick, and Claire Archer, she finds man-made language inadequate to her needs. But this man's world must press mothers into its service; therefore, the older doctor, commenting disapprovingly to the younger about "These neurotic modern women," commands that she be force fed and that her baby be brought to her.

After the birth of her child, the Young Woman becomes restless and is taken to a speakeasy by the Telephone Girl to meet the girl's married lover and his friend, Mr. Smith and Mr. Roe—or, more familiarly, Harry and the phallically named Dick, who will become the protagonist's lover. Smith presents sex as a mechanical business when, before the women enter, he asks Roe to take Helen off his hands so he can have sex with the Telephone Girl and be home to his wife by six. Correspondingly, business becomes a cover for sex when Smith says to the Telephone Girl: "Business is business. . . . I got a lot to do yet this afternoon—thought you might go along with me—help me out—how about it?"

Left with the charming Dick Roe, the Young Woman listens to his tale of using a bottle filled with pebbles to kill two Mexicans who had taken him captive because he had to "get free, didn't I?" He plants the idea of freedom in her mind and entices her to his basement apartment, where "no one will see you—coming or going." Its below-ground level symbolizes the subterranean nature of the Young Woman's awakening passion and the illicit nature, as society would judge it, of her action. Mistaking Roe's physical desire for love, she comes alive, speaking in sentences, singing, and even aggressively tickling him; she tells him: "I never knew anything like this! I never knew I could feel like this! So,—so purified!"

Her sense of freedom here contrasts with the confinement of the following scene, in which she and her husband, seated on opposite ends of the divan, silently read newspapers. After completing a business deal by telephone, Jones gives voice to the patriarchy's view: "The property's mine! It's not all that's mine! [*Pinching her cheek—happy and playful*] I got a first mortgage on her—I got a second mortgage on her—and she's mine!" The motif is reiterated in the exchange which soon follows:

HUSBAND:	A mother's a very precious thing. . . . And a child's a very precious thing. Precious jewels.
YOUNG WOMAN:	[*Reading*] Sale of jewels and precious stones.

Shortly, the Husband reads of a revolution in which no one was hurt and no prisoners were taken; instead "all [are] free." She sits staring ahead, thinking of her lover's stories of Mexico and hearing a chorus of voices in which Treadwell wreaks meaningful changes on the word "stones." The Husband's "precious jewels" becomes millstones, become the stones within the murder weapon her lover told of, become "head stones." The chant of "Stones—stones—stones" carries into the following scene, her trial for murder.

Episode 8, "The Law," is, except for the defendant, populated solely by men. They are the lawyers who defend and prosecute, the newspaper reporters who reveal the fallacy of the concept of "objective truth" by reporting contradictory yet not inaccurate versions of the events the audience witnesses, and, most important, the all-male jury who judge. Prompted by her lawyer, the young woman tells a story of "somebody—something . . . of two big dark looking men" who entered the bedroom and attacked her husband. When the state produces an affidavit from her former lover, she, eager to forestall a recitation of the intimate details of their relationship, confesses; her motive, she says, was "[t]o be free." As the Judge questions her further, Treadwell presents the most chilling sound of the play: "Young Woman begins to moan. . . . It is a sound of desolation, of agony, of human woe."

Awaiting execution in episode 9, "A Machine," the Young Woman rejects the prayers of the priest. Instead, she prefers the comfort offered by a spiritual sung by a black convict who, condemned like her, is also oppressed, also a victim of the patriarchy. As the song grows louder, the priest retreats into Latin, his words becoming totally unintelligible to the woman whom he is supposed to comfort. In questions that illustrate the patriarchal privilege of ownership and the way in which man's law, one which he attributes to God, imprisons woman, she asks how her sin of murder made her free and how her other sin, "that sin of love," can be wrong when it is all she "know[s] of Heaven." The priest, having no answer, urges her to confess to the paradigm of patriarchs, Almighty God.

At her execution, the Young woman cries out for "Somebody! Somebod—" but her voice is cut off. Throughout the drama, her alienation is palpable: she cannot breathe in the subway, she cannot eat in the scenes in her mother's home or in the hospital, where she gags at the mere sight of her husband. Her mechanical relationships with others lead to this same call in the soliloquy with which she ends episode 1; to her crying for her mother or for "Somebody—somebody" at the end of the honeymoon scene; and to her statement that it was "somebody—something" in the room that killed her husband. Almost as often, her alienation manifests itself in the inability or refusal to speak; she is voiceless at the close of the trial scene, at the point of execution, and in the hospital until she is left alone. Then her emotions erupt in a second soliloquy in which God metamorphoses into her husband, indicating the terrible power of the human patriarchy: "God . . . the Holy Ghost—the Holy Ghost—George H. Jones—oh don't—please don't!" Although she vows, "I'll not submit any more—I'll not submit," the drama is, as one 1928 reviewer noted, "a tragedy of submission" (as quoted by Andrea Stevens in her 10 October 1990 *New York Times* review). The Young Woman submits repeatedly to the engines of society, finally submitting to having a portion of her head shaved to accommodate the cap of the electric chair's apparatus, becoming a sacrificial victim to patriarchal justice.

While the Young Woman is powerless, the play as a statement of resistance makes its mark; perhaps that fact accounts for its run of only 91 performances. Like Crothers, Treadwell portrays marriage as a stifling institution, but Treadwell, going beyond Crothers, indicates that it induces rebellion and threatens both female and male, although unequally. It is not a coincidence that only a year after the premiere of *Machinal*, Sidney Howard wrote *Half-Gods* (1929), about which Barrett Clark noted: "He perceived what he thought to be a serious defect in the modern woman's attitude toward marriage and motherhood, and proceeded to remind her that her principal function, whether she liked it or not, was to bear and rear children."[9]

As Barbara L. Bywaters points out: "Emphasizing the average rather than the special woman, Treadwell implies that it is not the extraordinary "New Woman" of the suffrage movement that the patriarchal system has to fear but rather the outwardly docile, ordinary woman who can be transformed by the social pressures of the patriarchy to act. This accent on the ordinary constitutes the radical in Treadwell's work."[10] During the sensational 1927 trial that provided the rudimentary idea for *Machinal*, the press reported all the danger in the Ruth Snyder–Judd Gray murder case as threatening to men. Snyder was the "brains" behind the operation, a hypnotist, a "human fiend, a human serpent . . . a Circe" who transformed corset salesman Gray into her husband's murderer.[11] The threat is to the man who becomes murder victim or murderer, not to the woman driven to murder by the submission that constitutes a living death.

Despite being included in Burns Mantle's *Best Plays* series, *Machinal* was better received abroad than at home. In 1931 it was staged in London, Paris, and Moscow. Revived here in 1960 and 1990, the play continued to be misunderstood. Robert Brustein's sexist disdain evidences itself in a 1960 review in which he calls the play "one of those banal tabloid stories . . . about how a sensitive dish of cream is curdled in the age of the machine." While he does note that, "She is tried, convicted, and executed by a rigid and unsympathetic society which demands the submission of the *individual*"[12] (emphasis added; and read *woman*), he fails to acknowledge the import of the fact that the society is male and the individual forced to submit female.

Treadwell's vehement protest of female subjugation places her in the feminist tradition that stems from Warren's *The Group*. Behind what most critics preferred to see only as social criticism of the increasing division of labor and the consequent dehumanization of the machine age lies Treadwelll's stronger protestation against the roles the patriarchy, operator of the machinery of state, forces women to play.

Susan Glaspell's influence is readily observable. Both playwrights wrote about women who commit murder: Glaspell in *Trifles* and *The Verge*, Treadwell in *Machinal*. Both *Trifles* and *Machinal* are based on actual cases, and in each the husband is murdered in the marital bed. Both playwrights present the law as the ultimate patriarchal institution, which recognizes nothing of the inhumane circumstances prompting the women to violent acts. *Machinal* also contains echoes of *The Verge*. The Young Woman's call for "Somebody—something" to bring her rest recalls Claire Archer's desire for "Anything—everything—that will let me be nothing," and the mechanistic use of language in *Machinal* repeats the breakdown of linguistic form found in Claire's speeches. Finally, although Treadwell's use of the names Tom, Dick, and George for the men in her play seems to differ from Glaspell's naming Claire's lovers

Tom, Dick, and Harry, it must be remembered that George is George Jones and therefore as anonymous as any Tom, Dick, or Harry. Overall, the similarities are striking.

Treadwell, employing expressionism in a paradoxically understated manner that creates a disturbing dramatic tension, charges her dialogue with meaningful ambiguities. Her use of stage space and techniques goes well beyond that of Rice and O'Neill, whom she is accused of slavishly imitating, and instead anticipates the absurdists and avant-gardists who follow her. Her technical experimentation and virtuosity as well as the continuing salience of her themes merit greater attention.

The Playwrights of the Harlem Renaissance

The Harlem Renaissance (1910–1940), an outpouring of art, music, and literature from the black community, resonates with such names as W. E. B. Du Bois, Alain Locke, Langston Hughes, and Claude McKay. Equally deserving of recognition but lesser known are its black women, especially dramatists, who were influential in developing African American literature. White women who wrote dramas other than frothy comedy had trouble getting their plays produced, but black women were doubly disadvantaged, discriminated against because of both race and gender.

We might consider Sojourner Truth (1797[?]–1883) to be the first black feminist playwright. In her famous "Ain't I a Woman" address to the 1851 Woman's Rights Convention, she presented an audience with a performance piece that was created from life and that communicated an undeniable truth: being both black and a woman, she was not viewed as a human being but used as both beast of burden and producer of yet more free labor: "Look at me! Look at my arm! I have ploughed, and planted, and gathered into barns, and no man could head me! And ain't I a woman? I could work as much and eat as much as a man—when I could get it—and bear de lash as well! And ain't I woman? I have borne thirteen chilern, and seen 'em mos' sold off to slavery, and when I cried out with my mother's grief, none but Jesus heard me! And ain't I a woman?" In daring—using her own life as text—to seek and to speak for change, she is truly one of the mothers of black feminist drama.

At the outset of the Harlem Renaissance, black characters were portrayed onstage by white playwrights as exotic sex objects, tragic mulattoes, shuffling Stepan Fetchits, and violent criminals, stereotypes all.

The black women playwrights of the Renaissance provided truer images of African Americans. Because mainstream theater remained closed to them, they created their dramas for other outlets: contests sponsored by the magazines *Crisis* and *Opportunity*; the Negro little theater movement, which arose in the mid-1920s and included groups such as Du Bois's Krigwa Players, a theater group whose name is an acronym for the Crisis (Du Bois substituted the K for the C) Guild of Writers and Artists, and which included as actors many of the women playwrights of the Renaissance; and production by black colleges. Their dramas were of two general types: realistic dramas and "best-foot-forward" dramas, designed both to bring about social change and to provide genteel role models. Within these categories fell protest plays, folk dramas, antilynching works, even comedies. Working for change, black feminists, from Angelina Weld Grimké to Marita Bonner, confronted racism in all its guises and brought to the theater fully dimensioned black characters. Known mostly by black audiences in their era—Georgia Douglas Johnson's works were rejected by the Federal Theater Project, for example—they are now gaining recognition from a diverse audience.

Angelina Weld Grimké: Fighting Racism and Patriarchy

Angelina Weld Grimké (1880–1958) is often confused with her white grandaunt Angelina Grimké Weld, who became famous in the struggles for abolition and women's rights. Grimké's father, Archibald, was one of two sons fathered by Weld's brother Henry Grimké and born in slavery on his South Carolina plantation. Hearing of the young men when they were university students, Weld made them part of her family. Although she died the year before her grandniece was born, Archibald and Sarah E. Stanley, the white writer who became his wife, named their daughter for his aunt. Grimké grew up in Boston; she was usually the only black student at her schools. Her parents had separated shortly after she was born, and Grimké was brought up by her father. He seldom seemed satisfied with any of her very significant accomplishments and was a stern, demanding patriarch who made her feel she must earn his love.

Grimké became a teacher in Washington, D.C., where she frequented the famous S Street salon of writer Georgia Douglas Johnson. Earlier, she had a spiritual, if not a physical, lesbian relationship with playwright Mary Burrill. In 1896, Burrill expressed her feelings in a letter:

"Could I just come to meet thee once more, in the old sweet way, just come at your calling, and like an angel bending o'er you breathe into your ear 'I love you.'" Grimké's letters were also ardent. In one she writes: "Oh Mamie if you only knew how my heart overflows with love for you and how it yearns and pants for one glimpse of your lovely face."[13] Whatever the circumstances of her relationship with Burrill, Grimké never married. Bereft at the death of her father in 1930, she spent the remainder of her life alone.

Perhaps compensating for early separation from her mother, Grimké created affectionate mothers in her fiction and drama. Indeed, the family name in *Rachel* (1916), Grimké's sole published play, is Loving. *Rachel* is both propaganda and protest drama, and gave birth to like dramas authored by black women over the next 20 years. The first-known serious drama written by a black woman and performed publicly by black actors, *Rachel* carried a program note stating that it was "the first attempt to use the stage for race propaganda in order to enlighten the American people relative to the lamentable condition of ten million of colored citizens in this free Republic." Writing to two audiences, Grimké utilizes a "best-foot-forward" approach in presenting the well-educated, hard-working Loving family, offering her black audience role models while she presents to her white audience the horrors wrought by racism. In a subplot, Rachel speaks against the stifling manner in which girls are socialized and protests being subjugated by a male.

The drama concerns the Loving family, the mother, Rachel, and Rachel's brother, Tom. In the first act, Grimké denounces racism as Mrs. Loving tells her children about the lynching, 10 years earlier, of their father and half-brother. Although the family moved north to escape brutality, injustice continues. Rachel, educated as a teacher, and Tom, as an engineer, find themselves up against a "stone wall" of racism that limits their employment to jobs as seamstress and waiter. Far worse is the overt prejudice through which two weeks in a predominantly white school turn seven-year-old Ethel Lane, a "naturally sensitive" black girl into a child so frightened and withdrawn that her mother, aware the white world treats her as it does because the family is "poor, black [and by white standards] ugly," declares: "If I had another [child]—I'd kill it. It's kinder." (Rachel hears Ethel's story when her mother seeks to rent a flat in the Loving's apartment building.) Racism also pursues Rachel's adopted son, Jimmy; older white boys fling both stones and the epithet "Nigger" at him. When he says, "[W]hat they called me hurts and hurts" and asks "What is a 'Nigger,' Ma Rachel?" Rachel tries to pass the incident off as meaningless only to hear her child say: "You're only saying that, Ma Rachel, so I won't be hurt. I know. It wouldn't ache here like it does—if they didn't mean something."

Believing that "the loveliest thing of all the lovely things in this world is just being a mother," Rachel had looked forward to having children. Now she listens to her adopted son weeping as he wakes from nightmares; she swears, as Grimké reworks Proverbs 31:28, that "[N]o child of mine shall ever lie upon my breast, for I will not have it rise up, in the terrible days that are to be—and call me cursed." She explains her resolve to her suitor, John Strong: "If it nearly kills me to hear my Jimmy's crying, do you think I could stand it, when my own child, flesh of my flesh, blood of my blood—learned the same reasons for weeping? . . . I am afraid—to go—to sleep, for every time I do—my children come—and beg me—weeping—not to—bring them here—to suffer." As the play ends, she becomes the Rachel of Jeremiah 2:18, "weep[ing] for her children, refus[ing] to be comforted . . . because they were not." The curtain falls as the "terrible, heartbreaking sound" of the weeping of the unborn children continues.

Some critics reacted to Rachel's decision not to have children by claiming that Grimké advocated race suicide. To this charge she responded that the drama was addressed to white women whom she hoped to make "see, feel, understand just what [effects] their prejudice and the prejudice of their fathers, brothers, husbands, sons were having on the souls of the colored mothers everywhere, and upon the mothers that are to be, [so that] a great power to affect public opinion would be set free and the battle [against racism] would be half won."[14]

This appeal to cultural feminism makes it no surprise that Grimké also addresses sexism in her play. In act 1, the young Rachel slams doors, throws her schoolbooks on the table, and complains to Strong about the manner in which she is being socialized:

RACHEL: We don't mind climbing the stairs, particularly when we go up two or three at a time,—that is—Tom still does. I can't, Ma dear stopped me. (*sighs*) I've got to grow up it seems.

STRONG: It is rather hard being a girl, isn't it?

RACHEL: Oh, no! It's not hard at all. That's the trouble; they won't let me be a girl. I'd love to be.

Four years later, when Strong says he will take her to the theater, she responds testily:

> RACHEL: You talk as though I were a—a jelly-fish. You'll take me, how do you know *I'll* go?
>
> STRONG: You will.
>
> RACHEL: Indeed! . . . I wonder if you know how—how maddening you are. Why, you talk as though my will counts for nothing. It's as if you're trying to master me. I think a domineering man is detestable.

As he is leaving, Strong becomes paternal and calls her "little Rachel." When he proposes to her, he tries to entice her with a description of a dollhouse-like "little" flat he has rented and furnished for her, "even to the pins on the little bird's eye maple dresser." That Rachel, addressed here as "little girl" by the "big, strong man" who has prepared this home for her, fails to protest not having been consulted, testifies to the extent to which her spirit has been slain.

The play contains more declamation than dialogue, readily revealing in its style its date of composition. In March 1991, Tisch Jones "adapted the script to make it palatable to late twentieth-century audiences [and] . . . created a realistic depiction of early twentieth-century racial injustices."[15] Jones cut some of the lengthier speeches, eliminated several children's roles, and added period music and the poems of Paul Laurence Dunbar. The production proved the play to be more than a historical curiosity: "The drama depicts a part of the American experience that the stage too often neglects. It conveys the pain of feeling less than human. . . . Seventy-four years should not pass again before its next production" (Anderson, 386).

Mary Burrill: Controlling Bodies, Controlling Destinies

Broached in the 1870s by Elizabeth Cady Stanton as a means of women gaining control over their lives, birth control became a leading feminist issue in the early twentieth century. Mary Burrill (1879–1946) dramatized the problem in *They That Sit in Darkness* (1919).

Teacher and director as well as playwright, Burrill was born in

Washington, D.C. She earned two degrees from what is now Emerson College in Boston and returned to Washington to direct the School of Expression at the Conservatory of Music. A close friend of Angelina Weld Grimké, perhaps even her lover, Burrill inspired in her students a love for theater. May Miller, author of *Riding the Goat* (1930), flourished under Burrill's tutelage.

Burrill departs from the genteel tradition of Grimké. Her race dramas feature characters suffering from poverty as well as racism; their speech, in dialect, reveals the crushing weight imposed by this double burden. *They That Sit in Darkness* presents 38-year-old Malinda Jasper, who, despite a debilitating heart condition, has given birth to 10 children, 2 of whom died in infancy. She has recently given birth and, ignoring the instructions of the visiting nurse, has risen from bed to do the laundry that provides her family's subsistence. Her eldest daughter, Lindy, who is to leave the next morning for Tuskegee Institute, represents the hope of the family. When Lindy expresses doubts about leaving, her mother consoles her: "Nebber you mind, Lindy, Ah'm going be gittin' aw-right bime-by. Ah ain't a-goin' be stan'in in de way yo' gittin' dis edicashun. Yo' chance don' come, Lindy, an Ah wants ter see yuh tek it!"

The nurse, Miss Shaw, is shocked to find Mrs. Jasper out of bed. Patiently, Mrs. Jasper explains, "[I]t ain't *dyin'* Ah'm skeer't o' its *livin'*—wid all these chillern to look out fo'." When she suggests that God is punishing her and her hardworking husband, the nurse replies that she punishes herself by having a child every year. After pleading with Miss Shaw for help that goes beyond an admonition to "be careful," Mrs. Jasper dies, requiring that Lindy abandon her dream and step into her mother's place.

The metaphor of the title, drawn from Psalms 107:10—"Such as sit in darkness and in the shadow of death"—refers not only to the darkness of enforced ignorance but also the darkness of the Jasper family's skin. It is no accident that Burrill locates the two in her title; racism with its attendant poverty for the black is a crucial factor in this drama. Although Miss Shaw tells Mrs. Jasper that "the law forbids my telling you what you have a right to know," it is clear that the issue of birth control has never been colorless or classless and that well-off white women have had access to the information they need while poor black women, such as Malinda and Lindy Jasper, are trapped in an endless cycle of childbirth, poverty, and early death, a cycle suggested in the way Lindy's name recalls her mother's. The hope offered through contraception is denied them by a white patriarchy that limits access to birth control in order to ensure a supply of cheap labor. The play was published in the September 1919 issue of Margaret Sanger's *Birth Control Review;* Sanger, who understood well the issues involved, stated: "No woman can call herself free who does not own and control her body. No woman can call herself free until she can choose consciously whether she will or will not be a mother."[16] In devoting this special issue to "The Negroes' Need for Birth Control, As Seen by Themselves," she sought to empower black women and also illustrated her awareness of the strategic congruence of sex, race, and class in matters of fertility.

The other issues Burrill addresses in her drama rise from this wellspring. The malformation of the legs of Mrs. Jasper's newest baby, the hunger of all the children, the exhaustion of the parents—who "has tuh wuk so hard to give [the children] de li'l de gits dat we ain't got no time tuh look at'er dey sperrits"—all can be attributed to the enforced ignorance of poor black women concerning birth control.

Through Malinda's death and Lindy's entrapment, Burrill illustrates the futility of powerless women—a black washerwoman and a white nurse—attempting to gain a voice in the dialogue among powerful white men about women's fertility. Until women drive a wedge into this dialogue, Burrill implies, restrictions on birth control will be continued by a patriarchy that sees pregnancy as a means of punishing the women whom they feel exercise no sexual discipline and that sees the large numbers of children borne by the Malinda Jaspers as a validation of the myth of black women's insatiable sexuality.

Burrill's drama is as important for its protest against poverty and racism as for its use of authentic black dialect, which countered the sometimes unintelligible attempts of white playwrights to write black dialect. Like the dramas of her sister Harlem Renaissance playwrights, Burrill's works reflect the experience of American blacks in the first quarter of the twentieth century.

Georgia Douglas Johnson: Working for *Change*

Georgia Douglas Johnson (1880–1966), host of the famous S Street salon in Washington, D.C., where the intellectual elite of the Harlem Renaissance gathered, wrote history, race, folk, antilynching, African, and brotherhood plays as well as poetry and music. Among those attending the Saturday night conversations held in her home were sister poets and playwrights Marita Bonner, Angelina Grimké, May Miller, and Mary Burrill.

Johnson moved with her husband and two sons to Washington, D.C., in 1910. Following her husband's death in 1925, she worked as commissioner of conciliation in the Department of Labor. She also edited two magazines, the *Negro Woman's World Magazine* and the *Women's Voice*. In her "Catalogue of Writings," Johnson lists 28 plays, only a few of which are extant. Active socially and politically, she belonged to several Washington organizations concerned with improving the situations of women and minorities, as well as to the Crisis Guild for Writers and Artists. Through her association with W. E. B. Du Bois and the Krigwa Players, the playwrights who attended her Saturday salon, and Zona Gale, Johnson was motivated to write drama. Of this genre, she commented in the July 1927 issue of *Opportunity*, "I was persuaded to try it and found it a living avenue." Believing this "living avenue" to be an important vehicle for effecting social progress, she submitted six of her dramas—four antilynching plays and two historical works—to the Federal Theatre Project. None was accepted for production.

She had a far better response from the magazines that encouraged black playwrights. Winner of first prize in *Opportunity* magazine's 1927 competition, her folk drama *Plumes* is the story of the dilemma confronting Charity Brown as a result of the serious illness of her 13-year-old daughter, Emmerline. Bearing love in her very name, Charity faces a momentous decision: should she spend her $50 in life savings on an operation for her daughter—to be performed by a doctor she mistrusts and who cannot guarantee her daughter's life—or should she spend the money on a grand funeral, complete with plumed horses? According to local custom, a lavish funeral would demonstrate her love for her daughter; in Charity's view, it would also atone for the inexpensive funerals given—by economic necessity—to her husband and her daughter Bessie.

Bolstered by the support of her friend Tildy, who eases her pain by sharing her chores, Charity voices her misgivings about the doctor and finds omens of death in the coffee grounds Tildy reads for her and in the funeral procession that passes her cottage. Still, she delays her decision. When the doctor enters, marked by his standard English speech as much more educated than these women and thus differentiated by class—and perhaps by his race, which Johnson does not specify—he brings with him convictions of professional and gender superiority. He excludes the mother from her child's sickroom, responding to her protestation with, "You can't possibly be of any service." Thus the patriarchy silences her; she has no say about the doctor's examination. Furthermore, he ridicules her belief in the omen and insultingly ascribes her hesitancy to approve surgery for Emmerline to a lack of love. While Charity struggles to decide, the girl dies. Although Johnson spares Charity the agony of making a final decision, she deftly communicates the choices foisted on Charity by her poverty and at the same time suggests the comfort to be found in a community of women, here represented by the friend Charity addresses as "sister Tildy." Like Burrill who refers to the two dead children of Malinda Jaspers, Johnson, through the deaths of Bessie and Emmerline, underscores the high mortality rate among black children in this racist world bounded by poverty.

In *Safe* (1929), a woman about to deliver her first child is traumatized by hearing the shouts of a frenzied lynch mob and its 17-year-old victim calling for his mother. After giving birth to a healthy boy, Liza, maddened by what she has heard, strangles her newborn son while muttering repeatedly: "Now he's safe—safe from the lynchers! Safe!" The drama may have been inspired by Grimké's Rachel, who, on hearing of the lynching of her father and half-brother, responded: "How horrible! Why—it would be more merciful—to strangle the little things at birth."

The history play *William and Ellen Craft* (1935), like Johnson's *Frederick Douglas* (1935), details the escape of the enslaved protagonists to freedom in the North. Particularly pertinent are the disguises employed by the Crafts. Because Ellen is light skinned, she disguises herself as a white man, while William poses as a servant. Johnson's decision to dramatize this particular historic escape is quite telling, for the device of disguise itself suggests the freedom reserved for white males. In having William Craft teach his wife the "biggity" walk of a white man, Johnson symbolizes the self-assurance that is a concomitant of such freedom.

Johnson's finely structured dramas are emotionally taut. Her folk plays offer glimpses into the lives of poor rural blacks, lives far removed from and much more common than the lives of those who frequented her salon. Part of the tradition of social protest, Johnson's dramas brought the issues of lynching, rape, miscegenation, and the theft of the African American's human dignity to the attention of many. She focused her dramas on women, illuminating a recognition of the special dilemmas facing those who bore children who might not live to white men who likely raped them or to black men themselves imperiled by the white patriarchy.

May Miller: The Uses of History and Tradition

A native of Washington, D.C., May Miller (b. 1899) was the daughter of Kelly Miller, the prominent Howard University sociologist who founded the university's Moorland-Spingarn Research Center, and Annie May Butler Miller, a teacher. Eminent black writers, scholars, and other figures visited the home where Miller grew up studying Greek and Latin. At Dunbar High School, both Angelina Grimké and Mary Burrill were Miller's teachers; encouraged by Burrill, Miller wrote her first play in 1914. One of the "Saturday Nighters" at Johnson's salons and a member of the Washington branch of the Krigwa Players, Miller performed in the 1927 New York production of Johnson's *Blue Blood* and was at Johnson's bedside during the final hours of her mentor's life. To educate her own students, Miller began writing history plays; she, with Randolph Edmonds and Willis Richardson, "decided that black children needed plays and skits about their own history and heroes . . . and [they] wrote a total of 100 plays."[17] Like her sister playwrights, Miller was instrumental in smashing the stereotypes employed by white playwrights and bringing to the stage representative portrayals of African Americans, ranging from poor country folk to middle-class city dwellers.

Miller's history plays feature African, Haitian, and African American protagonists. *Harriet Tubman* (1935) presents one of Tubman's 19 trips from Canada to Maryland to free her fellow blacks through the Underground Railroad. In *Graven Images* (1929), a biblical play based on Numbers 12:1 ("And Miriam and Aaron spake against Moses because of the Ethiopian woman he had married"), Miller exposes sexism as well as racism. When the children play at worshipping the golden bull, the boys taunt the girls, telling them the bull "does not like girl children, . . . he does not want women to speak, [and they] must bow lower than we for [they] are girls." Eager to participate and knowing no other way of life, the girls bow to the dictates of these budding patriarchs.

Riding the Goat (1930) deals with a clash of values within the black community. The play opens with Ant Hetty, grandmother to Ruth Chapman, giving advice to Ruth's fiancé, Dr. Carter. This is, admittedly, an unusual role for a woman, especially one marked by her dialect as considerably less educated than Carter, but Hetty serves as a mentor whose function is to reveal to Carter and Ruth their places with the larger community. Carter, recently elected Grand Master of his social lodge, must be initiated by riding a goat in the annual parade. While he protests that both the ritual and the costume he is to wear are ridiculous, Hetty attempts to make him see the lodge as the glue that holds the community together. In a speech reminiscent of Johnson's *Plumes*, Hetty tells Carter of the magnificent funeral, complete with lodge members carrying swords and plumes, given her husband. Disregarding Hetty's message about the honor and dignity of the ceremonial role, Carter persists in seeing his role as an onerous duty, not a privilege, and exits, leaving his costume.

When Ruth confesses that she, too, sees no "sense in all that parading," Hetty warns that if Carter does not respect its customs, the community will reject him, imperiling not merely his income but the community's health. Feeling responsible for her people, Ruth relents; Carter returns but adamantly refuses to parade and snaps at Ruth: "You are so crazy about parading, it's really a pity you can't march yourself." Initially shocked, Ruth decides to stand in for her fiancé. As did Warren's Maria in *The Ladies of Castile* and Rowson's Fetnah in *Slaves in Algiers*, Ruth, donning Carter's costume and mask, disguises herself. While disguise is a time-honored dramatic device, it is much more than a plot point. Ruth's act reminds the audience that women disguise themselves so they may proceed in the world unmolested, move freely in the male arena of the public sphere, avoid being assaulted, or realize "unwomanly" ambitions. Here Ruth assumes the disguise to preserve for Carter a place in the community, even though doing so means she must step out of and thereby risk losing her own. Acknowledging what Ruth has done, Carter, who had seen the one-block journey as an unbearably long one to make while "foolishly" attired, makes the longer journey to empathy; his change of heart is signaled by a remark about "our parade." Ruth's act spans the generational and educational difference within the community, bringing Carter within its confines.

In 1986, May Miller received the Mister Brown Award (Brown managed the African Company theater troupe in New York from 1816 to 1823) for Excellence in Drama and Poetry from the National Conference of African American Theatre. Miller's dramas inculcated in the black community a sense of pride in its heritage; her history plays instructed young people, creating for them a usable past. The compassion, intelligence, and humor in her plays keep them relevant.

Marita Bonner: Drama and Revolution

Focusing on the restrictions placed on women, Marita Bonner (1899–1971) won first prize in an essay contest sponsored by *Crisis*. "On Being Young, a Woman, and Colored" appeared in December 1925, giving voice to both Bonner's desires and the frustrations arising from her gender and color:

> You know that—being a woman—you cannot twice a month or twice a year, for that matter, break away to see or hear anything in a city that is supposed to see and hear too much.
>
> That's being a woman. A woman of any color.
>
> . . . .
>
> You long to explode and hurt everything white; friendly; unfriendly. But you know that you cannot live with a chip on your shoulder even if you can manage a smile around your eyes—without getting steely and brittle and losing the softness that makes you a woman. . . .
>
> And you know, being a woman, you have to go about it gently and quietly, to find out and to discover just what is wrong. Just what can be done.

Born in Boston, Bonner graduated from Radcliffe College. She taught in West Virginia and Washington, D. C., participated in Georgia Douglas Johnson's Saturday night gatherings, and joined the Krigwa Players. Under Johnson's influence, Bonner began writing plays, proving herself an innovator in both style and thesis.

The Purple Flower, a radical response to the question of what can be done about white racism, won the 1927 *Crisis* prize for best play. A surrealistic work, the play utilizes innovative staging techniques. Breaking with the realistic representation found in earlier dramas by black playwrights, Bonner creates a bilevel, nonrepresentational setting. By actually situating the nonwhite characters in Nowhere and the whites on a high hill named Somewhere, Bonner illustrated the degree to which one's station in the world depends on the color of one's skin; by using white, yellow, brown, and black as the colors of those who have dropped through the Thin-Skin-of-Civilization, she widens her net to include oppressed people worldwide. Observing that thinking causes one to fall through that Skin, Bonner speaks against passive acceptance of the status quo, which, appearing to be a civilized humanity, veils inhuman racism. At the same time, the characters' falling through the Skin indicates that the time for thought is over; the need is for action. On the side of the hill, positioned to prevent access by the oppressed group of black people called Us, live the White Devils, who jealously guard against the Us's even approaching the purple "Flower-of-Life-At-Its Fullest," *"for if the Us's get up the hill, the Flower-of-Life-At-Its-Fullest will shed some of its perfume and then and there they will be Somewhere with the White Devils."*

The play opens with the White Devils' Song:

> You stay where you are!
> We don't want you to come up here!
> If you come you'll be on par
> With all that we hold dear.
> So stay—stay—stay—
> Yes stay where you are!

The Us's state their case. They have followed—to no avail—all the routes suggested by their leaders and the whites. They are "blind . . . and weary" from working, from "building for the White Devils in the heat of the noon-day sun." Bonner, noting that books tell the black Us nothing about how to get around White Devils (because "[t]he White Devils wrote the books themselves [and] you know they aren't going to put anything like that in there"), issues a call for more black writers to join the cause. Forbearance has led only to sexual assault and lynching. When offered gold, the White Devils refuse to "sell . . . even a spoonful of dirt from Somewhere!"

Hearing the Old Lady recount her dream of a dismembered White Devil, the Old Man decrees: "It is time then!" He calls for an iron pot and mixes in it the dust from the things the Us's have built for the White Devils, the books, and the gold. Next he calls for blood: "A New Man must be born for the New Day. Blood is needed for the birth. Come out, White Devil. It may be my blood—it may be your blood—but blood must be taken during the night to be given at the birth." To the character Finest Blood, who asks if there can be no other way, the Old Man responds:

> OLD MAN: No other way. It cannot pass. They always take blood. They built up half their land on our bones. They ripened crops of cotton, watering them with our blood. Finest Blood, this is God's decree: "You take blood—you give blood. Full measure—flooding full—over—over!"
>
> FINEST BLOOD: I'll go. [*He goes quickly into the shadow. Far*

> *off soon you can hear him—his voice lifted, young, sweet, brave and strong.*] White Devil! God speaks to you through me!—Hear Him!—Him!—You have taken blood; there can be no other way. You will have to give blood! Blood!
> [*All the Us listen. All the valley listens. Nowhere listens. All the White Devils listen. Somewhere listens.*
> *Let the curtain close leaving all the Us, the White Devils, Nowhere, Somewhere, listening, listening.*
> *Is it time?*]

Bonner calls for revolution. While this call for violent resistance may appear antifeminist, her urging blacks to move beyond passivity and claim their human rights is not; she has yet to be fully recognized as the forerunner of the militant 1960s dramas that threatened or portrayed such revolution.

Formally, Bonner's work exerted great influence; Kathy Perkins finds the roots of Adrienne Kennedy's surrealistic play *Funnyhouse of a Negro* (1962) in *The Purple Flower* (Perkins, 189). Ntozake Shange's 1975 *for colored girls who have considered suicide/when the rainbow is enuf* may be linked to Bonner's use of drum beat, dance, and song. Bonner pressed the boundaries of the drama, providing new ways of depicting age-old struggles. Because these struggles continue, her timeless allegory speaks even now with all its power.

Marita Bonner and all the other women of the Harlem Renaissance shared more than their race; educated, articulate, and daring, they challenged conventions in social philosophy and dramatic form. Bringing into drama authentic representations of blacks, they helped destroy the stereotypes fed by white playwrights. As feminists, they dared question the "naturalness" of race relations erected on an assumption of black inferiority; they envisioned new modes of being, which in turn informed both the civil rights movement of the 1950s and 1960s and the black arts movement of the late 1960s.

The Voices of Resistance

Overall, the varied voices of the feminist dramatists who began writing during the first wave of the women's movement illustrated the folly of expecting a single answer to the Woman Question. Through their lives and their dramas, they demonstrated the tremendous intelligence, power, and energy that had been pent up by the patriarchal doctrines that dictated women's inferiority to men and their place in a separate sphere. Dramatizing sexism, violence, war, and racism as well as the repressive and oppressive structures of home and government, they resisted the patriarchy and its power.

Unfortunately, the victory won in the cause of woman suffrage and the advent of the 1930s, a decade of economic upheaval, caused the tide of feminism to ebb. The weak economy forced women out of the marketplace as public and political sentiment decreed that jobs should go to men. These forces operated in the theater as well; in the 1930s, 1940s, and 1950s, fewer feminist playwrights found a place on the American stage.

4

Anticipating the Second Wave

Spurred by the Great Depression and World War II, a backlash against the economic, social, and political gains made by women came about in the 1930s and held sway until the 1960s. Having gained the vote, suffragists could not agree on new feminist issues to pursue. Unable to work in concert, they found their influence waning. Women's roles in the labor force and in professional fields dwindled while their numbers enrolled in colleges declined. In 1945, the Women's Bureau defined feminists as "a small but militant group of leisure class women [giving vent] to their resentment at not having been born men."[1] In *Sexual Politics*, Kate Millet describes this 30-year span as " 'the Counterrevolution' . . . the period when earlier feminist gains were neglected under the pressure of psychoanalytic theory and political reality, and when the twentieth-century version of the 'feminine mystique' was born."[2] The conservative forces that follow most reform movements exerted great pressure, affecting women's lives in the areas of education, employment, marriage, and childbearing.

As the percentage of women entering college fell, even prestigious women's institutions "rededicated themselves to producing the educated wife and . . . mother."[3] Only 25 percent of undergraduate females in the 1950s envisioned a lifetime of employment, while a number estimated at 60 percent dropped out, in most cases to marry (Ryan, 217). Medical and law schools enforced quotas, some as small as 5 percent, until 1945. Women's employment outside the home in these years presents a complicated picture. In general, women were discouraged from working during the Depression, wooed into the labor force during World War II, and encouraged to "retire" after the war.

The war produced striking change. While women who worked were once anathematized, they now found themselves welcomed to help meet an unprecedented demand for new workers. Opportunities beyond routine office work opened in business, factories, and even the professions. The large number of positions enabled black and immigrant women to move beyond the confines of domestic work. The size of the female labor force increased by more than 50 percent as more than 6 million women took jobs. As it had since the Revolution, war placed additional stress on women who worked both within and outside the home; many were also mothers, now bearing total responsibility for their children. Still, the propaganda war portrayed these women as simply doing their part on the homefront while the men fought the real battles; furthermore, women were expected, once the men returned, to relinquish both the economic self-determination and the independence that their employment had brought. Understandably, a majority of these women wished to continue working; to counter their desires, new propaganda campaigns glorifying the "feminine" were instituted to persuade women to return to the "normalcy" of their domestic roles as wives and mothers.

Psychology was one of the chief weapons in this campaign. In *The Psychology of Women* (1944), Helene Deutsch promulgated a theory based on the premises of "feminine-passive" and "masculine-active" personalities, a theory reminiscent of the philosophy of separate spheres popular 100 years earlier. According to Deutsch, "the role of everything female, from the ovum to the beloved, is a waiting one."[4] Her ideas were popularized by Ferdinand Lundberg and Marynia Farham in *Modern Woman: The Lost Sex*; they declared that for a woman to desire to be anything other than a wife and a mother was to "desire . . . the impossible, [to] desire to be a man," and found that "Feminism, despite the external validity of its political program and most (not all) of its social program, was at its core a deep illness."[5] Popular women's magazines disseminated these same views. Betty Friedan's survey of articles published in 1949 turned up such pieces as "Truly a Man's World, Politics,"

"Femininity Begins at Home," "Don't Be Afraid to Marry Young," "How to Snare a Man," and "Have Babies While You're Young."[6]

The decades from 1930 to 1960 mark a general retreat from feminism in American culture. Still, women learned from their wartime experience that they could do "man's" work; they learned, in other words, that there was nothing natural in the gendering of labor. This knowledge would help propel feminism's next wave.

The Theater: Mirroring Society

Conditions pertaining in society at large influence theater. As Honor Moore notes, "Women playwrights with important careers, few though they are, appear at times when a prosperous theatre is accompanied by relative freedom for women, especially women of the middle class."[7] As the New Woman left the wider stage of the American consciousness, she also departed from theater stages. There had always been fewer female than male playwrights, and condescension to those few women was readily apparent in such essay titles as "Ladies Who Write Plays" by Joseph Mersand and "Playwrights in Petticoats" by George Jean Nathan.[8] Feminist playwrights, in particular those interested in dramatizing the ethos that entraps women and hinders their development, morally, economically, and intellectually, became especially unwelcome in the years surrounding World War II.

Although a great deal of attention was directed toward feminist issues in the first third of the twentieth century, this attention resulted not in any lasting change but in a tacit decision to ignore both the "Woman Problem" and women who caused problems. Correspondingly, despite the award of Pulitzer Prizes to women and the large number of plays dealing with feminist issues, little change had been wrought in American theater. It appears that an almost unanimous decision was made sometime in 1930s to treat feminist dramas as if they'd all been titled *Trifles*. Overlooking Glaspell's irony, the male-dominated theater dismissed dramas of marriage, the double standard, family life, and spiritual and economic exploitation as the mere trifles that compose women's lives, as issues unworthy of serious dramatic consideration. Fewer feminists wrote for the theater, and most who did found it extremely difficult to get their works produced in a culture wherein financial backers were reluctant to risk money producing a play by a woman.

Dramatic Images of Women at Midcentury

Most of the women presented onstage from 1930 through 1960 by male playwrights are defined in relationship to men, and when not avaricious or evil are presented in connection with their sexuality or cast as intolerable burdens. In Sidney Kingsley's *Dead End* (1935), Kay rejects Gimpty, the poor man she loves, to become a rich man's mistress; female greed is also featured in Paul Green's *Johnny Johnston* (1936), which blames war on female consumerism. In *Come Back, Little Sheba* (1950), William Inge rouses sympathy for Doc Delaney, who failed to realize his dream of becoming a physician, but portrays Lola as a dowdy slob whose pregnancy trapped Doc into marriage and whose ambitions are not worth mentioning. Furthermore, the young college woman Marie leaves school immediately on accepting her rich boyfriend's proposal. That she does not wait to complete at least the current semester reflects the playwright's view that marriage is woman's goal. To Biff and Happy Loman in Arthur Miller's *Death of a Salesman* (1949), women are either virtuous like "Mom" or "pigs" and "strudel," commodities to be used or consumed. Eugene O'Neill perpetuates the age-old whore/madonna dichotomy with a vengeance. In *The Iceman Cometh* (1946), the whores who insist on being called "tarts" are presented as comic figures, while Hickey's murder of his wife, Evelyn, the embodiment of the self-sacrificing figure women are socialized to become, is presented as understandable, perhaps even justifiable. Hickey displaces his guilt on Evelyn, making a sin of a virtue and salving his guilty conscience by claiming her forgiveness of him merited her death. (In Anna Cora Mowatt's *Fashion*, Adam Trueman found woman's readiness to forgive an inherent and shameful weakness; 92 years later, Hickey finds it a capital offense.) In *A Moon for the Misbegotten* (1943), the virgin Josie Hogan feels she must play the whore for Tyrone because her overweight body does not conform to some male ideal of feminine beauty; O'Neill "compensates" her by presenting the Pieta-like scene in she which cradles the passed-out Tyrone in her lap. The irony of making a Christ figure of the drunken ne'er-do-well does not escape a feminist audience, nor does the fact that, within Josie, O'Neill conflates the two ancient stereotypes of women.

While critics lauded these portraits of women by male playwrights, they were not loath to discuss the shortcomings of female playwrights. In 1937, Mersand declared that women dramatists "rarely philosophize, their social consciousness is rarely apparent; . . . they don't raise you to the heights of aesthetic emotions. . . . If it is the privilege or the weakness of the daughters of Eve to write faithfully of simple things, our women have availed themselves zealously of that privilege" (Mersand, 153). Nathan remarked that "a woman dramatist seldom succeeds in mastering an economy of the emotions. . . that it is apparently very difficult for a woman playwright to see her leading characters with a complete objectivity. . . [and] that it appears almost impossible for a serious American woman playwright to handle a theme save she be positively committed that one side of it is absolutely right and the other side absolutely wrong" (Nathan 1941, 751–52). Despite such attitudes, during the three decades under consideration Pulitzer committees did award the prize for drama to Susan Glaspell in 1931 for *Alison's House,* to Zoe Akins for *The Old Maid* (1935), to Mary Chase for *Harvey* (1945), and to Ketti Frings for *Look Homeward, Angel* (1958).

As Sharon Friedman observes, "with the decline of feminist activity after the first quarter of the [twentieth] century, the 'New Woman' character and the related themes were no longer a conspicuous element in plays written by women . . . [and] feminist themes are not explicitly central concerns in their plays. . . . Nevertheless . . . the critic with a feminist lens may ascertain underlying issues of feminist concern that are linked to central themes."[9] Thus playwrights such as Lillian Hellman and Lorraine Hansberry, while not identifying themselves explicitly or exclusively as feminists, kept feminist issues alive on stage, often employing conventional dramatic structures that served as bridges to convey feminist thought from the 1930s to the 1960s.

Lillian Hellman: The Cut of Her Characters

Lillian Hellman (1905[10]–84) is the sole woman considered a major playwright during the 1930s, 1940s, and 1950s, an era when Eugene O'Neill, Arthur Miller, and Tennessee Williams reigned. Hellman was born in New Orleans, Louisiana, and spent the first six years of her life there. After her father suffered business losses, the family moved to New York to live with the family of Hellman's mother, Julia Newhouse Hellman. The exuberant and disputatious Newhouses would find their way into Hellman's plays, as would Max Hellman's two unmarried sisters, with whom the family stayed when they returned to New Orleans for six months each year. Hellman attended New York University from 1922 to 1924, leaving without graduating.

At 19 she became a reader for Horace Liveright, publisher of such writers as Faulkner, Hemingway, and Dreiser. In 1925 she married Arthur Kober, a press agent and publicist. During the seven years of her marriage she wrote short stories and book reviews, traveled abroad, and read play manuscripts for Ann Nichols (author of *Abie's Irish Rose* [1937]) and Herman Shumlin and scenarios for Metro-Goldwyn-Mayer. She met Dashiel Hammet, the creator of Sam Spade (*The Maltese Falcon*) and Nick and Nora Charles (*The Thin Man*) in 1931, and following her divorce from Kober in 1932 lived on and off with Hammet until his death in 1961.

Her success is documented not only by the plays themselves but also by the awards she earned. With the exception of *Days to Come* (1936), each of her plays was chosen by Burns Mantle as one of the 10 best plays of its season. *The Little Foxes* (1939) won the Pulitzer Prize, and *Watch on the Rhine* (1941) and *Toys in the Attic* (1960) New York Drama Critics Circle Awards. In 1962 she was elected vice president of the National Institute of Arts and Letters, which awarded her its Gold Medal for Drama in 1964. Named to the Theater Hall of Fame in 1973, she received both the Edward MacDowell Medal and the Paul Robeson Award of Actors' Equity in 1976. On 9 November 1975, "The Celebration of Lillian Hellman" was held as a benefit for the Committee for Public Justice, which Hellman, "alarmed at the abuses and excess of aggression of the FBI and the Justice Department in harassing dissenters from the Vietnam War,"[11] had founded as a watchdog on government. The evening combined speeches with the presentation of scenes from Hellman's dramas. As William Wright notes, "Few writers ever live to receive an outpouring of love and respect such as Lillian Hellman received that night" (317).

Hellman's involvement with the Committee for Public Justice stemmed from a sense that she had been betrayed by other liberals in the McCarthy era (Wright, 308). After Hammet was jailed for refusing to name those who contributed to the Civil Rights Congress ("a group ostensibly dedicated to protecting the voting rights of all threatened with disenfranchisement, but [whose] choice of causes proved the group was interested only in protecting the voting rights of Communists" [Wright, 216]), Hellman was subpoenaed to appear before the House Un-American Activities Committee. Prior to her appearance on 21 May 1952, she sent a now-famous letter to HUAC chairman John Wood; offering to cooperate with the committee according to the dictates of her conscience, she stated that she would discuss only herself. Refusing to save herself by hurting others, she declared, "I cannot and will not cut my conscience to fit this year's fashions," and concluded, "I am prepared to waive the privilege against self-incrimination and to tell you anything you wish to know about my views or actions if your committee will agree to refrain from asking me to name other people. If the Committee is unwilling to give this assurance, I will be forced to plead the privilege of the Fifth Amendment at the hearing."[12] As a result of her appearance, Hellman was blacklisted, kept from working in films for more then 10 years. Her chronicle of the McCarthy years appears in *Scoundrel Time* (1976), the third volume of her memoirs.

Often debated is the question of Hellman's feminism. Early in her career she informed a writer who had called her a leading female playwright: "I am a *playwright*. . . . You wouldn't refer to Eugene O'Neill as one of America's foremost *male* playwrights" (Wright, 85). Questioned about "the obstacles she might have faced as a woman writer for the stage," she replied, "Listen, I don't write with my genitals. Why should I have been at a disadvantage? Let me tell you one thing. The New York theater is so hard up for good plays, they'll take it from anywhere they can get it."[13] Inherent in this comment is a willed blindness to the prejudice against women playwrights, despite such evidence as the condescension epitomized in Nathan's "Playwrights in Petticoats." In a 1966 interview Hellman claimed, "There's certainly no barrier to women in the theater," and in 1976 she remarked, "I don't think I had any battle as a woman. I know I didn't get paid the same sums for jobs as men, that was an economic fight, not a battle as a woman."[14] While Hellman attributed the small number of women playwrights in her era to a lack of talent for the stage despite their success writing in other areas (Murray and Waldhorn, 77), one wonders on what, besides her gender, she thought her "economic fight" was based.

Patricia Meyer Spacks found that "Miss Hellman dreams of living successfully by masculine standards: honor, courage, aggression"[15] and Robert Brustein, writing in the 14 March 1960 issue of the *New Republic*, praised *Toys in the Attic* in masculinist terms as "constructed with all the rigidity and tensile strength of a steel girder." Even Nathan lauded her, in *Newsweek*, 27 February 1939, for what he assumed to be masculine characteristics: "a dramatic mind, an eye to character, a fundamental strength, and a complete and unremitting integrity that are rare among her native playwrighting sex." The gendering of such traits is, of course, capricious. Hellman deserves a place among the feminist playwrights of the era between the first and second waves of the women's movement. This is so not merely because her work meets the criteria of playwright Megan Terry—"Anything that gives women confidence, shows them to themselves, helps them to begin to analyze, whether it's a positive or a negative image, is nourishing"[16]—or because she is, to cite Vivian Patraka, "The Dramatist of the Second Sex."[17] It is also because she dramatized the inequities of a patriarchal, capitalist system; repeatedly exposed instances of injustice and oppression; and was committed personally and politically to change. As Brustein observes, "she never wavered in her conviction that theatre could be a force for change in what she considered an unethical, unjust, essentially venal world."[18]

She rewrote her earlier liberal feminist stance as "one of the boys" when, in *An Unfinished Woman* (1972), she asked, "Who the hell did I think I was, alone in a world where women don't have much safety?"[19] In the interviews collected by Jackson Breyer in *Conversations with Lillian Hellman*, issues central to feminism arise. She pointed out to Christine Doudna the stupidity of treating women as a monolith and agreed with Doudna that "Women *have* been put down, there's no question of that. For centuries and centuries." She observed that "[t]he big battle is equal rights" and, in a response to a question about young women having "an easier time of it" in 1977 than in 1927, demonstrated her awareness of the importance of race and class in determining who has the "easier time": "I'm not sure young women do have it easier. Yes, there are more jobs available, but for whom? I'm not sure negro women have it any easier than they did when I was growing up. I'm not sure poor women have it any easier" (204–5). In other interviews in the collection, Hellman called for "jobs for every woman who has to work . . . some kind of job for every woman who has to support children," labeled legal abortion "a very necessary, civilized, proper act," and placed her primary stress on "economic liberation. There must be equal pay for equal work." She raises the subject of woman's need for economic independence repeatedly.[20]

Many critics have noted that money is one of Hellman's major subjects. Examining the dramas from a feminist perspective, one can argue that her true subjects are woman's need for economic independence, which allows her to control her destiny, and the social constructs that prevent her from achieving such independence. The motifs arise again and again: in Martha and Karen's struggle to establish the Wright-Dobie School for Girls in *The Children's Hour* (1934); in Andrew Rodman treating Julie as an expensive possession in *Days to Come*; in Regina's being denied a share of the patrimony in *The Little Foxes*; in the life-or-death power of the Farrelly money in *Watch on the Rhine*; in Cassie's resentment of Emily and her money in *The Searching Wind* (1944); in the crippling effects of Marcus Hubbard's patriarchal tyranny in *Another Part of the Forest* (1946); in Sophie's blackmail of Nick and Nina in *The Autumn Garden* (1951); and, paradoxically, in the Berniers sisters' sacrificing their money to control Julian in *Toys in the Attic*. The era of Hellman's success was both post- and prefeminist, with the organized movement of the first wave having foundered on the success of the drive for suffrage and the second wave yet to swell. Looking back on the young woman she once was, Hellman commented on her "postfeminist" youth in *An Unfinished Woman*: "By the time I grew up the fight for the emancipation of women, their rights under the law, in the office, in bed, was stale stuff. My generation didn't think much about the place or the problems of women, were not conscious that the designs we saw around us had so recently been formed that we were still part of the formation . . . and I was too young to be grateful for how much I owed them in the battle of something-or-other in the war for equality" (45–46). Hellman admits that she and many young women of the 1930s thought that, with suffrage, the battle had been won. That Hellman, with her liberal feminist desire to be admitted into the male "universal," would not identify herself as a feminist yet would dramatize feminist issues to expose injustice and oppression is not difficult to comprehend. This, after all, is the woman who, when adapting Jean Anouilh's *The Lark* in 1955, "was convinced that Joan was history's first modern career girl, wise, unattractive in what she knew about the handling of men. . . . The wonderful story lay . . . in the miraculous self-confidence that carried defeated men into battle against all sense and reason, forced a pious girl into a refusal of her church, caused the terrible death that still has to do with the rest of us, forever, whenever her name is heard."[21] Hellman's feminism surfaces in her insight: she sees Joan's self-confidence as both curse in her own age and cause for celebration in ours, and announces the complicity of "the rest of us" in Joan's execution.

Hellman told Dramatists Guild members: "I can't remember what made me write my first play [*The Children's Hour*]. What made me write my second play and the others, was that I was a playwright."[22] The impetus for *The Children's Hour* came from Hammet, who gave her a copy of William Roughead's *Bad Companions* (1931) and suggested that the chapter "Closed Doors; or, The Great Drumsheugh Case" could serve as the basis for a play. The resulting work enjoyed the longest run of any of her dramas, 691 performances. That an accusation of lesbianism was one of its plot points led to the banning of *The Children's Hour* in 1935 in London; later that same year, the play was also banned in Boston and Chicago. The drama was revived for the stage shortly after Hellman's appearance before the House Un-American Activities Committee. Not surprisingly, most reviews read that production as a warning against the accusatory spirit of McCarthyism.

Based on Roughead's account of an 1810 trial in Scotland, *The Children's Hour* concerns two women, Karen Wright and Martha Dobie, friends since college, who have struggled for years to achieve their dream of making the Wright-Dobie School for Girls a success. On the threshold of that success, they are ruined by Mary Tilford, a student who, unhappy at being disciplined, manages to convince her grandmother, Mrs. Amelia Tilford, a major supporter of the school, that the women are lovers. The women bring suit and lose in court, primarily because their chief witness, Martha's aunt Lily Mortar, whom the younger women had pensioned off because they considered her a bad influence, does not return to testify in their behalf. Her testimony is crucial because the case is based, in large part, on a conversation overheard by several students, in which Lily, discussing Karen's upcoming marriage to Dr. Joe Cardin, Mrs. Tilford's nephew, tells Martha her fondness for Karen is "unnatural, just as unnatural as it can be." As the play ends, Joe questions Karen about whether there is any truth to Mary's accusation. Karen denies the accusation and sends him away; when she tells Martha, Martha "confesses": "I have loved you the way they said." Martha subsequently commits suicide, just prior to Mrs. Tilford's entering to tell the women that she now knows Mary lied and to offer, too late to save the school or Martha, "a public apology" and recompense.

Of primary interest to an exploration of the feminist subtext of the drama are the picture of female education; Karen's education in "mercy"; the issue of woman's need for economic independence; and society's attitude toward lesbianism. The play opens in the Wright-Dobie School for Girls, a country school for the daughters of the upper class. Mrs. Lily Mortar, formerly an actor, in a "dress too fancy for a classroom," now plays the role of teacher, presiding over "the sewing and elocution hour" for seven girls from 12 to 14 years old. As a student reads Portia's mercy speech from *The Merchant of Venice*, another, in a low monotone, conjugates Latin verbs. Here Hellman suggests that the daughters of the upper class receive, at best, a hybrid education, a curious *mélange* with no focus. This is unsurprising, for the Wright-Dobie curriculum "reflects the prevailing ideology among male educational officials in early-twentieth-century America, according to which young women's education should be different from men's. Since women were considered intellectually inferior to men, their education should prepare them for the only suitable career, that is, homemaking and childbearing."[23]

Portia's speech, with its call for mercy rather than retaliation, provides a major motif. By the play's end, both Lily Mortar and the town will be exposed as merciless, and Karen, who initially sides with a student in not "quite appreciat[ing]" Portia's speech, will herself be educated in mercy. Karen, despite losing the law suit, has not learned Portia's lesson by the time Martha confesses her love. Covering her ears and saying, "I won't listen to you," Karen is unable to express compassion. But Martha's suicide shocks her into recognizing her failure, enabling her, after the violent and bitter speech in which she informs Mrs. Tilford of Martha's death, to agree to let the older woman help her, "If," as Karen says, "it will make you feel better." Thus, what appear to many critics to be problems in the play—Karen's apparent disregard of Martha's death and her acquiescence to Mrs. Tilford—are really a working out of the mercy motif. Having witnessed what mercy's absence may engender, Karen swiftly moves to be merciful.

The drama emphatically underscores Hellman's belief in woman's need to be economically independent. When the women discuss Karen's upcoming marriage, Martha reminds Karen that "It's been so damned hard building this thing up, slaving and going without things to make ends meet . . . and now when we're getting on our feet, you're all ready to let it go to hell." While Karen insists that she won't leave the school, that "Joe doesn't want me to give up here," and that her marriage is "not going to interfere with [her] work," the audience would likely be—then and now—well aware of the conflicts facing women who combine marriage and career, aware enough to understand Martha's response: "It's going to be hard going on alone."

Mrs. Tilford, the Lady Bountiful who has "been so nice" to the younger women, needs to be reminded that all women are not so fortunate as she. Her nephew recasts Martha's words: "[T]hey've worked eight long years to save enough money to buy that farm, to start that school. . . . You wouldn't know about that. That school meant things to them: self-respect, and bread and butter, and honest work. Do you know what it is to try so hard for anything?" While Mrs. Tilford assuredly does not know, Hellman provides an interesting counterpoint in Agatha, the Tilford maid; as the other working woman in the play, she understands what it means to be tired because one has worked from early morning, and it is appropriate that she tell Karen, "I've always been on your side."

Shortly before Martha's suicide, Karen says they can go away, take a train somewhere, but Martha asks where they would go, where they would find "a job? Money?" Here we have a pithy instance of the single woman's need for her own means and a strong statement of how precarious her condition is when a lie can incense the supposed moral fiber of the townspeople and, overnight, take away her sustenance. There may be implicit in the town's attitude a sense of self-righteousness in depriving the women of their livelihoods. They have dared, after all, to assume positions of authority as headmistresses. Because of her engagement to Cardin, Karen is perhaps less to be feared than Martha, but both are beyond the average age for marriage, a fact that may have fueled the suspicions of the members of the ladies' clubs, leading them to wish, subconsciously perhaps, to punish the transgressors who stepped out of their proper roles.

This same desire undoubtedly lies behind the reactions to the accusation of lesbianism on the part of the town, the play's audience, and its critics. It is here that Hellman's feminist ideas have most often been questioned. Did she retain the accusations of lesbianism in Roughead to draw an audience? Did she view the accusation as a lie? Does Martha's suicide indicate Hellman's cavalier refusal to deal with the issue she has raised? Does the suicide indicate Hellman's lack of mercy, her failure of compassion?

Although lesbianism was a sensational subject in 1934, *The Children's Hour* was not the first Broadway play to deal with it. *The Captive*, a translation of Edouard Bourdet's *La Prisonniere*, was produced in 1926. While this drama garnered good reviews, its run was brief; the police closed the production and arrested the female actors. Eight years later, several female actors, either recalling what had happened to the cast of *The Captive* or fearing that the play would generate career-damaging controversy, refused the roles they were offered. Additionally, when the drama was nominated for a Pulitzer Prize, William Lyon Phelps, a professor at Yale and member of the Pulitzer Prize Committee reportedly refused to see the production. When the 1934–35 Pulitzer went to Zoe Akins for *The Old Maid*, most theater people felt that Hellman lost only because of her subject matter. Yet one of the biggest problems raised by the play concerns just that: Is the subject matter of *The Children's Hour* lesbianism, or is it the lie Mary tells?

In act 2 Karen tells Mrs. Tilford, "[T]here isn't a single word of truth in anything you've said. We're standing here defending ourselves—and against what? Against a lie. A great, awful lie," while in act 3 Martha tells Karen: "*I have loved you the way they said.*" When Karen insists, "You are guilty of nothing," Martha replies, "I've been telling myself that since the night we heard the child say it; I've been praying I could convince myself of it. I can't. I can't any longer. It's there. I don't know how, I don't know why. But I did love you. I do love you. I resented your marriage; maybe because I wanted you; maybe I wanted you all along; maybe I couldn't call it by a name; maybe it's been there ever since I first knew you—" Karen insists that the charge is a lie and that Martha, "tired and sick," doesn't know what she is saying. In the original third act, Martha was more explicit, "recall[ing] her fascination in watching Karen undress when they were in college."[24] Hellman, one sees, is challenging her audience by dramatizing the attitude toward lesbianism held by Mrs. Tilford and other upper-class residents of that Ur-town of Puritan America: Lancet, Massachusetts. The words "sick" and "unnatural" oscillate through the drama, shifting signifieds depending on the speaker. Mary, Mrs. Mortar, Martha, and Mrs. Tilford are variously described as sick; Mrs. Mortar first uses the word "unnatural." Mrs. Tilford later trembles to hear it whispered by Mary as she accuses her teachers of what Hellman here presents as the "love that dare not speak its name" because of the social, personal, and economic risks entailed.

Reviewing *The Collected Plays* in the *Saturday Review* of 12 August 1972, Alex Szogyi noted of *The Children's Hour*: "Its shames no longer seem capable of eliciting any moral opprobrium, and yet—who can tell—another more prudent age may some day come upon us." That more prudent, or rather prudish, age arrived in the 1990s. A 1993 anti–Equal Rights Amendment campaign in Iowa linked women's issues with lesbian and gay rights to defeat Iowa's ERA initiative, and specific antigay initiatives were enacted in Colorado and Oregon. Added to this mix were the fear, anger, and violence generated by the debate in the first six months of 1993 over allowing self-proclaimed homosexuals to serve in the U.S. military. No longer does *The Children's Hour*, "this most outspoken and revolutionary play in its time . . . seem so old-fashioned," as Falk noted in the more enlightened year of 1978 (Falk, 41). Like the feminists who have seen backlash erode the gains made in the first and second waves of the women's movement, gay men and lesbians in the last decade of the twentieth century face anew the cruel treatment that Hellman dramatized in 1934.

Did Hellman mean Martha to be a lesbian, or did she intend the play to focus on the lie? Ultimately, the question matters less than does the overwhelmingly negative response of the townspeople to even the accusation of homosexuality. Despite much commentary to the contrary, it is not Hellman but the town, Mrs. Tilford, Joe, and even Karen who kill the lesbian. But it is Hellman who, through Martha's despairing suicide, hoped to "challenge the convention of a society that destroys those who deviate from its mores—in this instance, sexual" (Falk, 36). Although the drama appears at first glance to endorse only a heterosexual ideology, it does not; as Mary Titus points out: "If in the play that society, mustered by Mrs. Tilford, brought on Martha Dobie's suicide, outside the play another society forced the playwright to murder the lesbian in her text, and perhaps in herself. In both worlds the result is the same: isolation and grief, not a renewed, happily heterosexual social order."[25]

Hellman's refusal to provide such a closure has been met with various responses. While complaining that Hellman, once having established her situation through a "mastery of exposition" did "not know what to do with it," and so "the play went to pieces in the last Act," Arthur Hobson Quinn proposed what one might call the manly solution: "In real life, the doctor whose fiancée has been attacked would have insisted upon immediate marriage which would have put an end to the scandal."[26] Helene Keyssar faults the drama for "refut[ing] its own potential for disruption."[27] Others have faulted the play because it merely dramatizes the problem and its effects rather than calling for change. It is useful to remember that in its 1952 revival the play was seen as a commentary on the McCarthy era, an era of a politics of backlash against the social liberalism of the 1930s.

The Children's Hour, Hellman's longest running play, was followed on stage in 1936 by her shortest: *Days to Come* ran only one week. The consensus among reviewers was that Hellman had attempted to portray too much for any one play. Six years later, in her introduction to *Four Plays*, she agreed, saying that she had ruined what might have become a good play because she had made the "amateur's mistake: everything you think and feel must be written *this* time, because you may never have another chance to write it."[28] Although overwrought, *Days to Come* speaks to issues of injustice and oppression and suggests that conditions would be different in a society less stratified by distinctions of sex and class. Equally important, it contains the seeds of several later dramas: "the ruthless infighting of the Hubbards [in *The Little Foxes* and *Another Part of the Forest*]; the well-intentioned befuddlement of the families of *Watch on the Rhine* and *The Searching Wind*; the jettisoning of lifelong lies of *Toys in the Attic* and *The Autumn Garden*" (Wright, 111–12).

After the failure of *Days to Come* came the success of *The Little Foxes*, which opened in New York on 15 February 1939, ran for 410 performances, and toured the United States for two years. Produced in Moscow in 1945, the play had successful revivals in a 1967 New York production directed by Mike Nichols and a 1980 tour of several cities that starred Elizabeth Taylor and earned $1 million.

The characters are derived from Hellman's mother's family, the constantly squabbling Newhouses. In *An Unfinished Woman* she tells of her uncle Jake's reaction to her pawning his gift to buy books: "So you've got spirit after all. Most of the rest of them are made of sugar water" (5), words which became part of Regina's final line in *The Little Foxes*. Many reviews focused on the performance of Tallulah Bankhead as Regina. Of the play itself, *Time* found that Hellman "makes her plot crouch, coil, dart like a snake," and *Life* named it "the year's strongest play" (Wright, 135). Nathan observed in the 27 February 1939 issue of *Newsweek*: "From first to last, 'The Little Foxes' betrays not an inch of compromise, not a sliver of a sop to the comfortable acquiescence of Broadway or Piccadilly, not the slightest token that its author had anything in her purpose but writing the truest and most honest play on her theme that it was possible for her to write."

Set in a small southern town in 1900, the drama exposes the infighting among the wealthy Hubbards—Ben, Oscar, and their sister, Regina Hubbard Giddens—as they scheme to reap millions in profits by collaborating with William Marshall, a wealthy northern textile manufacturer, to bring "the machines to the cotton." Often categorized as a scathing portrayal of capitalist greed, *The Little Foxes* is also a drama of women's lives in which Hellman focuses on such concerns as economics, woman's status as chattel to be disposed of at the discretion of the patriarchy, and the convergence of race and class as well as gender in determining one's destiny.

Left out of her father's will, Regina marries Horace Giddens, not for love but because she was "[l]onely for all the things I wasn't going to get." Regina never truly becomes a Giddens, and, because she is a woman, has never been a Hubbard either, as Ben makes clear when he proposes a toast to their new venture, "Hubbard *Sons* [emphasis added] and Marshall, Cotton Mills." Although Keyssar complains that Regina "reifies images of the business woman as a cold and calculating narcissistic creature" (29), Regina is forbidden, because of her class and gender, to be in business; she controls no money of her own and, to ensure her share in the pending deal, must convince her banker husband Horace, ill in a Baltimore hospital, to invest. Regina also sends her daughter, Alexandra, to bring Horace home, imparting to Alexandra a message hinting at reconciliation. Regina and Horace have been estranged for years. Denied Regina's bed, Horace had a series of affairs. When Regina bids Alexandra to tell Horace that she "miss[es] him very much," she appears to be offering to take him back. Making sex Regina's currency, Hellman exposes the conditions underlying the status of upper-middle-class women in the South in 1900. While it is true that Regina connives to secure a larger share of the profits, it is worth remembering that her tutors have been not other women but her brothers.

Characterized by Richard Moody as a woman of "aggressive bitchiness" (84), Regina actually suffers from her economic dependence. Excluded from patriarchal privilege, from its systematic distribution of spoils that metes out authority, power, and money to men, she ultimately implodes and, rather than bring him his medicine, stands by watching as Horace dies. He had just revealed to her that her brothers excluded her from the deal by stealing his bonds and that he intended to do nothing about it. Outraged at having been made powerless once again, Regina "murders" Horace; like Glaspell's Minnie Wright and Treadwell's Helen Jones, she symbolically slays the system that oppresses her while seeking to become a subject in her own right.

Hellman also focuses on woman being denied the right to self-determination by addressing her status as chattel. At Ben's behest, Oscar married Birdie Bagtry to bring her plantation and its cotton into the family. As Ben so crassly tells Marshall, "Twenty years ago we took over [the aristocrats'] land, their cotton, and their daughter." This takeover makes Birdie, in Oscar's words, "a miserable victim of headaches" brought on by drinking as a means of escape. Beaten down and shamed, she hides her face after Oscar berates her about chattering to Marshall; like the classic victim of the battered woman syndrome, she covers for her abuser. Although she cries out when Oscar slaps her, she lies for him by telling Alexandra, "Nothing happened. I only—I only twisted my ankle." In an earlier scene, when Ben persuades Oscar to accommodate Regina and accept a smaller share by hinting at a marriage between Alexandra and Oscar's son Leo, Birdie literally rises against the scheme, getting up from the table to protest that Alexandra is too young. Interestingly, Regina indicates a willingness to consider the idea, this probably

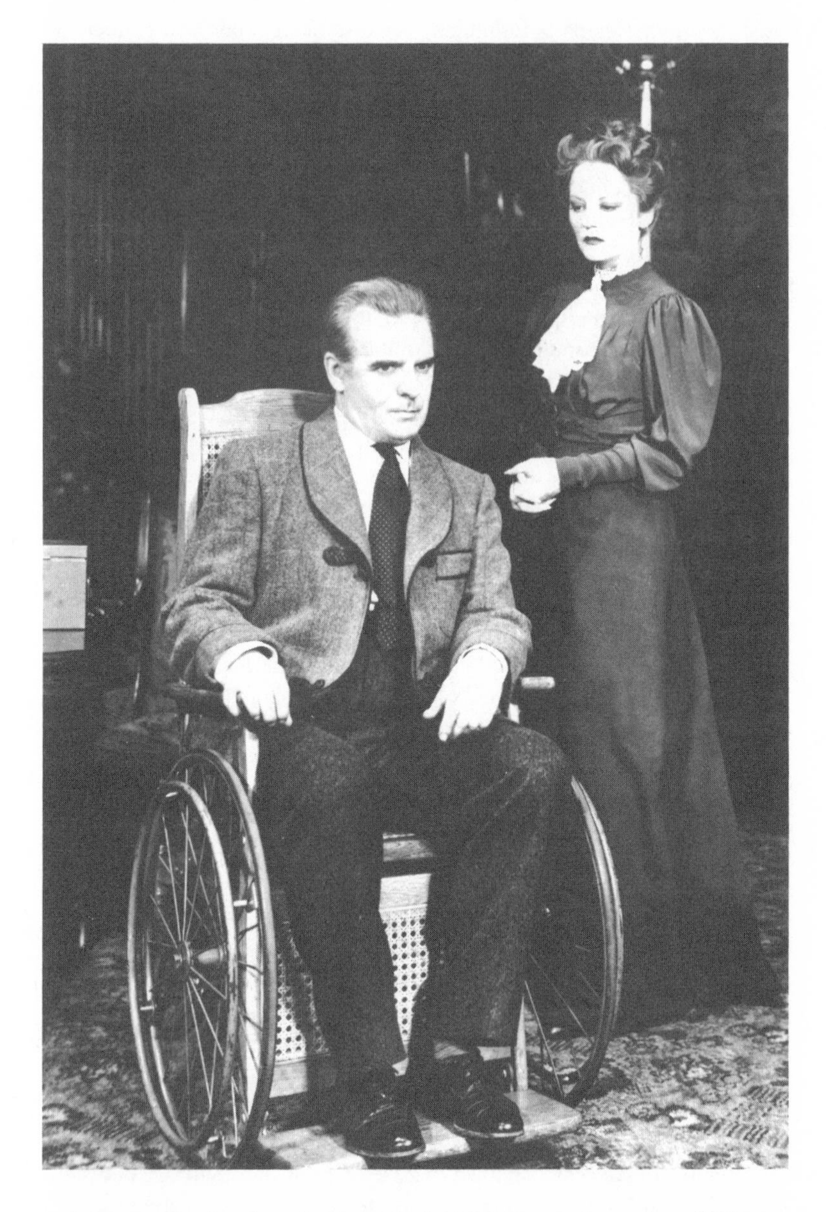

Tallulah Bankhead and Frank Conroy in the 1939 New York premiere of Lillian Hellman's *The Little Foxes. Photograph courtesy of Harvard Theatre Collection, The Houghton Library.*

being one of the few times when a woman is directly dramatized as being part of the agency of the patriarchy's exchange of women (although for reasons ranging from parsimony to survival, they have historically been forced to cooperate, as Warren illustrates in both *The Ladies of Castile* and *The Sack of Rome*). Finally, this threat to Alexandra motivates Birdie to confess her alcoholism and warn her niece about the foxes' plans. Thus, this "weak" victim tries, at least, to become an agent for change.

The Little Foxes also incorporates vital commentary on class, race, and gender as determinants of status. Ben, countering Marshall's description of the Hubbards as aristocrats, claims the aristocrats could not adapt to the "new ways," but the Hubbards learned those ways and "learned how to make them pay." Their plans for their factory include instigating a wage competition among the members of the underclasses. Ben claims: "[T]here ain't a mountain white or a town nigger but wouldn't give his right arm for three silver dollars every week, eh, Horace?" Horace, seeing through this plot to promote racism, replies: "Sure. And they'll take less than that when you get around to playing them off against each other. You can save a little money that way, Ben. And make them hate each other just a little more than they do now."

In Addie, the Giddens's black housekeeper, Hellman concentrates the focus of race, gender, and class and illustrates the falseness of the white male's assumptions about those he labels inferior. In this realist drama, Addie occupies a subservient position as a domestic. Rather than bequeath Addie the money to take Alexandra away, Horace must hide it; otherwise, as Addie says, "A nigger woman in a white man's will! I'd never get it nohow." But, by making Addie the moral center of this drama, Hellman balances somewhat the black woman's powerlessness in the world at large. Addie tells Horace of the foxes' plan to unite Leo and Alexandra; she has the insight to realize that the town's black people are "use [*sic*] to believing what Ben orders," and she condemns the immorality of the Hubbards, who "got mighty well-off cheating niggers." Although Addie is denied a life of her own when she promises Horace to take Alexandra away from the foxes, it is through Addie that Hellman pronounces the theme of the play, the complicity of most in the evil wrought by the foxes: "[T]here are people who eat the earth and eat all the people on it like in the Bible with the locusts. And other people who stand around and watch them eat it. [*Softly*] Sometimes I think it ain't right to stand and watch them do it."

Hellman hints at hope for the future through a confluence of races. When Alexandra tells Regina that she will not accompany her to

Chicago, Alexandra repeats Addie's words and vows to fight the foxes of the world. Thus Hellman suggests that a better future may arise from the interaction of the wisdom of an oppressed black woman and the energy of a young white woman.

The Little Foxes is a complex drama, combining social themes of corruption and greed with a focus on the wrongs done to women and blacks by a patriarchy determined to retain its power. Charlotte Goodman suggests that *The Little Foxes* had significant influence on Miller's *All My Sons* (1947) and on Williams's *The Glass Menagerie* (1945) and *A Streetcar Named Desire* (1947).[29] Produced frequently at colleges and by amateurs, it remains an American classic.

The citation that accompanied the New York Drama Critics Circle Award for *Watch on the Rhine* (1941) read: "To Lillian Hellman for *Watch on the Rhine*, a vital, eloquent and compassionate play about an American family suddenly awakened to the danger threatening its liberty" (Moody, 133). The play ran on Broadway for 378 performances, toured the United States, and was produced abroad in London and Moscow.

Set in the living room of the Farrelly country house, 20 miles from Washington, D.C., in spring 1940, the play concerns the awakening of Fanny Farrelly, matriarch of the household, and her son, David, to the evil of fascism. Fanny's daughter, Sara, absent from home for 20 years, returns with her husband, Kurt, and their children. Kurt is actively engaged in the struggle against fascism. Another guest, Teck de Brancovis, is a Roumanian count who seeks preferment from the Fascists. Hellman brings the battle in Europe into an upper-class American living room, as Teck recognizes Kurt, threatens to expose him, and attempts to blackmail him. Although Fanny pays Teck, Kurt, knowing he cannot trust Teck to keep silent, kills him. After securing a promise of two days' silence from the Farrellys, Kurt returns to Europe to try to free some fellow Resistance workers, leaving the American family, in Fanny's words, "shaken out of the magnolias."

The play begins as an upper-class comedy of manners of the type written by Crothers. But Hellman contrasts the manners and way of life of the American Farrellys and the European Mullers in a style reminiscent of Warren's *The Blockheads* and Mowatt's *Fashion*. When Teck recognizes Kurt, the play, like Glaspell's *The Verge*, changes form, becoming a serious drama. This is also the only Hellman drama to employ a male protagonist.

The play is of interest in assessing the feminism in Hellman's work largely for what Vivian Patraka labels reversion.[30] Because Hellman "wanted to write a play about nice, liberal Americans whose lives would be shaken up by Europeans, by a world the new Fascists had won because the old values had long been dead" (*Pentimento*, 186), she reverted to patriarchal ideology instead of "going against norms she challenged in other plays" and left "no space in the form, content, or ideology of *Watch on the Rhine* for female resistance" (Patraka 1989, 139). Thus Fanny, although witty, sharp-tongued, and assertive, lives by the philosophy of her dead husband, Joshua, present in the large portrait that dominates the set. Sara is a subservient, submissive wife, and her daughter, Babette, a highly feminized 12-year-old who delights in cooking, sewing, and wearing pretty dresses. Determined to arouse Americans to the perils of nazism, Hellman sacrificed her feminist convictions. Patraka points out the tension this abandonment caused Hellman by suggesting that the women's roles in the "Julia" episode of *Pentimento* are the mirror image of the women's roles in *Watch on the Rhine*. In "Julia," Patraka argues, "politically committed, ordinary women taking grave risks are foregrounded." *Watch on the Rhine* is the "engineered, fixed, logical text," she suggests, and "Julia" "is its disruptive, repressed text" (Patraka 1989, 139, 141).

Its orthodox gender roles may well have helped the play find favor with critics and audience. But Hellman's theme here differs little from that in *The Little Foxes*; she is still condemning those who refuse to become involved in combatting evil. Brooks Atkinson praised her because "[s]he chose sides in the gravest problem of the western world while most people temporized. Not only her mind, which is formidable, but also her heart was involved in this play about the nobility of antifascism."[31]

The Searching Wind also dealt with fascism. The people judged here are the observers, those who stand around and watch the earth being eaten, or those who, disbelieving in the power of any individual to affect history, make this philosophy "an excuse," as Sam Hazen tells his grandfather Moses Taney, "to just sit back and watch; nothing anybody can do makes any difference, so why do it?" The play had a successful New York run of 318 performances and missed winning the New York Drama Critics Circle Award by only one vote, this latter fact perhaps reflecting the generally poor quality of the season rather than the drama's excellence.

In *Another Part of the Forest*, Hellman undertook an investigation of the Hubbards' youth, shedding light on what had made them foxes. That cause was, it appears, their living in the house of the father, a house built on treason and murder. The heritage of patriarch Marcus Hubbard will not be the visitation of punishment for his sins on his children but, as seen in *The Little Foxes*, their repetition of the father's sins. In this prequel, Hellman situates the rise of the Hubbard fortune in Marcus's making unconscionable profits on the salt he sells during the Civil War and leading Union troops to a Confederate camp where the southern troops are slain. As the drama opens, these events are 15 years past; Marcus presides over his family in a pseudo-Greek house wherein he indulges his pretensions to culture. Regina, at 20, is in love with Confederate veteran John Bagtry, Birdie's cousin, who is in love with war; Ben and Oscar are clerks in their father's business. Their mother, Lavinia, who feels guilty even for marrying Marcus, knows of his treason. As the play ends, she divulges the evidence to Ben, who grasps this weapon to assume his father's place as family patriarch.

Not so successful as *The Little Foxes*, *Another Part of the Forest* nonetheless ran for 191 performances. About this drama, the first she would direct, Hellman said, "I had always planned *The Little Foxes* as a trilogy. . . . In 1946 it seemed right to go back to their youth, their father and mother, to the period of the Civil War. I believed that I could now make clear that I had meant the first play as a kind of satire. I tried to do that in *Another Part of the Forest*, but what I thought funny or outrageous the critics thought straight stuff; what I thought was bite they thought sad, touching, or plotty and melodramatic" (*Pentimento*, 197). Nevertheless, Hellman clearly demonstrates anew how the rule of the patriarchy wreaks injustice and oppression on women as she deals with such issues as women's economic dependence, silencing, and commodification.

Lavinia has spent a year waiting for Marcus to keep his promise to discuss her going to teach in a school for black children and somehow atoning for the guilt she feels both for marrying Marcus and keeping his secret. In act 1 he silences her, telling her, "Try to act like you're not crazy." Earlier, after betraying the troops, he had had her examined to establish both her "insanity" and his alibi. As Hellman brings retribution to Marcus, Lavinia speaks, revealing his treason. She also speaks for Coralee, her black maid and caretaker, who has been silenced by race and class as well as gender. While Lavinia assumes her right to usurp Coralee's self-determination in claiming her as a traveling companion, she tells Marcus that he will have to provide for Coralee's "kinfolk."

As Friedman notes, "[t]he social and economic powerlessness of [the] women puts them at a disadvantage" (83). Coralee's presence is all but obliterated, Lavinia is threatened with institutionalization and thereby silenced, while the three young women, Regina, Birdie, and the prostitute Laurette, are all commodified. Regina, wishing to marry John Bagtry and go to Chicago, tempts him by using her beauty and sexuality, the only capital she owns. When Ben outwits his father and gains control, he tells Regina: "[W]hat is in your room, is yours. Nothing else. And save your time on the talk. No Chicago, honey. No nothing." Like his father before him, the new patriarch simultaneously takes away woman's voice and reminds her that she has no rights, that she is a legal nonentity. Ben intends to marry Regina to the wealthy, socially superior Horace Giddens (here Horace is upgraded in terms of financial and class position from the clerk Regina says in *The Little Foxes* that he was when they married) and through this exchange of Regina bridge a social gulf and establish a financial connection for himself.

Not understanding that she cannot use as security something she does not own, Birdie Bagtry comes to Ben seeking a loan on her family plantation. Birdie acts heroically, overcoming both her shyness and her distaste for the Hubbards in an attempt to save her family. Ben sees Birdie's request as a way to secure working capital for his own investment and, more important, by marrying her to Oscar, to bring the land and the cotton to the Hubbards. As Regina, paraphrasing Ben's line from *The Little Foxes*, had told John: "[Your cousin Birdie] [k]nows full well [Papa] could buy and sell Lionnet on the same morning, its cotton and its women with it—"

While Ben schemes to marry Birdie to Oscar, Oscar is in love with the town prostitute, Laurette Sincee. Ironically, because of her business, Laurette is the only one of the three marriageable young women who can control her own destiny,[32] and when Oscar fails to secure money from Marcus to set them up in housekeeping she rejects him. Part of Hellman's point here is that although Laurette alone carries the title of prostitute, by its treatment the patriarchy prostitutes each young woman.

Rather than be penniless, Regina sides with Ben. She is on her way to becoming the murderer seen in *The Little Foxes*, yet "Hellman's discourse reveals that [Regina] is more sinned against that sinning: . . . [she] exposes the corrupting influence of young Regina's patriarchal family and social environment on her character, thus shifting the blame from the individual to the lack of moral values in her environment" (Georgoudaki, 76). Furthermore, "her behavior is largely a response to the limited options of a woman's life, particularly the obstacles that leave her economically dependent" (Friedman, 83). Even here, Hellman does not reward Regina; at the drama's end she sits down next to Ben, placing herself near, but not in, a position of power.

Another Part of the Forest is a plot-driven drama whose characters are less fully dimensioned than those of its predecessor in the Hubbard saga; it relies too heavily on such melodramatic devices as guns and secret or hidden papers. Still, it remains an effective illustration of both the early days of Hubbard avarice and the limited circumstances of women's lives.

Unlike its predecessor, *The Autumn Garden* is a character-driven slice of life; it ran in New York for 101 performances and placed third in the voting for the Critics Circle Award in 1951. Her aunts' boardinghouse provided both source and setting for this drama of midlife in which the major characters face the inner conflicts that surface as they enter their autumn years; as they lose their illusions they discover the reality of their wasted lives.

Toys in the Attic (1960) was Hellman's final original drama. Its run of 556 performances is surpassed only by that of *The Children's Hour*. Attempting to develop Hammet's suggestion that she write a play about a man, Hellman discovered, "I can write about men, but I can't write a play that centers on a man. I've got to tear it up, make it about the women around him, his sisters, his bride, her mother and—" (*Pentimento*, 206). So the play became the story of the sisters Anna and Carrie Berniers, two middle-aged, unmarried women who share their childhood home, work at sales and clerical jobs, and devote their lives and their finances to their younger brother. Unlike that of the earlier plays, the focus on money here involves women who sacrifice the independence their labor could bring them to support a man's schemes. "Hellman has taken many of the traits traditionally regarded as ideal for mothering—generosity, patience, self-denial—and as satisfying for the mother, and turned them around to show how both giver and receiver may be undermined by their unjudicious use. In doing so she anticipates the reemergence of feminist ideas about the constricting nature of conventional maternal roles" (Patraka 1977, 190–91).

Hellman's original dramas mark her as a woman-conscious playwright who gave voice to feminist themes while publicly eschewing the title of feminist. The plays she wrote over four decades continue to be revived. Moody gives her "top billing in the record of American playwrights of the Roosevelt and postwar years" and remarks, "Among her contemporaries only Tennessee Williams and Arthur Miller have matched her record; they alone belong in her league" (Moody, 350,

1). The plays are strong, complex, and demanding, the work of the consummate craftswoman.

In her use of feminist themes she provides a link between Rachel Crothers, whose social problem themes she continued, and Marsha Norman, who stated, "Quite simply, I owe [Hellman] a great debt," in the May 1984 issue of *American Theater* magazine. Hellman's dramas are a cultural hall of mirrors, reflecting the prejudices and conventions of the era in which she wrote, balanced by the weight of her perspective. She brought onstage the subjects of lesbianism, fascism, capitalism, racism, and the patriarchy's abuse of power, just as she also illuminated the ways in which patriarchal institutions restrict woman's opportunities and retard her development. She does not presume to solve the problems she dramatizes, but neither does she cooperate in reestablishing male power. Furthermore, her "characterizations of women may appear harsh [but] she affords her audience the opportunity to explore the conditions of a woman's life which may lead to manipulating, possessive and 'emasculating' behavior" (Friedman, 83).

It is fitting that this woman who saw theater as "a vehicle for social commentary, psychological insight, and, above all, sharp incisions into the diseased body of a corrupted society" (Brustein, 46), who sought to disconcert and discomfort her audiences, became herself the subject of drama. In January 1986 Zoe Caldwell enacted Hellman in William Luce's monodrama *Lillian*. "I found it very painful," said Caldwell in a preopening interview on 1 January 1986 with the *New York Times*, "because Lillian Hellman is a difficult person to have inhabit you." In May 1993, *Cakewalk*, a play about Hellman by her last lover, Peter Feibleman, premiered at the American Repertory Theatre in Cambridge.

Beah Richards: Forging Connections

Beah Richards (date of birth unknown), born in Mississippi, matriculated at Dillard College. She moved to New York in 1951, where she made her off-Broadway acting debut in *Take a Giant Step* (1954). Claudia McNeil's understudy for the role of Lena in *A Raisin in the Sun* (1959), Richards played the part on tour. She has played numerous roles onstage, including Addie in Mike Nichol's revival of *The Little Foxes*, in television dramas, and on film. She received an Oscar nomination for her role as Sidney Poitier's mother in *Guess Who's Coming to Dinner?* (1967).

Although known primarily as an actor, Richards is also a playwright; her best-known work is *A Black Woman Speaks* (1950). Richards may have been moved to write this play almost as much by her career as by her race and gender. As Omofolabo Ajayi-Soyinka notes, "Black theatres . . . mostly produce the works of male playwrights who write few good roles for women. Deprived of performing opportunities, women become solo performers creating theatre from nondramatic sources, performing excerpts from prose and poetry, about historic personalities, and do character and interview performances."[33] Richards created *A Black Woman Speaks* out of the history of her race and her life as a woman. In the tradition of Sojourner Truth and Angelina Weld Grimké, Richards addresses white women, seeking to forge an alliance against the white patriarchy that seeks to make black and white women, despite their gender bond, enemies. It is disheartening that so many of the issues incorporated in this 1950 composition remain points of contention. Empowered, she says, by the blood of lynch mob victims—a link to the dramas of the women of the Harlem Renaissance—Richards establishes her right to critique "white womanhood," envisioning it as it "should be, when it stands tall in full equality," but notes that that day would also usher in a womanhood "void of color and class." In contrast, she continues, the purity of white womanhood is a notion promulgated by white supremacists and sustained on the flesh of the black women whom the white men rape.

Richards informs white women that they, too, are slaves; "the difference is degree." Illuminating the status of all women as chattel, Richards's Black Woman speaks of the white women being "sold . . . here / even as [white men] sold me." Chiding these women for not fighting, she states, "I'm fighting now for our unity," and bids for unity in life—or death: "So we share a mutual death / at the hand of tyranny." The speaker points out that white women were purchased with flattery and vanities, thus "robbed of name, voice and authority," and in the face of that silence endured their "pink . . . economic slavery" by "set[ting their] minds fast / on [black] slavery."

White society's sexual double standard was exacerbated by slavery, which condoned, even institutionalized, the rape of the black woman whose half-white sons were sold to assuage the jealousy of the scorned white woman. Yet this same white woman commanded the black woman to nurse her children. Not even the poor white women, potential allies in their class as well as their gender, would join hands so "we, being the majority, could long ago have rescued our wasted lives." Instead, they fed on Klan hatred, attempting to forget their poverty by condoning, even supporting, orgies of brutal violence wreaked on blacks.

Speaking of "naked bodies on . . . calendars," the Black Woman categorizes white women's sexual commodification as "the depravity they would reduce you to" and reminds her audience that "white supremacy is your enemy and mine." Richards ends her performance piece with an invitation: "If you will fight with me, then take my hand, / that our land may come at last to be a place of peace / and human equality." Long after *A Black Woman Speaks* has ended, the resonances of literal and economic slavery, the cruelty of the lash and of the marriage market, the tyranny of "beauty," the dehumanization of sexual objectification, the monstrous violence of rape, murder, and lynching ring in the listener's ears. When aired on television in 1975, the performance piece, first presented for Women for Peace in Chicago in 1950, won an Emmy. It is a dramatic watershed, looking back to Truth and Grimké and ahead to Hansberry.

Lorraine Hansberry: Herald of the Second Wave

"I was born black and a female," Lorraine Hansberry (1930–65) said in addressing a 1959 black writers conference.[34] She thus acknowledged the significance of these immutable aspects of her identity, of being always already black and female. This double consciousness marked her writing, which she produced in the midst of the burgeoning civil rights movement and which heralded the second wave of the women's movement.

Hansberry was born in Chicago, Illinois, to Nannie (Perry) and Carl A. Hansberry. Her mother served as a ward committee woman; her father, a realtor, made what seemed to his black neighbors tremendous wealth by renovating, then renting or selling kitchenette apartments similar to the one in which *A Raisin in the Sun* is set. Moving his family into a "restricted" area, Carl Hansberry challenged the restrictive real estate covenants through which white owners agreed not to sell to blacks. Years later Hansberry recalled "howling mobs" surrounding her home; a brick being thrown through a window with such force that, after narrowly missing her, it became embedded in the opposite wall; and her "desperate and courageous mother, patrolling our house all night with a loaded German luger, doggedly guarding her four children, while my father fought the respectable part of the battle in [the U.S Supreme Court]."[35]

At home Hansberry met black leaders, including Paul Robeson, Jesse Owens, and Duke Ellington. She spent two years studying English, drama, art, and stage design at the University of Wisconsin, where, profoundly moved by a production of Sean O'Casey's *Juno and the Paycock*, she wrote: "The melody was one that I had known for a very long while. I was seventeen and I did not think then of writing the melody as I knew it—in a different key; but I believe it entered my consciousness and stayed there" (*Young*, 65).

In 1950 she moved to New York City and began working for *Freedom*, a radical black newspaper published by Paul Robeson. She also studied in a seminar on African history conducted by W. E. B. Du Bois. In 1953 she married Robert Nemiroff, and they moved to Greenwich Village, where she began writing in earnest. In 1957 she read the script of *A Raisin in the Sun* to music publisher Philip Rose, a friend, who decided to produce it. He engaged Sidney Poitier to play Walter Younger and Lloyd Richards as director. Richards was Broadway's first black director and subsequently director of the Eugene O'Neill Center, artistic director of the Yale Repertory Theatre, and dean of the Yale School of Drama. Unable to secure a Broadway theater, the company counted on good out-of-town notices, and on 11 March 1959 the play, the first by a black woman to be produced on Broadway, opened.

Its success brought Hansberry a fame that would provide a platform for her political activism. She became an active supporter of the Student Non-Violent Coordinating Committee's work to defeat segregation in the South and wrote the text for SNCC's photo book *The Movement: Document of a Struggle for Equality* (1964). Despite a grandmother born in slavery and an "uncle . . . lynched in the infamous Elaine, Arkansas, riot of 1919" (Brown-Guillory 1988, 68), Hansberry wrote the disinherited of both black and white races into her call for justice in a speech delivered at a rally to abolish the House Un-American Activities Committee. That her concern was justice, not race per se, is evident also in her desire, as announced in the July/August 1979 issue of the *Black Scholar*, to create a community theater for Harlem that would celebrate the cultural heritage of the African American people and "also utilize all and any forces of the Western heritage of that same people in the arts."[36] She added that she would name this stage the John Brown Memorial Theatre of Harlem. As Steven R. Carter notes, "The consciously paradoxical act of naming a black community theatre after a white man emphasizes the consciously paradoxical nature of Hansberry's world view and art. She was a fighter for her race who insisted on 'the oneness of the cause of humanity'" (Carter, 187).

In *A Raisin in the Sun*, Hansberry "prophetically embodied the Afro-American spirit that was soon to engulf the nation in a historic movement for social change [and provided] a catalyst for the emergence of a new movement in black theatre."[37] As protests led by the NAACP, SNCC, and Dr. Martin Luther King, Jr., grew, so did the Blacks Arts movement; Amiri Baraka, Ed Bullins, and others followed Hansberry's lead; Adrienne Kennedy, in *People Who Led to My Plays*, tells of abandoning playwriting until, "with Lorraine Hansberry's success, I felt reawakened. I read every word about her triumph and took heart."[38]

Hansberry died of cancer at 34. Her published work consists of five plays, numerous speeches, poems, essays, and newspaper articles, and the text for *The Movement*. Remaining unpublished are several film- and playscripts, portions of a novel, and adaptations. *To Be Young, Gifted, and Black*,[39] a dramatization of her plays, letters, and essays compiled by Nemiroff, found success both on Broadway and on national tours.

As a herald of the second wave of the women's movement, Lorraine Hansberry lived and wrote a feminism not widely recognized in her lifetime and one inseparable from her identity as an African American. In an unpublished essay on Simone de Beauvoir, she states her position:

> Woman like the Negro, like the Jew, like colonial peoples, even in ignorance, *is incapable of accepting the role with harmony*. This is because it is an unnatural role. . . . The station of woman is hardly one that she would assume by choice, any more than men would. It must necessarily be imposed on her—by force. . . . A status not freely chosen or entered into by an individual or group is necessarily one of oppression and the oppressed are by their nature . . . forever in ferment and agitation against their condition and what they understand to be their oppressors. If not by overt rebellion or revolution, then in the thousand and one ways they will devise with and without consciousness to alter their condition.[40]

Also cognizant of class issues, Hansberry warned against "an illusion . . . that our country is made up of one huge sprawling middle class whose problems, valid though they are as subject matter, are considered to represent the problems of the entire nation and whose values are thought

Antoine Rashell (left) and Brent Jennings in the 1983 Goodman Theatre production of Lorraine Hansberry's *A Raisin in the Sun. Photograph by Lascher, courtesy of The Goodman Theatre, Chicago, Illinois.*

to be not only the values of the nation but, significantly enough, of the whole world!" ("Negro Writer," 5).

Hansberry spoke as she wrote; in an interview published posthumously in the November 1984 *American Theatre* magazine, she anticipated the resurgence of the women's movement, noting, "Obviously the most oppressed group of any oppressed group will be its women, who are twice oppressed. So I should imagine that they react accordingly: As oppression makes people more militant, women become *twice* militant, because they are twice oppressed." Hansberry located this oppression in the social construct of "woman." In a letter to a friend, she commented on its use in *After the Fall*. Finding Arthur Miller "incapable of indicting the social order" that destroyed Marilyn Monroe, Hansberry writes, "the concept of 'woman' which fashioned, warped and destroyed a human being such as Marilyn Monroe (or 'Audrey Smith' or 'Jean West' or 'Lucy Jones')—*daily* IS HIDEOUSLY WRONG—and she, *in her repudiation of it*, in

Jackie Taylor and Brent Jennings in the 1983 Goodman Theatre production of Lorraine Hansberry's *A Raisin in the Sun. Photograph by Lascher, courtesy of The Goodman Theatre, Chicago, Illinois.*

trying tragically to RISE ABOVE it by killing herself is (in the Shakespearean sense)—right. Such a life as hers was an affront to *her humanity.*"[41]

Women are central to Hansberry's dramas, in which her "portrayals of women challenged prevailing stage stereotypes of both black and white females and introduced feminist issues to the stage in compelling terms."[42] These dramatic characters joined the real women who marched in the parade she described in the September 1963 edition of *Ebony* magazine: "It is indeed a single march, a unified destiny and the prize is the future. . . . Above all, in behalf of an ailing world which sorely needs our defiance, may we as Negroes or women never accept the notion of—'our place.'" In her first and most successful drama, Hansberry presents in Lena, Ruth, and Beneatha Younger women who refuse to be relegated to "their place."

A *Raisin in the Sun* enjoyed a run of 538 performances on Broadway, won a special award for its film version at the Cannes Film Festival in 1961, and was televised by the Public Broadcasting System's *American Playhouse* in 1989 in a version that restored most of the cuts made for various reasons in the Broadway original. When the New York Drama Critics Circle recognized her work over competition from O'Neill's *A Touch of the Poet* and Williams's *Sweet Bird of Youth,* Hansberry became the first black, the fifth woman, and the youngest American to win its award for best play. Reviews were enthusiastic. In the 28 March 1959 *New York Times,* Brooks Atkinson found the play to be "honest" and added, "A *Raisin In The Sun* has vigor as well as veracity and is likely to destroy the complacency of any one who sees it." Harold Clurman, in the 4 April 1959 issue of the *Nation,* described it as "an honestly felt response to a situation that has been lived through, clearly understood, and therefore simply and impressively stated." On 22 March 1959 the *New York Herald Tribune*'s Walter Kerr discerned the social and political qualities of the play, commenting that the playwright "reads the precise temperature of a race at that time in its history when it cannot retreat and cannot quite find the way to move forward. The mood is forty-nine parts anger and forty-nine parts control, with a very narrow escape hatch for the steam these abrasive contraries build up. Three generations stand poised, and crowded, on a detonation cap."

Friedman notes a connection between Hellman and Hansberry, declaring that, like Hellman, "Hansberry is [a] playwright whose awareness of a feminist perspective, particularly as it illuminates the experience of black women, is demonstrated in relation to social issues" (73). Among these social issues is one that was of utmost importance to the women playwrights of the Harlem Renaissance: lynching. Like Grimké, Johnson, and Burrill, Hansberry reminds her audience of the perils of instant white "justice," as Lena Younger recalls her not-so-distant past: "In my time we was worried about not being lynched and getting to the North if we could and how to stay alive and still have a pinch of dignity." Even as Hansberry recalled the past, she pointed toward the factors fueling the coming revolutions in black and feminist consciousness, incorporating into the play such issues as the link between Africa and African Americans, racism, threats to the black family's survival, assimilation, the generation gap, abortion, feminism, and male/female relationships. The effect on black audiences was electric. James Baldwin wrote, "I had never in my life seen so many black people in the theater. And the reason was that never before, in the entire history of the American theater, has so much truth of black people's lives been seen on the stage" (*Young,* x).

The plot focuses on the Younger family, three generations

crowded into a kitchenette apartment on the Southside of Chicago, and on the dreams engendered in each member by a $10,000 life insurance settlement. Walter Lee, a chauffeur, hopes to become part-owner of a liquor store; his sister Beneatha wants help with medical school tuition, while Lena, Walter's mother, and Ruth, his wife, dream of escaping the ghetto by buying a home where there is room for all, fresh air, and sunlight. After making a down payment on a house in a white neighborhood, Lena, realizing Walter's need to control his own life, gives him the remaining $6,500. Although she tells him to put half in the bank for Beneatha's education, Walter naively entrusts all the money to his dishonest partner, who flees with the cash. In a desperate effort to atone for his error, Walter decides to accept the previously rejected offer of the white neighborhood's representative to buy out the family. As he rehearses his Uncle Tom act for Mama, she tells him: "Son—I come from five generations of people who was slaves and sharecroppers—but ain't nobody in my family never let nobody pay 'em no money that was a way of telling us we wasn't fit to walk the earth. We ain't never been that poor. . . . We ain't never been that—dead inside." She insists that his 10-year-old son witness the sellout. His mother's steel enters Walter's spine and, instead of accepting the bribe, he informs Lindner that the family will, indeed, be moving to Clybourne Park. As the play ends, the family members pack their worn furniture and deferred dreams and prepare to face the threats, fears, and possible violence awaiting them in their new home.

Although Walter acts as spokesman, it is the women in the family who move him beyond his devotion to the material aspect of the American Dream and beyond the sexism that allows him to view himself as castrated by the women in his family rather than by racism and materialism. Mama, described as possessing "the noble bearing of the women of the Hereroes of Southwest Africa" and sometimes deferentially addressed as "Miss Lena" by her daughter-in-law, Ruth, appears at first to be the stereotypical matriarch. She has worked as a domestic, sees marriage as a woman's role and destiny, claims that because her grandson is "a little boy [he] ain't supposed to know 'bout housekeeping," objects to the idea of selling liquor, and clings to a conservative Christianity. Her dream, since marrying Big Walter, has been to escape the "rat trap" of the ghetto, where her grandson literally finds it sport to watch the janitor corner and kill a rat. Now she plans to take the life insurance settlement and fulfill that dream, not only for herself but also for her family, a family breaking apart as Walter berates Ruth for failing to support his dreams and quarrels with Beneatha over her aspiration to become a doctor. Seeing her children setting at each other like rats in a trap, Mama puts a down payment on a house where "there's a whole lot of sunlight."

Mama does not act arbitrarily but only for what she considers the good of her well-loved family; she does not wish to control her children and her grandson for the sake of maintaining power, but only to continue to provide growth and opportunity for them. That she, along with her husband, had done so in the past is evident when she points out to Walter Lee, "You ain't satisfied or proud of nothing we done. I mean that you had a home; that we kept you out of trouble till you was grown; that you don't have to ride to work on the back of nobody's streetcar." Here Mama becomes the embodiment of consciousness raising, the representative of the Civil Rights movement as it was also embodied in the real-life heroics of another determined black woman, Rosa Parks.

On the other hand, Mama is not blind to Walter's needs. She makes him trustee of the remainder of the insurance money, and even when he loses it to his crooked putative partner continues to love him, because "the time to love somebody the most . . . [is] when he's at his lowest and can't believe in hisself 'cause the world done whipped him so!" She responds to Lindner's appeal that she urge her son not to insist on moving by making Walter's status as new head of the household official: "My son said we was going to move and there ain't nothing left for me to say."

While Lena's deference to her son, reminiscent of Crothers's Rhy McChesney ceding her self-determination to her brother Clem to make a man of him, is appropriate to a woman of Lena's generation, Walter's sister, Beneatha, makes no concessions as she resists pressures from family and suitors to surrender her dreams. As her mother refuses to accept a rat-infested, cockroach-ridden ghetto as her place, Beneatha refuses to accept the subservient position often seen as "natural" for women. From childhood she has dreamed of being a doctor, and her brother's telling her to "go be a nurse like other women—or just get married and be quiet" only strengthens her determination. Though two attractive young men pursue her, Beneatha will not be pushed into accommodating their patriarchal ideas of what she should be. The wealthy African American assimilationist George Munchison values her for her good looks and tells her, "You're a nice looking girl . . . all over. That's all you need, honey, forget the atmosphere. . . . I don't go out with you to discuss the nature of 'quiet desperation' or to hear all about your thoughts." Joseph Asagai, a Nigerian, also vies for Beneatha's affection. Asagai's position is ambiguous; he sometimes laughs at Bennie and answers her protest about his inability to understand "that there is more than one kind of feeling which can exist between a man and a woman" by insisting that "[b]etween a man and a woman there need be only one kind of feeling" and that "[f]or a woman it should be enough." Yet he counterpoises this sexism with a refusal to allow her to rationalize surrendering her dream merely because Walter has lost the money. He answers her metaphysical question about where we all are going and why we all are bothering by reminding her of what she already knows. His "I live the answer" speech repeats the feminist philosophy Hansberry stated: "Man is unique in the universe, the only creature who has in fact power to transform the universe. Therefore, it [does] not seem unthinkable to me that man might just do what the apes never will—*impose* the reason for life on life" (*Young*, 11). Beneatha finds Asagai's response and the man himself attractive, but insists on taking time to think, thus remaining consistent with Hansberry's portrayal of her as a young woman who will control her own destiny. Here Hansberry, like Hellman, invests hope for the future in the rising generation.

Ruth occupies a midpoint between Mama and Beneatha. Like Lena, Ruth works as a domestic and suffers the indignity of employers who refer to her as "my girl." She is a loyal wife to Walter, doing his bidding by speaking to Lena about investing in the liquor store. Like her mother-in-law, Ruth sees marriage as woman's destiny and is not above encouraging Beneatha to marry George Munchison because of his money. Yet Ruth is not altogether trapped in thinking dictated by the patriarchy. Faced with the prospect of bringing another child into the already overcrowded Younger apartment, Ruth, without consulting anyone, reluctantly makes a down payment on an abortion. Much as she wants her child, Ruth also knows that she has the right to control her body. Ultimately, she is spared from taking what she sees as this painful step; when Lena buys the house, Ruth expresses her joy at being able to continue her pregnancy by shouting "PRAISE GOD!" When Walter loses the money, Ruth promises Mama, "I'll work twenty hours a day in all the kitchens in Chicago . . . I'll strap my baby on my back if I have to and scrub all the floors in America." Thus she expresses both her own agency and the urgency of the family's need to leave the ghetto.

All three women, while nurturing different dreams, exhibit strength of spirit, will, and mind. Through them, Hansberry refutes the view of women as lesser beings, properly subject to the will of men.

And once Walter recognizes the nature of his true legacy, he pays homage to these remarkable yet ordinary women. Initially, Walter perceives the insurance money as his inheritance; through the proposed investment in the liquor store, he dreams of multiplying this $10,000 into a sum that will buy Chryslers and Cadillacs, a home complete with gardener, and an education at one of "the great schools in America" for his son. The insurance money represents to Walter a piece of the materialistic America Dream. Only after the money is lost does Walter come into his true legacy: the promise of America that lies in freedom, the right of self determination, and the right to live where one chooses. This legacy, too, has been too long delayed; racism leads whites to attempt to buy the blacks' freedom and, failing that, to intimidate them through fear. When he spurns Lindner's offer, Walter has learned that, in fact, money can be squandered or lost to a cheat, but, though blacks are forced to fight for it, the truly valuable legacy—freedom—remains. Here Hansberry asserts humankind's right to a decent home and a comfortable standard of living while she rejects the blatant materialism that drove Walter's earlier vision. Freed of that distorted dream, Walter acknowledges to Lindner not only the flesh of the father that purchased the $10,000 dream but also his wife and his mother, who do "domestic work in people's kitchens," and his "sister [who's] going to be a doctor," the women who live the more precious dream.

The Drinking Gourd (1960) was to be the first in a series of dramas commissioned by producer Dore Schary for NBC to mark the centennial of the Civil War. The network executives found Hansberry's honest treatment of slavery too controversial and decided against presenting not only her drama but the entire series. In 1965 Nemiroff tried to get the play produced. Despite assembling a cast that included Florence Eldridge, Frederic March, and Claudia McNeil, he was turned down by Hallmark Playhouse, CBS Playhouse, and NBC's Experimental Theatre. Two scenes were broadcast in 1967 in the WBAI radio program "Lorraine Hansberry in Her Own Words," and in 1972 one scene was televised when NET aired *To Be Young, Gifted, and Black*.

The drama's title comes from the song "Follow the Drinking Gourd," which, like the spiritual "Steal Away," also included in the play, provided slaves with coded information. The Drinking Gourd was the blacks' name for the North Star, which pointed the way north on the Underground Railroad. While songs specifically criticizing the master, such as "Raise a Ruckus," were prohibited, the code songs passed unnoticed. Ironically, Zeb Dudley, overseer on Hiram Sweet's plantation, encourages the slaves to sing in the fields. As the play ends, Hiram's son Everett, hearing the slaves singing "Steal Away," asks, "The singing is pretty tonight, isn't it?"

To frame the drama, Hansberry employed a narrator who provides background about the slavers of the West Coast of Africa and the middle passage, then sets the drama in the context of nineteenth-century patriarchy: "Please do not forget that this is the nineteenth century. It is a time when we still allow little children—white children—to labor twelve and thirteen hours in the factories and mines of America. We do not yet believe that women are equal citizens who should have the right to vote. It is a time when we still punish the insane for their madness. It is a time, therefore, when some men can believe and proclaim to the world that this system is the—*highest form of civilization in the world.*" It is "this system," especially its "peculiar institution" of slavery, that Hansberry profiles with an unflinching eye.

The drama is set on the plantation of Hiram Sweet. His oxymoronic name, combining "exalted brother" and "sweet"-ness, provides a paradigm for Hiram's worldview. He does indeed see himself as exalted but also feels he is benevolent. Hiram pictures himself as a self-made man who, starting "with four slaves and fifty dollars," wrested a fine plantation from the bare ground. One of those four slaves was Rissa, Hiram's cook and the mother of two sons, one of whom has already followed the Drinking Gourd northward. Hannibal, the other son, is, despite prohibition and dire penalty, learning to read. As it must, "this system" exacts its toll, leaving Hiram dead, Hannibal blinded but making his way north, and Rissa alone.

Hiram, aging and ill, cedes control to his son. Intent on increasing production, Everett hires the poor white Zeb Dudley to drive the slaves. Here Hansberry inserts class into the racial mix, already brilliantly focused on in the opening scenes, which contrast the beauty of Hiram's home and sumptuousness of his meal with the grimness of both habitat and food in the slave quarters. Zeb sees his children going hungry and, despite his preacher's exhortation to follow the example of his father, who, "Didn't call anybody master and caused none to call him master," falls prey to Everett's promise of salary and bonuses. Soon he is a tool of the patriarchy, lashing stripes across Hannibal's face; Dudley acts because he can: "That's right, for *nothin'!*" And when they discover Hannibal at his reading lesson, Zeb, under orders from Everett, uses the butt end of the same whip to gouge out Hannibal's eyes.

Rissa, learning of this horrific maiming, rebukes the elder Sweet, who begs her forgiveness by claiming, "Other men's rules are a part of my life" with "Why? Ain't you *Master*? How can a man be master of some men and not at all of others—." This once docile slave, who had compromised with the "system" and quietly obeyed her master because she knew of other plantations where life was harsher by far, becomes a different woman. In her query she calls the patriarchy itself into question: in ministering to her wounded son, she steals Hiram's gun, a gift from his father, stealing the symbol of the potency of the patriarchy; by refusing to heed Hiram's plea for help as he lies dying outside her cabin, she symbolically murders him in an act representative of the wished-for death of both slavery and the slaveholder, as symbolized in the white patriarchy. Now a Hansberry woman joins those of Glaspell and Treadwell in slaying the oppressor. As Rissa acts to save her son rather than the master, Hansberry also demolishes the myth of the submissive, forgiving Black Mammy, ever loyal to her white charges. Despite the drama's intensity and honesty—or perhaps because of these factors—it seems unlikely that the work will ever be produced in the medium for which it was created.

In 1964, *The Sign in Sidney Brustein's Window*, Hansberry's second stage play, reached Broadway. Reviews ranged from Rex Reed's glowing encomium in the 29 October 1964 *New York Express* that "I shall never, as long as I live, hope to see such perfection in the theatre again" to Marvin Gottfried's scorn about "the triviality of it all" in the 16 October 1964 *Women's Wear Daily*. Part of the problem mirrors that in Hellman's *Days to Come*; both playwrights pursue too many issues. *The Sign in Sidney Brustein's Window* deals with the solipsism of the intellectual, the need for commitment, race, the oppression of women, existentialism, psychoanalysis, patriarchy, political opportunism, betrayal, anti-Semitism, and the sexual double standard. It is notable as the drama in which Hansberry introduces a homosexual character. She had "by this time . . . become comfortable with her own lesbianism."[43] She had also linked homophobia and sexism, theorizing that "there may be women to emerge who will be able to formulate a new and possible concept that homosexual persecution and condemnation has at its roots not only social ignorance but a philosophically active anti-feminist dogma."[44] Through gay playwright David Ragin, Hansberry recognized the pain connected with having to conceal one's sexuality, but she also indicated impatience with special pleading when Sidney remarks, "David, please get over the notion that your particular 'thing' is something that only the deepest, saddest, the most nobly tortured can know about. It ain't—it's just one kind of sex—that's all."

In *Les Blancs*, a drama she began in 1960, Hansberry dramatized her anticolonial, antiracist stance. Although one scene of the play was presented in an Actors Studio Writers Workshop staging in 1963, no complete production took place until 1970, when Nemiroff "synthesiz[ed] the scenes already completed . . . [drew] upon relevant fragments from earlier drafts and creat[ed], as needed, dialogue of [his] own to bridge gaps, deepen relationships or tighten the drama along the lines [he and Hansberry] had explored together."[45]

The drama, which highlights the connection between colonialism, racism, and sexism and the patriarchy, makes its strongest statement about race. Hansberry sets down what is arguably the first statement in American drama concerning the intersection of these elements. The Europeanized African Tshembe Matoseh, who has returned to Africa for his father's funeral, calls "race—racism . . . a device. No more. No less. . . . An invention to justify the rule of some men over others." He nevertheless points out to the white journalist Charlie Morris that

> a device *is* a device, but . . . it also has consequences; once invented it takes on a life, a reality of its own. So, in one century, men invoke the device of religion to cloak their conquests. In another, race. Now, in both cases you and I may recognize the fraudulence of the device, but the fact remains that a man who has a sword run through him because he refuses to become a Moslem or a Christian—or who is shot in Zatembe or Mississippi because he is black—is suffering the utter *reality* of the device. And it is pointless to pretend that it doesn't *exist*—merely because it is a *lie!*

Hansberry then employs the device and the lie to illustrate that bloody revolution—like that forecast by Bonner in The Purple Flower—is probably inevitable because freedom is "the only possible manner of life on this planet."[46]

Hansberry moved marginalized peoples to the center of the stage. Her black women and men, white women, and gay men convey to the audience truths they have perceived from their vantage points on the edges of society. Proving that the truth of black lives could command audiences both black and white, she also spoke in her plays for women who, like her Iris Paradus Brustein, were "chafing at the bonds" placed on them by the patriarchy. Hansberry seized historic moments and, working dramatic alchemy, transformed these times into art that both captured and transcended the particular.

Pathways to a Feminist Future

Lillian Hellman, Beah Richards, and Lorraine Hansberry wrote in an era characterized by the economic upheaval of the Great Depression, the universal horror of World War II, the blossoming of suburbia, and, with Hansberry, the Civil Rights and the renewed Women's movements. These three decades—1934 to 1964—were not decades of great social awareness, yet these playwrights carried forth the social concerns of earlier feminist dramatists, maintaining thereby a dramatic platform that would, in the following three decades, support a new generation of feminist playwrights who would strive even more overtly to transform both stage and society.

5

The Second Wave: A Multiplicity of Concerns

Under the veneer of 1950s complacency, a new consciousness simmered among women. Buoyed by a self-confidence developed when many managed homes and jobs during World War II, women who had apparently accepted the retreat from feminism and careers ordained by the return of the men did not forget that their earlier success had proven there was no "natural" gendering of labor into men's and women's work. Like their foremothers who underwent change during America's earlier wars, these women incubated ideas that formed the basis of the second wave of the women's movement. Of course, women's absence from most history, written as it is by men, concealed their common cause with Abigail Adams, the abolitionists, the suffragists, even their mothers or grandmothers who might have had similar experiences during World War I. Feminists have been forced by this absence to keep reinventing the wheel, that is, a feminist consciousness, defined by Gerda Lerner as: "(1) . . . the awareness of women that they belong to a subordinate group and that, as members of such a group, they have suffered wrongs; (2) the recognition that their condition of subordination is not natural, but societally determined; (3) the development of a sense of sisterhood; (4) the autonomous definition by women of their goals and strategies for changing their condition; and (5) the development of an alternate vision of the future."[1] Since the late 1960s, feminist theorists have labored to ensure that, despite conservative backlash, the principles of sexual equality and the history of the struggle to bring about that equality are not again eclipsed, that women will retain possession of feminist consciousness and a usable past.

The second wave of the women's movement concerned itself with multiple issues. Under the banner of equal rights, women worked to effect equality between the sexes in such areas as education, employment, wages, the family, child rearing, and government. As their precursors in the first wave had learned to organize in the abolitionist movement, many women of the second wave received their education in the Civil Rights movement, recognizing that sex, as well as color, led to a denial of rights. Equally important to the reawakening of American feminist consciousness was the 1963 publication of Betty Friedan's *The Feminine Mystique*. While much of what Friedan articulated had been said before, her focus on "the problem without a name" helped women realize that they were not alone, that others felt imprisoned by a society that circumscribed their lives according to their biology. Some perceived that the "problem" was social, not personal, and thus began the journey to women's realizations that "the personal is the political" and that the solution to the "problem" is political.

In 1961, President Kennedy established the Commission on the Status of Women. Its 1963 report demonstrated that women were victims of discrimination and recommended action in education and counseling, home, community, employment and labor standards, social security for widows, paid maternity leave, and equality under the law. The recommendations, while startling to many, asked for far less than women would soon demand for themselves. Women who had worked on state and national commissions grew weary of rhetoric followed by inaction. In 1968, at the third National Conference of State Commissions on the Status of Women, several delegates attempted to submit a resolution demanding that laws against discrimination be enforced; when they were told that the conference would accept no resolutions, they perceived the need for organization. This was the genesis of NOW, the National Organization for Women, formed "[t]o take action to bring women into full participation in the mainstream of American society NOW, exercising all the privileges and responsibilities thereof in truly equal partnership with men."

The women of the 1960s and 1970s, like their foremothers in the suffrage and temperance movements, paraded to protest inequality and used street theater to attract media attention. For example, "At the 1968 Miss America pageant," a group of radical young women "crowned a live sheep, tossed objects of female torture—girdles, bras, curlers, issues of the *Ladies Home Journal*—into a 'freedom trashcan,' and auctioned off an effigy: 'Gentlemen, I offer you the 1969 model. She's better every year. She walks. She talks. She smiles on cue. *And* she does housework.' "[2] While demonstrations called attention to the widespread perception of women as sex objects, women continued working in other areas. In 1970 NOW filed discrimination complaints with the Office of Federal Contract Compliance against 1,300 corporations; by 1971, the Women's Equity Action League had filed discrimination complaints against more than 250 academic institutions. Women confirmed, with statistical evidence, that their educations had been damaged by gender stereotyping. To countervail such damages, women lobbied for legislation outlawing sex discrimination in public schools and most colleges, which Congress passed in 1972.

The resurgent feminism of the 1960s and 1970s also challenged patriarchal privilege within families. As inexpensive oral contraceptives became available, birth rates fell; women, with and without children, employed outside the home gained some economic independence and no longer felt constrained to remain in unhappy or abusive marriages. Also, the age at marriage rose for women and more women remained single altogether.

By 1980, more than half the women in two-parent families were employed outside the home. New models for families came into being as males were urged to become active participants in child rearing. In the 1976 edition of *Baby and Child Care,* Dr. Benjamin Spock declared the father's responsibility to be as great as the mother's. In the 1980s and 1990s, new definitions of family arose: the "molded families" of second marriages, the two parents of the same-sex families of gay or lesbian partners, the single-parent family, and other variations of the so-called "ideal." By the mid-1990s, some states were extending health care and other benefits to unmarried domestic partners. By 1991, according to the U.S. Census, men with wives employed outside the home were the primary caregivers for 20 percent of children age five and younger. The Family Leave Act of 1993 guaranteed leave for childbirth or family illness to wife or husband. Clearly, feminism had had an impact.

Praxis: Transforming Stage and Society

The playwrights of the second wave sought to transform both the stage itself and the society it reflected. In the 1960s, off-Broadway revues, regional theaters, and newly created feminist theaters began producing plays by women in large numbers. These works were characterized by significant structural and thematic innovations. The playwrights melded the comic with the serious, blended musical and conventional theater, combined individual and social themes, and frequently replaced the traditional plot utilizing climax, recognition, and through-line with circular or contiguous structures and scenes of transformation. Gender roles were blurred, inverted, or abolished, and many dramas resisted closure. Emulating Alice Gerstenberg, Susan Glaspell, and Sophie Treadwell, feminist dramatists began using expressionistic techniques to portray the female psyche, to dramatize and explore women's oppression and the uniqueness of their fragmented lives. Others discovered ways to dramatize woman's reawakened feminist consciousness. These playwrights sought, through a praxis of the stage, to transform actor, audience, and world by using drama to promote women's awareness of their situation and to assist them in imagining alternatives to their oppression. These playwrights desired not only to dramatize women's experiences but also to change the conditions of their lives.

Agents of Change

When asked by the *New York Times* on 20 May 1973, "Where Are the Women Playwrights?" Rosalyn Drexler replied, "They are deployed about the city waiting to make their move. They have already learned how to take apart and put together their typewriters in a matter of minutes, and how to keep them clean and well lubricated. At a signal . . . all women playwrights will shoot the vapids and proceed to a secret rendezvous where a secret store of explosive topics is waiting to be used. With proper handling, each sentence will find its mark." Her tongue-in-cheek metaphor holds seeds of truth. The feminist playwrights who had left or been turned away by the commercial theater had found homes in the cafés and studio theaters of off- and off-off-Broadway, in regional and feminist theaters. Yet except by scholars who began analyzing feminist drama in the mid-1970s, these playwrights were largely ignored. Even though seven women dramatists won Obies (the Obie Award was established by the *Village Voice* in 1956 to honor excellence in off-Broadway drama) between 1958 and 1978, the 10 plays included in Ross Wetzsteon's *The Obie Winners: The Best of Off Broadway* are by male playwrights. Ignoring Pulitzer Prize winners *Crimes of the Heart* (Beth Henley, 1981), *'night, Mother* (Marsha Norman, 1983), and *The Heidi Chronicles* (Wendy Wasserstein, 1989), *Time* selected plays by male dramatists only for its January 1990 best-of-the-decade issue.

To combat such ignorance and indifference, women have formed alliances designed to make it known that, in Julia Miles's words, women playwrights "exist, they are talented, and they are ready to enter the mainstream theatre."[3] In 1978, partly in reaction to learning that only 7 percent of the playwrights produced in funded nonprofit theaters from 1969 to 1975 were women, Miles founded the Women's Project at the American Place Theatre in New York. While Miles identifies neither herself nor the Women's Project as specifically feminist, the Women's Project has produced works by Maria Irene Fornes, Emily Mann, and many other feminist playwrights. By 1985, with a membership of approximately 200 playwrights and directors, the Women's Project had reviewed more than 4,000 scripts and presented 150 rehearsed readings. By 1994, it had produced 70 plays and published 5 anthologies. While its now 400 members have received numerous fellowships and grants, in her mission statement artistic director Miles says, "We measure our success by the increased courage and energy women are bringing to the stage. . . . A more tangible measure is the increase in the numbers of women working in the theatre from approximately 6 percent to 7 percent for playwrights and directors [in 1978] to three times that number [in 1994]." Other organizations that have promoted women playwrights include the Women's Program of the American Theatre Association, the Women and Theatre Program, Women's Interart Theatre, the Women's Theatre Council, and the Committee for Women of the Dramatists Guild. In 1989, the First International Women Playwrights Festival and Conference was held in Buffalo, New York; the third met in July 1994 in Australia.

Negative images of women continued to predominate onstage. The vacuous but castrating Mommy of Edward Albee's *The American Dream* (1961) is an appropriate ancestor to the male-devouring Martha of his *Who's Afraid of Virginia Woolf?* (1962). The white Lula of Amiri Baraka's *Dutchman* (1964) uses her sexuality to lure, ensnare, demean, and murder Clay. Women are presented as marginal creatures by David

Mamet, Sam Shepard, David Rabe, and Israel Horovitz. Even as diegetic characters, women are debased by Mamet's males. In *American Buffalo* (1975), Teach labels Ruthie a "vicious dyke" who has "not one loyal bone" in her body. Shepard's female characters are beaten to insensibility (*A Lie of the Mind*, 1985) and raped (*The Tooth of Crime*, 1972), while in Rabe's *Goose and Tomtom* (1981) Lulu is tied up, blindfolded, hung in a closet and periodically raped by Tomtom, who says, "I love to bang 'em, man. They got the plumbing, you know what I mean." As Susan Smith Harris concludes, "The very fact of the commercial success of these three writers points to a domination of a patriarchal, phallocentric theater system."[4] Horovitz's Margy Burke, the title character of *The Widow's Blind Date* (1989), is gang-raped by men whose motives range from desiring to take her virginity to punishing her for being a whore, but who blame her for their crime. Countering such images and stereotypes by resisting the identities they posit and thus recovering womanhood is one task of the feminist playwright.

The vanguard of the feminist playwrights of the second wave actually preceded the onset of the women's movement in the 1970s. Writing in the early 1960s with wit, insight, courage, and determination, playwrights such as Megan Terry, Myrna Lamb, Adrienne Kennedy, Rochelle Owens, and Rosalyn Drexler produced works in a flowering that was anticipated in the plays of their foremothers. Inspired by both the Civil Rights and anti–Vietnam War movements, these pioneers used the stage to illustrate that the violence of rape, inequality, and the assumed inferiority of women were human, as well as women's, issues. To experience the transition from being the other to being the center was the heady experience these playwrights offered female audiences.

Alice Childress: From the 1940s to Tomorrow

In April 1994, the New WORLD Theater at the University of Massachusetts produced *Florence* in tribute to Alice Childress (1920–94), whose career spanned six decades, from the original staging of *Florence* in 1949 to the 1994 production. Born in South Carolina, Childress moved to Harlem where she was raised by her grandmother; she left high school in her junior year to earn her living. At 19 she helped found the American Negro Theatre and worked there as a playwright, actor, and director for 12 years. She credits her grandmother with exposing her to art, encouraging her to write, and taking her to the Salem Church where, at Wednesday night testimonials, she learned to be a writer. "[P]eople, mostly women, used to get up and tell their troubles to everybody," she recalled. "I couldn't wait for person after person to tell her story. . . . That's where I got my writing inspiration."[5]

Her *Gold through the Trees* (1952) was the first play by a black woman to be professionally produced. *Trouble in Mind* (1955) won the first Obie Award for the best original off-Broadway play. Asked about the "firsts" attached to her name, Childress commented: "I never was ever interested in being the first woman to do anything. I always felt that I should be the 50th or the 100th. Women were kept out of everything. [Being first] almost made it sound like other women were not quite right enough or accomplished enough, especially when I hear 'the first Black woman.' When people are shut out of something for so long, it seems ironic when there's so much going on about 'the first' " (Brown-Guillory 1987, 68). Childress viewed race as the dominant factor in her life and work: "Being a woman adds difficulty to self expression, but being Black is the larger factor of struggle against the odds. Black men and women have particular problems above and beyond the average, in any field of endeavor."[6] She also decried "people who say, 'I'm not a *black* playwright, I'm a playwright who *happens* to be black.' Like they're some goddamned accident! You know? Happenstance. I am a woman and I am black. . . . The person who says, 'I'm not a woman playwright,' or 'I'm not black, I'm a writer who happens to be black,' et cetera, is deluding herself."[7] Her dramas address the difficulties of the struggle against racism and sexism, legacies of a white patriarchy that doubly oppresses black women. Rather than concern herself with a genteel middle class, Childress wrote, as did Georgia Douglas Johnson and Mary Burrill, of the lower economic class.

In *Florence*, the title character, like Glaspell's Bernice, Minnie Wright, and Allison, is present only diegetically. *Florence* was reviewed for *Freedom* by Lorraine Hansberry, who called Childress a "leading black woman playwright" and characterized her as "our first" and "our best."[8] Segregation is very much in evidence in the set, a railroad station waiting room divided by a low railing that separates the "Colored" and "White" sections. Presumptions of race superiority are apparent in rest-room signs: "white ladies" and "white gentlemen," but "colored *women*" and "colored *men*." Two black women, mother and sister of the title character, enter. Marge urges Mama to insist that Florence, struggling to become an actor in New York, return home. Differences within the

Julia Rosenblat and Natasha Springer in The New WORLD Theater's 1994 production of Alice Childress's *Florence*, directed by Celia O. Hilson. *Photograph by Edward Cohen, courtesy of The New WORLD Theater, University of Massachusetts at Amherst.*

race, even within the family, become evident as Marge speaks of Florence seeking a salesgirl's job at Strumley's where "they don't hire no colored folks" and declares, "She must think she's white!" Marge has internalized the oppression accorded her by whites and consequently "lowered" herself, while Florence aspires to achieve more than her hometown can offer.

After Marge leaves, Mrs. Carter enters. Like Florence, this white woman left home to become an actor. When Mama asks Mrs. Carter to help Florence, the white woman gives Mama the telephone number of a director and permission to use her name as a reference. Gradually it becomes clear that Mrs. Carter is recommending Florence not for a role in the director's new musical but for a job as her maid. This self-proclaimed liberal reveals her prejudice and ignorance not only by calling the 50-year-old porter "Boy" and by saying that mulattoes wish to be white or to die but also by assuming Florence's inferiority.

When Mrs. Carter leaves, Mama tears up the paper bearing the director's name and mails Florence the check that was meant to pay her fare home, enclosing a note exhorting her to "keep trying." As she leaves the station, Mama rests her hand for a moment on the railing, calling attention to it as a symbol of the Jim Crow laws enacted by the white patriarchy. While Marge with her notions of "place" and Mrs. Carter with her assumptions of superiority reinforce patriarchy by oppressing another woman, Mama hopes to boost Florence over that barrier.

Like *Florence*, the Obie Award–winning *Trouble in Mind* concerns the theater; it utilizes a play-within-a-play through which Childress castigates the treatment of black actors by white directors and the stereotyping of black characters by white playwrights, which she underscores in the black women characters' names: Petunia and Ruby. Because the producers wished to make sweeping changes in the script, Childress refused a Broadway option.

Deriving its title from a blues song, *Trouble in Mind* deals with the conflict within Wiletta Mayer, a strong black woman who has spent 25 years in the theater. Finally given a leading role, she struggles over the incompatibility between her desire to be an actor and the inaccuracy of her role, that of a mother who sends her son out to face a lynch mob. Challenging the white director by asking if he'd send his son to be murdered, she leads him into exposing his bigotry. As the company is dismissed with promises of telephone calls for the next day's rehearsal, she knows she will not be called. The play ends with Wiletta telling the doorman, "Henry, I've always wanted to do somethin' real grand . . . in the theater . . . to stand forth at my best"; she then "recites beautifully from Psalm 133." The effect is powerful. Wiletta has done something grand in the theater by confronting the hypocritical director; she follows this with a second grand action, offering the audience the alternative vision of the psalm: "Behold how good and how pleasant it is for brethern to dwell together in unity."

Childress reveals the sexism and racism of the white male-dominated theater. The director harasses, touches, and intimidates the white ingenue, who, in a bit of nascent feminism, tells him "Girls . . . girls . . . can go to the Yale drama." Although she uses the word "girls," she asserts herself by telling him that she is not a sex object but an actor who has "finished the Yale drama course." She thus implies that she deserves his respect. Donald T. Evans, writing in the February 1971 edition of *Black World*, finds the play a harbinger: "*Trouble in Mind* . . . begins with the hassle of the Black artist. She shows the difficulty of working in *the man's* theater and maintaining one's integrity and identity. She shows why the Black Arts Movement had to come about." In both *Florence* and *Trouble in Mind*, Childress offers a feminist critique of the theater as an institution, illustrating its rigidity, class consciousness, racism, and sexism.

Class differences within and between the races also play a large role in *Wedding Band: A Love/Hate Story in Black and White*. In 1963 the play was given a rehearsed reading and optioned for Broadway, but because this drama of interracial love was considered too controversial and Childress refused to compromise her vision, it was not produced. In 1966, the University of Michigan staged it, and in 1972, with Ruby Dee and James Broderick in the leading roles, *Wedding Band* was produced by the New York Shakespeare Festival. Clive Barnes in his *New York Times* review of 27 November 1972 found the writing "rather old-fashioned in its attempt at Ibensite realism," a charge rebutted by Rosemary Curb: "Far from being 'old-fashioned,' the writing in *Wedding Band* offers the authenticity of the regional dialect in the diction of the period. Necessarily, the dialogue sounds stilted to a contemporary ear. Although Childress's realism owes much to Ibsen and Chekov, it cannot for that reason be dismissed as out-of-date. After all, realism has proved to be a successful mode for most of what are considered the great American tragedies."[9]

The drama concerns the 10-year love affair of Julia and Herman, who are forbidden from marrying by South Carolina's antimiscegenation laws. Around this couple, Childress weaves a plot studded with striking intersections of race, class, and gender. Pursued by the law and society's disapproval, Julia moves often; as the play opens, she has just moved into a backyard neighborhood of three houses owned by Fanny. The occupants of the other houses are Lula and Mattie, two women formerly abused by their husbands. Mattie married Delroy, who "used to beat the hell outta me . . . tried to stomp me, grind me into the ground . . . callin' me such dirty names" and internalized his abuse, becoming "shame[d] to look at myself in a mirror," but thinking herself unworthy to leave. After he "run off," she met and began living with October, a loving, gentle man now in the merchant marines. State law forbids divorce, so despite a private marriage ceremony and an 11-year relationship, Mattie is deemed ineligible to collect October's allotment; the law penalizes her for the violence of her "legal" husband. The patriarchy's attempt to regulate women in the name of the sanctity of family life results only in making Mattie poverty-stricken.

Mattie survives by taking care of a white child, Lula makes and sells paper flowers, and Julia sews for a living. Fanny, whose father built the rental houses that support her, counts herself above them and responsible for "representin' her race in-a approved manner." When Herman is stricken with influenza while visiting, Julia sends for his mother and sister to bring him home; they arrive, but his mother refuses to take him until she can do so under cover of darkness. In the interim this woman, who describes her son as a man who "makes pies and loves a nigger," crosses the race line to make common cause with Fanny, who serves her tea. Fanny, afraid of the statute that makes it illegal for Herman to be in Julia's bed, offers to corroborate the mother's cover story: "My son comes to deliver baked goods and the influenza strikes him down." When Fanny tells Herman's mother, "We're just poor, humble colored people . . . and everybody knows how to keep their mouth shut," the white woman calls her "Friend Fanny." This title is not extended to Julia; Herman's mother addresses her son's lover as "nigger whore" and "dirty black bitch," while Julia calls her "White trash! Sharecropper!" As Childress illustrated in *Florence*, enforced separation of the races leads to anger, fear, and hatred. Linking racism and sexism, Childress commented in an interview with Rosemary Curb: "*Wedding Band* dealt with a black woman and a white man, but it was about black women's rights. . . . The play shows society's determination to hold the black woman down through laws framed against her. There are similar laws framed against white women, and, of course, unwritten laws. I never run out of subject matter for writing about women's rights—particularly black women, but white women too, which I have included in *Wedding Band*" (Curb, 59).

In 1969, *Wine in the Wilderness*, was commissioned by WGBH television in Boston as part of its series *On Being Black*. The play takes place in the apartment of Bill Jameson, an artist who is painting a triptych on black womanhood. The tail end of a riot can be heard in the street. Once again Childress highlighted the conflation of racism, classism, and sexism in a drama that presents in its protagonist Tommy (for Tomorrow Marie) a vibrant, independent black woman who demands the dignity due her.

Bill opens his door to Oldtimer, who wishes to hide the "leavin's" he picked up after looters abandoned them. Bill answers Oldtimer's question about his work by explaining that the painting before them consists of three canvases on black womanhood; two are completed, "Black Girlhood," depicting a little girl in her Sunday best, and "Wine in the

Wilderness," which depicts *"a beautiful woman, deep mahogany complexion . . . cold but utter perfection, draped in startling colors of African material."* Bill enthuses: "There she is . . . 'Wine In The Wilderness' . . . regal, black womanhood in her noblest form." This majestic figure is Bill's ideal; he pictures his "black queen" looking down from the wall of a public building, showing "the messed up chicks in the neighborhood . . . what a woman oughta be." Here Childress offers a striking instance of the sexism inherent in man's propensity to "create" woman as he thinks she ought to be. Even more sexist is Bill's description of the woman he will depict on the third panel: "She's gonna be the kinda chick that is grass roots, . . . I mean she's underneath the grass roots. The lost woman . . . what the society has made out of our women. . . . She's as close to the bottom as you can get without crackin' up . . . she's ignorant, unfeminine, coarse, rude . . . vulgar . . . a poor, dumb chick that's had her behind kicked until it's numb." Bill's sense of male superiority is evident in both his description and his willingness to blame "the society" for this woman's plight, without ever thinking of who might be doing at least some of the kicking. Worse still is Oldtimer's response when Bill tells him that his friends Sonny-man and Cynthia found the ideal model. *"Full of laughter,"* Oldtimer says, "[W]hen she get here let's us stomp her to death." Tacitly acceding to this violence, Bill says only, "Not until after I paint her."

Sonny-man and Cynthia are professionals, he a writer and she a social worker; their extreme class consciousness is apparent in their patronizing treatment of Tommy, who thinks they have brought her primarily to meet Bill and only incidentally to pose. Childress creates a tension between their understanding of Tommy and what Tommy reveals of herself. Wearing a mismatched outfit and a wig and carrying a brown paper bag, Tommy appears to be Bill's "messed up chick." She asks for no money, only Chinese food. When the men leave to get the food, Tommy tells Cynthia she likes Bill and thanks her for bringing them together. Reacting out of guilt, Cynthia says, "Oh, Honey . . . Tommy, you don't want a poor artist." Tommy senses that Cynthia is "tryin' to tell me I'm aimin' too high lookin' at Bill," and asks, "What's wrong with me?" Becoming a mouthpiece of male sexism, Cynthia tells Tommy to be less brash and more feminine, to "let him do the talking. Learn to listen. Stay in the background a little. Ask his opinion." She is willfully complicit in silencing another woman.

When Bill and Tommy are alone he recites a litany of what is wrong with "our women"; his complaints include women wanting to be "great brains" and wanting to "latch on" to a man. He bemoans the existence of the matriarchy and a lack of femininity, finally advising Tommy: "Yall throw them suppers together, keep your husband happy, raise the kids." Because she has heard some of the same advice from Cynthia and still wishes to please Bill, she agrees to pose, but spills a soda on her shirt. While changing into the African wrap Bill offers her, Tommy overhears Bill boasting on the telephone about the magnificent woman to whom he is "beginnin' to have this deep attachment." He is speaking of his already completed portrait, but Tommy, thinking he speaks of her, is "*awakened to feelings of being loved and admired.*" She removes her wig, fluffs her hair and appears in the African wrap, astounding Bill with her metamorphosis. She reveals her personal history and a good bit of black history, history she has lived through black social groups, such as the Eastern Star, and her church. Gradually, their mutual desire leads them to bed.

In the morning Oldtimer arrives and inadvertently reveals that Tommy was to be the messed-up chick, not "Wine in the Wilderness." Justifiably angered, feeling used yet again, Tommy lectures Bill, Sonny-man, and Cynthia, telling them they prefer history and pictures to "us . . . that's alive and walkin' by you on the street . . . you don't like flesh and blood niggers. . . . [W]hen you run into us livin' and breathin' ones . . . then you comin' on 'bout how we ain' never together. You hate us, that's what! *You hate black me!*" She points out the falseness of their reliance on class stratification: " 'The' masses. Tryin' to make out like we pitiful and you got it made. You the masses your damn self and don't even know it. . . . When [whites] say 'nigger,' . . . they mean educated you and uneducated me. They hate you and call you 'nigger,' I called you 'nigger,' but I love you." Preparing to leave, she asserts the truth: it is not the majestic portrait, but she herself, "alive and kickin," who is the true "Wine in the Wilderness." Stunned by the truth, Bill sees the falseness of his earlier vision and plans a new triptych with Oldtimer and Cynthia and Sonny-man flanking Tommy, "so all the little boys and girls can look up and see you on the wall. And you know what they're gonna say? 'Hey, don't she look like somebody we know?'" The real woman who "came through the biggest riot of all, . . . somethin' called Slavery," becomes both "Wine in the Wilderness" and role model as Childress replaces the sexism of which even women are guilty, the racism that can occur within a race, and the classism that serves only to separate with the "we-ness and us-ness" of real people.

Over the six decades in which her dramas were produced,

Childress offered strong feminist statements to challenge the status quo. Protagonists such as Mama and Tommy rise above the despair proffered them. Tommy and Wiletta dare speak against damaging stereotypes, whether held by white theater directors or black artists and social workers. As Gayle Austin notes, "Increased production of plays like Childress's, which are a critique of representation in themselves, could lead to a tradition of women writing plays that question the images men have constructed."[10] Alice Childress brought feminist drama from the 1940s to tomorrow, igniting possibilities inherent in the future for her sister dramatists.

Megan Terry: "Mother of American Feminist Drama"

Named the "Mother of American Feminist Drama" by Helene Keyssar (Keyssar, 53), Megan Terry (born 1932) has written more than 60 plays, been translated into every major language, and produced internationally. Born in Seattle, Terry began working with the Seattle Repertory Playhouse at 14; artistic director Florence James's technique of having the actors write biographies of what their characters were doing offstage, was, Terry says, "one of the things that got me into writing."[11] In 1966, she held a writer-in-residence fellowship at the Yale School of Drama. She has taught theater and given seminars in playwriting across the country.

Moving to New York in 1956, she worked in several theaters and in 1963 joined Joseph Chaikin at the Open Theatre, where she served as playwright-in-residence and ran the playwrights' workshop. Eight of her dramas were produced there, the most notable being *Viet Rock: A Folk War Movie* (1966). In the early 1970s she began working with the Omaha Magic Theatre, and in 1974 moved to Omaha and became playwright-in-residence, performer, composer, designer, and photographer. Her book, *Right Brain Vacation Photos—New Plays and Production Photographs, 1972–1992*, highlights the production of 25 of her works as well as dramas by Rosalyn Drexler, Rochelle Owens, and Maria Irene Fornes. Since its founding in 1968, the Omaha Magic Theatre, "which typically mocks and demystifies patriarchal sites and practices,"[12] has produced more than 100 plays and musicals.

According to Jill Dolan, "Many contemporary feminist theatre makers, such as Megan Terry . . . , left the experimental theatres to form their own groups when their invisibility in the male forums was articulated by the American women's liberation movement."[13] Terry, who acknowledges that "the women's movement enabled me to leave New York and give up that whole careerism business—the man's world of career stuff," defines feminist drama as "[a]nything that gives women confidence, shows them to themselves, helps them to begin to analyze whether it's a positive or negative image" (Jenkins, 329). Her dramas confront sexism, gender roles, the repression and oppression of women, and sexist language with the intent of disrupting what the patriarchy claims as the natural order. As a teacher, Terry acquaints her students with feminist dramatists: "I taught Emily Mann's *Still Life*. . . . My students were *outraged* that they'd never heard of this play, nor the work of Maria Irene Fornes, nor Roz Drexler, Rochelle Owens, Adrienne Kennedy, . . . Ntozake Shange, . . . Tina Howe. They knew none of these people, and they were getting their master's degrees!" (Betsko and Koening, 385).

Common to many feminist dramatists is "the strategy of transformation" (Keyssar, xiii); Terry is often credited with introducing it onstage. Transformation itself is variously defined as a training technique for actors, a means of dramatizing the instability of character, a disruption of the conventions of realist theater and the status quo that those conventions support, thus a means of "throw[ing] the spectator's focus onto society and the way it maintains oppressive roles and attitudes" (Savran, 241). Transformation is thus seen as a means of "inspir[ing] and assert[ing] the possibility for change" that can bring about "transformation of the self and the world" (Keyssar, xiv). Strindberg's expressionism may be an influence; in the preface to *A Dream Play* (1902), Strindberg wrote, "Anything may happen, anything seems possible and probable. . . . The characters split, double, multiply, vanish, solidify, blur, clarify." Strindberg's influence is discernible in Terry's remark, "I was more crazy about Strindberg and Ionesco and Sartre" than about other modern Europeans (Savran, 245). In Terry's transformations, too, anything may change and, "These changes occur swiftly and *almost without transition*, until the audience's dependence upon any fixed reality is called into question. A member of our audience once said that these continual metamorphoses left him feeling 'stationless,' which is precisely the point."[14]

Transformation in feminist drama also has roots in women's psychology and life experience. Julia Kristeva, Hélène Cixous, and Luce Irigaray all write of the fluidity of woman's experience and find her reality to be other than the binary thinking characteristic of phallic logic.[15] That her time is so open to interruption is reflected in the abrupt changes of character, scene, and event found in transformational drama. Action frequently proceeds not in a linear manner but by contiguity, a principle described by feminist theorists as a nearness that creates a work "constantly in the process of weaving itself, at the same time ceaselessly embracing words and yet casting them off to avoid becoming fixed, immobilized."[16] Terry works in the tradition of Glaspell, who also eschewed linear development. Claire's intent in *The Verge* in dealing with her plant forms applies equally well to feminist playwrights' experiments with dramatic structure: "I want to break it up! If it were all in pieces, we'd be . . . shocked to aliveness. . . . There'd been strange new comings together—mad new comings together."

Terry's first transformational drama, *Calm Down Mother*, was produced in 1965. The play, written because "there were no parts for women" (Savran, 253), is often cited as the first truly feminist American drama. Its three characters, identified only as Woman One, Woman Two, and Woman Three, are variously parts of a plant form; two delicatessen clerks and a customer; a woman filled with anger; a writer; two friends and the dying mother of one; nursing-home patients; a subway door; call girls; sides of a triangle; a mother and her daughters; and three amused gentlewomen. As the play begins, the plant splits and from it emerges Margaret Fuller, who asserts that she knows who she is because, "My father addressed me not as a plaything, but as a living mind." The transformations that follow expose the ills resulting from the institutionalized sexism of American society. The writer, for example, thinks, "Maybe if I keep talking and writing . . . I won't seem so small, at least not so small to me." A woman who has just escaped an "impossible marriage" is questioned about restraining orders. Women as victims of society's stress on them as sexual beings appear in the nursing-home patients whose nurse signals their superfluity—"Your cream's all gone. Time for the heap"—and in the young woman pressured by priests into abandoning birth control. Her sister, who refuses to "sit there in the church every Sunday, kneeling and mumbling and believing all that crap that those men tell you," is disowned by her mother, herself a victim of patriarchal religion. As the play ends, the three at once confirm and confront the idea that anatomy is destiny as they progress from proclaiming, "The eggies in our beggies [*sic*] are enough," to turning their backs on the audience in its representation of sexist society and asking, in unison, "ARE THEY?" Although beaten down by sexist assumptions, woman's mind and spirit as initially represented by Margaret Fuller rise to resist being apprehended merely as a medium for reproduction.

Terry's best-known play, *Viet Rock: A Folk War Movie*, "was translated into every major language and was proclaimed in every major, and many minor, cities all over the world" (Betsko and Koening, 382). Terry directed the play, which has the distinction of being both the first rock musical ever staged—featuring such songs as "The Viet Rock" and "War Au Go Go"—and the first to deal with the Vietnam War.[17]

Visual image dominates as troops parachute onstage, mortars fire, a heap of dead bodies "pulse[s] like a giant beating heart," and actors lying in a circle on the floor "form a giant flower or a small target," which becomes by the play's end "a tangled circle . . . the reverse of the beautiful circle of the opening image." Terry, driven by "anger at the destruction and the confusion [caused by the war], turned that anger into an examination and discussion and catalyst" (Savran, 249). The opening song is followed by a voice reciting a series of clichés that prepare for the events to come, parodies of scenes in B war movies: the induction examination, the brutal drill instructor, letter writing, and slaughter. To the transformations brought about by changing characters into different characters, Terry adds a second type in which "actors replace actors within the framework of a single scene. The richness of *Viet Rock* depends largely on the interweave between these two basic modes of transformation."[18] The transformation of American women into South Vietnamese soldiers and the G.I.'s distrust of these soldiers because "they're awful little" underscore the patriarchy's fear and distrust of the Other, whether the difference be gender or race.

The Sergeant's monologue mocking war protestors endorses the patriarchy's validation of war as evidence of love and manhood: "Since when is it not honorable to die for your country? Spill your blood, boobies. That's the highest form of love. Give your blood for others. . . . Yes, boys. War is hell, with a hell of a lot of blood to spill for the hell of a lot of love you have for your hell of a country!" In imitation of blood shed by women in childbirth, according to this myth, the blood shed in the violent lovefest of war begets men. It is no coincidence that military literature frequently describes war as the rebirth of a country or that one of Mussolini's favorite sayings was, "What war is to men, so maternity is to women."[19]

Respite from battle and (purchased) love become dangerous as Saigon Sally's, the R and R bar, is blown to bits. The lines that arise from the resulting heap of dead bodies conclude with "Who needs this.

Who needs war. Who needs this shit. . . . WHO WHO WHO—!" The actors then enter the audience, communicating by "look and touch" the obvious answer to Terry's question.

War also figures prominently in Terry's 1970 Obie Award–winning drama *Approaching Simone*. A striking departure from her usual dramaturgy, it focuses on a specific character. Her depiction of Simone Weil is not solely one of an ethical mystic and philosopher whose pursuit of questions of justice and faith represent a moral force; Terry's Simone is she who was dubbed the "red virgin" and "the categorical imperative in skirts," a woman who was teacher, factory worker, combatant in the Spanish Civil War, trade union activist, and writer. While Simone identifies profoundly with the suffering of the impoverished and persecuted, Terry demonstrates the suffering Simone underwent as a woman. Weil seeks to transcend self; she is presented as a woman-defined or self-defined woman, not as one whose identity rests on her relationship with a man. Terry told Phyllis Jane Wagner that women "need to know that a woman can make it and think clearly in a womanly way. All the heroes are dead or killed or compromised, and women *need* heroes. That's why I wrote *Approaching Simone*."[20] For Terry, this female hero exists as "opposition to the patriarchal Judeo-Christian mythology on which Simone was raised, a kind of counter-mythology-female, pacifist, nurturing and strong" (Savran, 241).

The play begins with the five-year-old Simone insisting on carrying her share of the family's luggage and progresses through her life of self-sacrifice. Teaching, promoting liberal causes, supporting the French Army and the Resistance, she strives to remake the world. Finally, after 34 years of rejection and disappointment, she withdraws; in sympathy with the French suffering under Nazi rule, she refuses to eat and achieves spiritual transcendence in death.

The larger part of Simone's "defeat" may be laid to her society's sexist assumptions and its insistence on preserving constructed gender roles. When a visitor tells Simone's mother that Simone's brother is "the genius, and [Simone] . . . the beauty," the young girl recoils "*as if slapped by an unseen hand*"; an ensuing scene, "Simone at Fourteen—When and Why She Wants to Kill Herself," shows Simone suffering from severe migraine and being tortured by the allegorical embodiments of "*her self-doubt, self-loathing, and pain and anguish*," who tell her she is talentless, stupid, awkward, and possessed of a miserable body and a mind that cannot move. As she is reminded that she is "nothing but a girl . . . only a girl," there arises from the auditorium "Taunts . . . in three languages, equivalent to 'You're nothing but a stupid cunt.' " Reduced to mere sexuality, Simone declares she does not wish to live, but her will is revived by a Singer who urges:

> ANYONE CAN KNOW TRUTH
> DESIRE, DESIRE
> ONLY MAKE THE EFFORT OF ATTENTION
> FOCUS ON THE DARK INSIDE YOUR HEAD
> UNTIL IT LIGHTS YOUR WAY.

Subsequent scenes present Simone confronting the systematic devaluation of women: as an innovative young teacher who wishes to teach her students how to live, she is fired for flouting patriarchal orthodoxy; in the factory she is assigned a subordinate order of work and told she is "paid not to think"; and, threatened with jail for distributing an illegal newspaper, she is labeled "crazy" when she welcomes the opportunity to be placed in the same cell with prostitutes.

Terry also uses Simone to demonstrate the confluence of language, gender, and war. When Simone, for once using her gender, offers to head a group of frontline female nurses, "a small group of women exerting day after day a courage of this kind with a maternal solicitude," she is told that women must not be exposed to the dangers of the front, for they are the very reason "we men leave for the front to defend our homes and families." With the battle in the background, Simone explains the "unreal character" of war: "For our contemporaries the role of Helen [in the Trojan War] is played by words with capital letters. If we grasp one of these words, all swollen with blood and tears, and squeeze it, we find it is empty. Words with content and meaning are not murderous. When empty words are given capital letters, then men on the slightest pretext will begin shedding blood. . . . To clarify thought, to discredit the intrinsically meaningless words . . . might be a way of saving human lives." She tells the truth to the wounded and dying—"War is unreality itself . . . war is affliction"—and then mounts the platform of the staging as others beseech her to eat. Refusing, she dies as a "*pin spot on Simone [dims] slowly, slowly, slowly, slowly to black.*" From Simone's initial appearance, in which she reverses the gaze and "silently stares at the audience," to this startling final image, Terry crafts a new representation of woman.

Because she believes the artist must critique society, Megan Terry and the Omaha Magic Theatre have done "one show a year to give voice to community concerns."[21] Among these dramas are *American King's English for Queens* (1978), an examination of gender bias in language; *Goona Goona* (1979), an expose of spouse and child abuse; *Kegger* (1983), a study of alcohol (mis)use by young people; and *Head Lights* (1989), a dramatization of the pain of illiteracy.

Eschewing male careerism and moving to Omaha, Terry has become a vital force in moving theater beyond the confines of realism and naturalism. She "challenges the hegemony of the consciousness of the intractable individual that had so dominated American drama in the 1950s" (Savran, 241). For five decades she has provided inspiration for feminist dramatists by living true to her artistic creed: "Art is about taking action. I believe in taking creative action. Theatre reminds you that you can transcend this discrete unit, the body, by combining imaginatively with your community in reacting with, for, and to the presentation on the stage that is meaningful to the community."[22]

Maria Irene Fornes: From the Absurd to the Oppressed

Maria Irene Fornes's career began with *The Widow* (1961). In 1982 she was awarded an Obie for sustained achievement in the theater; her total of seven Obies is unique among women in the theater. Born in Cuba in 1930, Fornes emigrated to America in 1945. She studied painting, spending some time in Paris, where she was profoundly moved by Roger Blin's 1954 production of Samuel Beckett's *Waiting for Godot*. In a memorial tribute, she remarked, "I more than just admire Beckett. He had a personal impact on me; he provided me with a new vision. . . . I was illuminated by it."[23]

The author of more than 30 plays, Fornes also teaches playwriting, designs scenery and costumes, and, like Crothers, Sophie Treadwell, Hellman, and Terry, directs her own plays. She also directs the INTAR Hispanic Playwrights-in-Residence Laboratory. A founding member of New York Theater Strategy, she served as president, fund-raiser, production coordinator, bookkeeper, and secretary; this work interfered with her playwriting for six years, a drought that ended with the production of *Fefu and Her Friends* (1977).

Fornes identifies herself as a feminist: "To be a feminist I think means that you follow a political process that has a development and you are part of the development and you adhere to it. I am a feminist in that I am very concerned and I suffer when women are treated in a discriminatory manner because I am a woman."[24] Furthermore, Fornes invites "the audience to view the underside of patriarchal culture through women's eyes. . . . Fornes's mirror reflects disturbing images of patriarchy in general and of male behavior in particular."[25]

Returning full-time to writing and directing with *Fefu and Her Friends,* she examined women and their roles, investing her dramas with sympathy, empathy, and compassion. *Fefu* brought her Obies for writing and direction. The plot of this challenging drama centers on eight women who meet at Fefu's home to plan a fund-raising event. Although it is 1935, these women, untouched by the Great Depression, seem at first comfortable and self-sufficient in this domestic setting that functions as a concretization of woman's sphere. Although the play's action stretches from noon through the evening, Fefu's husband, Phillip, remains outside, seen by some of the women but not the audience. Fefu tells her friends that Phillip "married me to have a constant reminder of how loathsome women are," and begins to reveal the pernicious effects of the patriarchal control that looms just outside, keeping woman both nervous and in her place. Her metaphor of the stone in damp soil illuminates the state of male/female relationships: "that which is exposed to the exterior . . . is smooth and dry and clean. That which is not . . . [the] underneath, is slimy and filled with fungus and crawling with worms. It is another life that is parallel to the one we manifest. It's there. The way worms are underneath the stone. If you don't recognize it . . . [*whispering*] it eats you." The arrival of Julia, confined to a wheelchair by a surreal hunting accident in which she was not hit by a bullet but fell anyway, underscores the manner in which patriarchal control devours both body and spirit.

In part 2, the action and the audience are split. Four scenes are performed simultaneously, and the audience, divided into four parts, rotates among them. Denied the distancing provided by the transparent "fourth wall" of the stage, the audience enters the play's environment. In the study, Cindy tells Christina about a terrible dream in which she meets, at a dance, a young doctor whom she has consulted. They dance in a circle; then the doctor curses her. When she says "Stop and listen to me" so strongly that he does stop, everyone looks at her admiringly. While she struggles to form the words "Respect me," the doctor trembles in "mad rage," and another man tells her to leave before the doctor kills her. The dream indicates the dizzying dance of appropriate female behavior in the face of male authority, an authority outraged to the point of murder when the woman dares assert herself, even over so personal and urgent an issue as her health.

This revelation is followed by a more terrible instance, as the audience enters the bedroom where Julia naps. In her dream hallucination, she recounts how the "judges" clubbed her, broke her hands, robbed her of sight, and silenced her: "They tore my eyes out. They took my voice away." Yet she smiles because to stop is to "get clubbed because they love me. They say they love me. I go along with that because if I don't . . . [*with her finger she indicates her throat being cut*]." Her head moves as if she is being slapped, as she is coerced into saying her prayer: "The human being is of the masculine gender. The human being is a boy as a child and grown up he is a man. Everything on earth is for the human being, which is man. . . . Women are Evil.—Woman is not a human being. She is: 1—A mystery. 2—Another species. 3—As yet undefined. 4—Unpredictable; therefore wicked and gentle and evil and good which is evil." Finishing the prayer, she moves as if slapped until she says, "I believe it." Julia's paralysis symbolizes her internalizing this message, a recanting of her integrity "because she wanted to live." Julia's mattress lies on the floor; as the audience looks down on her, Fornes's staging communicates viscerally the defining power of the male gaze, of the invisible judges who hurt "out of love." Seeing from without and within, the audience becomes aware of its complicity in upholding the patriarchal system.

In part 3, Fefu urges Julia to fight the impending surrender to death she sees in her eyes, but Julia responds by wishing that no harm come to Fefu, an affirmation of Julia's earlier revelation that the judges have their eyes on her friend. Releasing her hold on Julia, Fefu takes her gun outside to clean it. As she shoots and kills a rabbit, blood appears on Julia's forehead; Fefu reenters saying, "I killed it . . . I just shot . . . and killed it . . . Julia . . . ." and the women surround Julia. The ending is open and ambiguous. What has Fefu killed? Has she exorcised the demon of the judges' control, or has she killed Julia because her compromise is "contagious"? Or does the ending signal a "world . . . blown apart," which Fefu forecast as a result of women finally "recogniz[ing] each other"?

Joan Larkin in the June 1978 *Ms.* said: "I am disappointed to see women yet again as sacrificial victims who cannot endure their strength. In the end I find that the images in the play that remain strongest are those of women's self-loathing. Not that in our writing we must deny our demons—but I fear, finally, that this play loves them more than our powers." Fornes describes this reaction as a problem between herself and some feminists. To those who see her dramas as loving woman's demons more than her powers or as offering woman no exit from the trap, Fornes responds: "I don't romanticize pain. In my work people are always trying to find a way out. . . . Some people complain that my work doesn't offer the solution. But the reason for that is that I feel that the characters don't have to get out, it's *you* who has to get out" (Savran, 55). Fornes's creed sets the praxis of the stage in action.

At times Fornes's comments about her plays can be unsettling, as is the case with *The Conduct of Life* (1985), which explores the interconnections among gender, class, and power. Orlando, an army lieutenant in a Latin American country, declares in his opening soliloquy, "Man must have an ideal, mine is to achieve maximum power. That is my destiny." In scene 2 he has become a lieutenant commander, rising by dint of the torture he administers to political prisoners, degrees of which he also inflicts on his wife, Leticia, his maid Olimpia, and Nena, the 12-year-old destitute street girl whom he makes his sex slave and repeatedly rapes. Fornes's comments stand in unbearable tension with the action her drama embodies. Invoking the class structure of her play, Fornes says of the servant that she has a job she must keep to survive and therefore cannot tell Orlando she's going to leave (Savran, 68). Still, Olimpia, moved by Nena's suffering, does repeatedly punch Orlando in one scene, threatening to kill him in his sleep.

About Orlando, who sexually tortures Nena so severely that her screams rising from the cellar are audible in the house, Fornes says, "[H]e's in love with a child." This "love" manifests itself in the assaults that Orlando rationalizes to Nena: "What I do to you is out of love. Out of want. It's not what you think. I wish you didn't have to be hurt. I don't do it out of hatred. It is not out of rage. It is love." Telling Nena that this sexual violence is his gift to her, Orlando claims, "It is a desire to destroy and to see things destroyed and to see the inside of them.—It's my nature." His explanation accords with Octavio Paz's explication of " '*chingar*' as the verb that defines masculine and feminine roles as played out in the Mexican/Chicano male psyche: *chingar* then is to do violence to another, i.e., rape. The verb is active, masculine, cruel: it stings, wounds, gashes, stains. . . . The person who suffers this action is passive, inert, and open, in contrast to the active, aggressive, and closed person who inflicts. The *chingon* is the macho, the male; he rips open the *chingada*, the female, who is pure passivity, defenseless against the exterior world."[26] While the text exposes the brutality of this cultural myth, Fornes's calling it "love" can be explained only by her desire to indict the entire system: "There is an oppression in that play, but it's not Orlando, who is just a peon in the political system. It's the generals" (Savran, 68).

Fornes's vital, provocative drama has exercised significant influence on experimental theater for four decades. Like other feminist dramatists, she has been largely ignored by mainstream theaters and critics, but, through plays that "deal very often with the oppressed and some kind of oppression, emotional or political, plus the desire to free one's self from any kind of oppression,"[27] Fornes, by critiquing the hierarchy, dramatizes the hope of a more humane, compassionate world.

Adrienne Kennedy: "A Growth of Images"

Adrienne Kennedy (born 1931) was raised in a racially mixed suburb of Cleveland. Her parents were active in the black community. Attending racially and ethnically mixed schools, Kennedy did not experience the sting of racism until she attended Ohio State University, where she encountered overt racial hatred from the women in her dormitory. "The white students on campus did not socialize nor interact in any fashion with black students. This experience made an indelible mark on her sensibility and engendered anger and hatred for racism which would find compelling expression in her plays."[28] Kennedy is best known for her complex, enigmatic dramas, which have been translated into several languages and have been produced in Paris, London, and Rome.

The Great Lakes Theater Festival staged her first full production in Cleveland when it held the first Adrienne Kennedy Festival in 1992, during which the play it had commissioned, *The Ohio State Murders*, received its world premiere. Calling her writing "a growth of images," Kennedy stated, "Autobiographical work is the only thing that interests me. . . . I see my writings as being an outlet for inner, psychological confusion and questions stemming from childhood."[29] If self is the subject of her expressionistic, surrealistic dramas, sui generis but also in the tradition of Marita Bonner's *The Purple Flower*, Glaspell's *The Verge*, and Treadwell's *Machinal*, that self is infinite, containing woman, man, god, and beast; it is also a template for the experience of the African

American woman. As epilogue to her autobiography, *People Who Led to My Plays* (1987), Kennedy writes, "My plays are meant to be states of mind" (*People*, n.p.). An avant-gardist, she fashions her poetic dramas through arresting verbal and visual imagery. Like Terry, she changes scenes at a rapid pace. Her characters often split into several selves and her drama's form is often equally fragmented. She writes in a non-Western, circular time and may utilize sets simultaneously or superimpose them one upon the other. From herself as subject, Kennedy spins a thread that winds through her oeuvre, connecting the plays through shared characters and themes.

Kennedy frequently speaks of the women of her family—mother, aunt, and grandmother—as heroes and inspiration. bell hooks, discussing Kennedy's feminism, comments that "there is an emergent perspective on women's identity . . . that can be read as linked to a growing political concern in the fifties and sixties with female identity—with women's efforts to come to voice—to establish a writer's identity, and this concern is there in Kennedy's work."[30] hooks also celebrates Kennedy's autobiography for "[d]ocument[ing] . . . the harsh nuances and textures that characterize [black women's] relationships to many white women" (183), something that Beah Richards and Childress also document. In a comment foreshadowing reaction to Anita Hill's testimony before the 1991 Senate Judiciary Committee hearings on Clarence Thomas's nomination to the Supreme Court, Susan E. Meigs wrote that Kennedy's "characters represent the community of women, largely excluded from the political mechanisms of black protest, who are nonetheless expected to sacrifice gender issues for racial concerns."[31] For Kennedy, as for Childress, "the history of race . . . is the predominant question of my existence."[32] Significantly, Kennedy identifies Childress as a "great inspiration" (Betsko and Koening, 257). She also credits Lorraine Hansberry's success as inspiring: "I had abandoned playwriting . . . because I thought there was no hope; but with LH's success, I felt reawakened" (*People*, 109).

Funnyhouse of a Negro (1964) was written while Kennedy was in Ghana accompanying her husband on a research trip. If Tommy in Childress's *Wine in the Wilderness* is, in Bill's word, "together"—sure of herself, knowing who she is—Kennedy's Sarah is her polar opposite. In the multicultural chaos of *Funnyhouse*, Sarah fragments into four selves: the Duchess of Hapsburg, Queen Victoria Regina, Jesus, and Patrice Lumumba. Daughter of a woman who "looked like a white woman" and a father who is "the darkest one of us all," Sarah isolates herself in her room. Surrounded by artifacts of the dominant white culture, she writes poetry imitative of Edith Sitwell and has what she describes as her "vile . . . nigger" dream of herself and her white friends living "in rooms with European antiques, photographs of Roman ruins, pianos and oriental carpets." Although she "long[s] to become even a more pallid Negro" than she is, she cannot prevent her father, whom she characterizes as the "wild black beast" who raped her mother, from knocking on her door and begging "forgiveness for . . . being black." All of Sarah's selves speak of the black man as their father; all intend to kill him or believe they have already done so.

Describing the various sets as "my rooms," Sarah tells why she fantasizes about the Hapsburg chamber, the room in Victoria's castle, the hotel where she imagines killing her father, and the jungle; they are "the places myselves exist in." But, she adds, "I know no places. That is, I cannot believe in places. To believe in places is to know hope and to know the emotion of hope is to know beauty. It links us across a horizon and connects us to the world. I find there are no places only my funnyhouse." A culture that insists on identities established on the basis of either/or offers no room for the mulatto, for one who is both and thereby more. Sarah, who begins the play "faceless . . . with a hangman's rope about her neck," ends by hanging herself. She appears to be one more tragic mulatto, like the character cited by Mrs. Carter in *Florence*, killing herself because she is not white. Kennedy, however, does not wish to promulgate this white myth any more than did Childress. Sarah's death, announced from the outset by the noose, becomes a call for the creation of new spaces, for the accommodation of new identities beyond the prison of white patriarchy's binaries.

In *A Movie Star Has to Star in Black and White* (1976), Kennedy continues to deal with representation and transformation. Clara, identified as a playwright and quoting lines she "wrote" for Kennedy's second drama, *The Owl Answers* (1965), keeps vigil at the bedside of her comatose brother while she works through problems in her marriage by projecting herself into scenes from the movies *Now Voyager*, *Viva Zapata*, and *A Place in the Sun*. The drama testifies to Kennedy's lifelong fascination with film, film stars, and fame, yet it also graphically presents the conundrum of the representation of minorities. Clara's life is the subject and she narrates her own drama, but in a unique manner. She is present in the reenactment of the films, sitting in the boat behind the actor playing Shelley Winters in the scene from *A Place in the Sun*, for example. But Clara, who "plays a bit part" in this story of her life, does not speak. The movie images speak for her, delivering not lines from the movies but from Clara's story. Although Kennedy's protagonist remains subsumed by the white majority, she is neither killed nor, as in *The Owl*, transformed into a nonhuman being, and thus moves closer to speaking for herself.

With *The Alexander Plays*, a quartet centered on the character Suzanne Alexander, a writer, Kennedy continued her "autobiography." No longer strained through white masks or voices, Suzanne Alexander speaks for herself. The first play, *She Talks to Beethoven* (1989), is set in Ghana; as she anxiously awaits the arrival of her husband who vanished two days earlier, Suzanne reads from a diary that has been written on Beethoven, the subject of her current project. So strong is Beethoven's presence for her that he appears; they converse about creativity and fame, and she discovers messages from her missing husband in the notebooks the deaf composer used for communication. When David returns, Suzanne asks if he sent Beethoven; in a voice not unlike Beethoven's, David replies, "I knew he would console you while I was absent," marking the interconnectedness of love, creativity, and art. Parts 3 and 4 of Kennedy's quartet, *The Film Club* (1992) and *The Dramatic Circle* (1992), deal with David's later disappearance; the first is Suzanne's monologue, the second its dramatization.

The most important of the four plays, *The Ohio State Murders*, premiered at the Great Lake's Festival's Adrienne Kennedy Festival in 1992. Beginning as a monologue in which Suzanne rehearses the talk she is to give on the genesis of the violent imagery in her work, the play enlarges into a restaging of Suzanne's memories of her undergraduate days. Kennedy's own pain at the prejudice she experienced living in a dormitory is searingly present in Suzanne's story. More shocking is the tale of the betrayal of this gifted young woman enrolled at the university in an era when minorities had to qualify to become English majors by taking "trial courses." The rage that imploded to split Kennedy's earlier protagonists as they turned inward is directed outward at a patriarchy that employs its privileged status to flatter, seduce, abandon, and murder. Declaring Suzanne's work "brilliant," white professor Robert Hampton seduces her. When she becomes pregnant, he insists he could not be responsible. Later he kidnaps and kills one of her infant twins; several months later, posing as a researcher, he imprisons the baby sitter, murders his second daughter, and kills himself.

In an indictment of patriarchy, both white and black, Suzanne explains that the university protected Hampton by keeping the story out of the papers and by circulating a tale that "a white professor had wandered into the Negro section of Columbus and was killed." Her own father, who had contacts with state politicians, also lobbied the papers "to bury the tragedy." The entire tale of a woman's betrayal, and specifically the murders of her baby daughters, became, as Suzanne remarks in a brilliant understatement, "the main source of the violent imagery in my work."

Whether related by visual images that are achingly visceral or narrated with a straightforwardness that exists in ironic counterpoint to the content of the narrative, Adrienne Kennedy's plays are minefields. These dramas, especially the earlier works, are indeed the abstract poems she once labeled them, allegorical abstractions presenting in tangibly affecting ways challenges to the twin pillars of racism and sexism on which patriarchy is balanced. Perhaps if her work were produced in mainstream venues with greater frequency, those pillars might crumble. Important in both subject and structure, Kennedy's "highly complicated plays introduce students of drama to experiments in dramatic form, decentered subjects, and postmodern fragmentation that unfailingly indict the symbolic workings of racism and misogyny. . . . There are few North American playwrights who have brought together a study of the symbolic construction of racism and sexism so powerfully."[33]

Rosalyn Drexler: The Art of Experimentation

Like Kennedy, Rosalyn Drexler (born 1926) is an experimental writer, a classification she also ascribes to life: "Life is experimental because it is changing from moment to moment, and you're never quite sure of the result, but you know something is happening and you are going in an organic direction. Only death is non-experimental. There's nothing more to work with."[34] Drexler gave herself much to work with in a life that includes work as playwright, novelist, singer, painter, wrestler, masseuse, waitress, playground director, and sculptor. Her experience as a wrestler, for example, informs the plot of *Delicate Feelings* (1984). Drexler won Obies for her first play, *Home Movies* (1964), for *The Writer's Opera* (1979), and for three one-act plays, collectively titled *Transients Welcome* (1984). Puns, double entendre, literary allusions, and non sequitur abound in her work. She acknowledges Ionesco as another self (Lamont 1993, viii); several critics also detect the zaniness of the Marx Brothers in her dramas. Her works have been identified as theater of the ridiculous, absurd, collage, and farce; she describes them as "inside out . . . things that most characters only think are given voice and spoken in my work," and feels she has experienced discrimination "because of the kind of noncommercial work [she does]" (Betsko and Koening, 132 and 129). Rosette Lamont calls her destabilization of discourse a "semiotics of instability," within which she deconstructs the "naturalness" of male/female relationships in which the woman is presented as always already inferior. Instead, "Woman as the desiring subject is central to most of her work"[35] She also exposes the tactics of the patriarchy; in *She Who Was He* (1976), Thutmose, Queen Hatshepsut's husband, arranges her murder, "then attempts to erase her name from history, has servants chipping away at obelisks raised in her honor, removes her name from scroll and tomb" (Betsko and Koening, 130).

Raunchiness and humor mark *Home Movies.* In what might be seen as a twentieth-century version of *Fashion*, Mrs. Verdun holds calling hours in her bedroom for guests who include homosexual poet Peter Peterouter, the sneering, stuttering intellectual Charles Arduit, the sly priest Father Shenanagan, Sister Thalia, and John the Truckdriver. Peter, acknowledging his homosexuality, also claims that an encounter in a gymnasium with the missing "well hung" patriarch left him "covered with the rash." Mr. Verdun arrives home literally encased in a large wooden closet delivered by John. He then "breaks his way out of the closet [and] prances around." He tells Mrs. Verdun, "My hormones are in top form" and, singing a sadomasochistic song, they go behind the curtain. In Drexler's hands, the portrait of the controlling patriarch becomes one of the first comic portrayals of bisexuality on the American stage.

The Bed Was Full (1964) was staged in 1983 by the Omaha Magic Theatre, which also presented *Room 17C* (1983), *The Line of Least Existence* (1987), and *The Heart That Eats Itself* (1988). *The Bed Was Full* parodies farce. A wife suspected of infidelity is pursued by a paranoid detective as people literally fall from overhead ramps into bed. In the midst of the absurdity, Drexler limns a male-dominated society in which violence imperils woman's attempts at self-determination, as is illustrated by the model Kali being kidnapped at gunpoint by Joel, who desires her as his model and muse.

In *Occupational Hazard*, the 1992 version of *The Heart That Eats Itself* (1988), Drexler contemplates the nature of art and artist. She calls this adaptation of Kafka's "A Hunger Artist," "a portrait of the artist as suicide" (Lamont 1993, x). Using the play as a vehicle for social critique, Drexler adds a flashback scene illustrating the sexual harassment of Emma by the Official of the Review Board of the Accident Compensation Authority, the agency for which the Artist works before leaving to pursue his calling. As she shoves the Official away and chokes him with her legs he feels only pleasure, then forces her to take money, with the threat, "And remember, mum's the word. Your future depends on it."

Drexler's primary concern is the role of the Artist as one compelled to "sacrifice . . . comfort and nourishment for art," while his comfortable, complacent bourgeois audience questions whether what he does even qualifies as art. Art as business manifests itself in the artist's being caged—partly because, as the Impresario notes, "Nothing sells tickets faster than misery!"—and in the souvenirs pushed on the crowd. The Baker, exemplifying an audience that seeks merely amusement and reinforcement of its own comfortable assumptions, quotes a critic's description of the show as "a laugh a minute romp defining the human condition." Pushing "deeper into the heart of darkness alone" during his life, the Artist, as he lies dying, explains that his art is artless, that he starved himself because he could find no food he liked. Thus Drexler, via Kafka, demonstrates that the artist cannot be other than she or he is, nourished by the lack that consumes, in pursuit of what the Doctor who attends the Hunger Artist describes as "something that does not exist."

Subversive and liberating, Drexler's work spans more than 30 years, yet remains largely unknown. Exposing the fallacies of patriarchal constructs and experimenting with dramatic form by expanding the possibilities of representation, Drexler startles and often discomforts her audience as she "deconstructs the art form to reveal the turmoil of the real" (Lamont 1985, 77).

Rochelle Owens: ''Challenging the Categories''

Asked about the dramatist's function, Rochelle Owens (born 1936) responded, "To improve the well-being of the human psyche by revealing the multitudinous levels of human experience. To get rid of the false, dangerous and sanctimonious images the society inevitably is fixated on. To inspire and generate the possibility of authentic awareness of the sacred obligation of being alive."[36] This advocate of theater as praxis was born in Brooklyn, where she attended public schools, and later studied at the New School for Social Research. A sponsor of the Women's Interart Center, Owens also helped establish the theater arts magazines *Scripts* and *Performance*, served on the advisory board of *Performing Arts Journal*, and taught drama at the University of Oklahoma.

She calls her early work "protofeminist [in] structure and dynamics. Protofeminist because it preceded the wave of political and sociological consciousness of the late seventies. Many women were writing incredible plays which pointed up a warped, sexist reality. . . . I think our work, beyond being avant-garde (that means getting rid of old structures, finding new meaning and creating new forms) also had an aware sensibility of the paradox and the inherent—almost genetic—cellular injustice between the sexes" (Betsko and Koening, 346). As one of several women playwrights responding to the question, "Where Are the Women Playwrights?" in the 20 May 1973 issue of the *New York Times*, Owens noted that while many women were writing for the theater, few were being produced, adding, "[T]hat sad fact is just a part of the general cultural attitude toward the female—women viewed in a particular framework are made invisible and totally ignored . . . [a woman who] dares to write [a] play . . . must have guts of steel and great forbearance to transcend the devious undermining, the negative expectations, and a mountain of other assaults on her sensibilities." In a later interview, she remembers being reviewed as "a housewife who writes plays." Such blatant sexism is among the subjects of her dramas, as are power, bestiality, scapegoating, love, murder, and theater itself—all part of her strategy of "challenging the established categories of theater" (Betsko and Koening, 344, 347).

Owens's *Futz* (1961), ostensibly a tale of bestiality concerning Cy Futz's passion for his pig, Amanda, proves to be a tale of scapegoating and misogyny when viewed under a feminist lens. Futz lives far from town and carries on his porcine amours in the privacy of his barn; to observe this "Satan" at his "abominations" with the pig he calls his "wife," the townsfolk must go to his farm. As Cy protests, "I wasn't near people. They came to me and looked under my trousers all the way up to their dirty hearts. They murdered my *own* life." The women in the play, having suffered years of being branded sluts and bitches, agree that "no woman is good" and acquiesce in their own oppression. In the 10 February 1968 *New Yorker*, Edith Oliver called *Futz* "a witty, harsh, fanciful, and touching dramatic poem," but, like other critics, overlooked its feminism. In a 1978 interview, Owens stated, "When *Futz* and my other plays were first produced, there was absolutely no feminist perspective on the part of the critics and intellectuals who had either read or seen my work. Thus, these plays were often seen as a cry for freedom for males. You see, the women were invisible. There were women in the plays obviously. The women's story was there. But the critics didn't see it. They all had blinders on. That's why feminism is so important."[37] In 1967 *Futz* won Obies for writing, directing, and acting.

The title character of *Chucky's Hunch* (1981), Owen's Obie Award–winning monologue, is a misogynistic failed artist, envenomed with scorn and hatred for the ex-wife to whom he addresses the letters that compose his monologue. He insists on his superiority: "I'm an artist, remember—an abstract expressionist that is. And you're just a housewife," and in that insistence, he typifies the "self-pitying male that a lot of women recognize as having known, married or lived with at one time or another. These men always regard women as support systems of one kind or another; nurturer, mother, sex object, muse, and scapegoat, if necessary. The very last thing they want in a woman is a competitor" (Betsko and Koening, 352).

Owens frequently employs poetic, even surreal metaphors in her plays, and she often incorporates violence to underscore the damage done to women by a patriarchal system. Committed to both reforming and re-forming the theater, she acknowledges feminism as vital to these tasks: "My writing is feminist because it has much to do with my personal and social identity as a woman in a patriarchal culture, and because it resists in both form and idea the absolute power of organized doctrine, principles, and procedures. One ought to question the assumptions of the culture which created the social role of women" (Coleman, 20). In challenging those assumptions, Owens prompts audience and reader to pursue challenges of their own.

Myrna Lamb: "One Ultimate Revolution"

In her introduction to *The Mod Donna and Scyklon Z: Plays of Women's Liberation* (1971), Myrna Lamb (born 1935) writes: "There are many valid revolutions which we must support. . . . And there is one ultimate revolution which encompasses them all, and that is the liberation of the female of the species."[38] Lamb feels the feminist movement has enabled women to see "themselves differently . . . as potential artists, not merely cooks and bottle-washers"; she wants her drama to effect social change and is "very hurt when people interpret [her] work as purely personal and psychological and don't see the political . . . substructure."[39] She helped found the New Feminist Repertory Theatre, which in 1969 premiered three of her one-act dramas—*But What Have You Done for Me Lately?* and *The Serving Girl and the Lady*, and *In The Shadow of the Crematoria*—an event that Honor Moore describes as a "breakthrough in feminist theatre" (Moore, 499).

In *But What Have You Done for Me Lately?* a male lawmaker implanted with a pregnant uterus offers to the female physician who performed the implant all the reasons why the fetus must be aborted. She counters each protest by echoing the responses made by the patriarchy as it exerts control over women's bodies in the name of religion or humanity; recalling her own unwanted pregnancy, she disparages "righteous male chauvinists of both sexes who identif[y] with the little clumps of cells and g[i]ve them precedence over the former owners of the host bodies." To the Man's protestations, the physician responds, "If one plea is valid, then they might all be. So you must learn to accept society's interest in the preservation of the fetus, within you, within all in your condition." She informs him that as a legislator he killed women, careers, spirits, love, and self-respect. Finally, she agrees to take his case before a board "composed of many women, all of whom have suffered in some way from the laws you so ardently supported." The board decides, "[o]ut of compassion for the potential child and regarding qualities of personality and not sex that make you a potentially unfit mother, . . . that the pregnancy is to be terminated." Written, Lamb admits, as a polemic, *But What Have You Done For Me Lately?* is a powerful statement of woman's right to self-determination.

While other playwrights of the second wave wrote plays that were feminist in philosophy, orientation, and subject matter and utilized antirealist structure and techniques such as transformation and nonlinear time schemes, held by many to be essential to feminist drama, Lamb made feminism itself her topic in *The Mod Donna: A Space-age Musical Soap Opera with Breaks for Commercials* (1970). On the surface a tale of mate swapping that satirizes the "new morality" of the 1970s, *The Mod Donna* incorporates issues of class status and capitalism into its plea for women's liberation. *The Mod Donna* intersperses choric songs and "commercials" dramatizing the dilemmas of women's everyday lives into the narrative of the capitalist "boss couple," Chris and her husband, Jeff, and the underling couple Donna and Charlie. Lamb details in the commercials and songs the ways in which women are bombarded with such messages as "Be desirable," and "Food is love / . . . So pick up that trusty kitchen tool." In the main plot, Chris, fearing her marriage going stale, has Jeff bring Donna, wife of Charlie, general manager at

Jeff's business, into their home and their marriage. Chris convinces Jeff he needs a child to validate his manhood, persuades Donna to bear that child, then decides her marriage has been revitalized and tells the pregnant Donna that she is no longer needed. When Donna refuses to leave, Chris gives Charlie pictures of Donna performing various sex acts with Jeff. Inflamed, Charlie, refusing even to recognize the role Jeff, his employer and master in the capitalist system, plays in Donna's seduction, wields a blunt instrument in what the stage directions call a "symbolic execution" of Donna, a graphic illustration of the manner in which capitalism seizes on women as scapegoats and consumes not only their labor but the women themselves. As the drama ends, the chorus sings of "Our true need / LIBERATION."

Because the play portrays marriage as exploitative and a trap for women, it drew predictable protests from some male reviewers. John H. O'Connor of the *Wall Street Journal* described it as "merely anti-sex. . . . The implications, far from being liberating, are disturbingly puritanical." *Newsday's* George Oppenheimer waffled in his patriarchal outrage: "It is so inept a plug (for women's liberation) that I left with a conviction that maybe we were wrong allowing women to vote" (*Plays of Women's Liberation,* back cover). But in the 4 May 1970 *New York Times* Clive Barnes found it a "pertinent and stimulating offering. . . . basically a political play . . . [which] raises the issues of women's liberation in a persuasive manner." In the 7 May 1970 *Village Voice,* Dick Bruckenfeld admired Lamb's courage and wit but called her drama's logic neither masculine nor feminine, "just dangerous." His review is an example of critics' oft-displayed inability to break the boundaries of such binary thinking as masculine/feminine and recognize that Lamb's logic is ungendered and liberating for all.

Celebrated by Vivian Gornick in the 28 May 1970 *Village Voice* as the "first true artist of feminist consciousness," Lamb is important for literally bringing liberation onstage. Her work with the New Feminist Repertory Theatre spurred the development of feminist theaters nationwide. Although her plays have a somewhat unfinished quality, Lamb's dense drama conveys, through probing questions and evocative images, emotion powerful enough to move others to enlist in the "ultimate revolution."

Jane Chambers: Dramatizing Lesbian Desire

The best-known plays of Jane Chambers (1937–83) bring onstage the representation of the lesbian and of lesbian desire, not by an outsider—as is the case in Hellman's *The Children's Hour*—but by a member of the community. Born in South Carolina, Chambers studied acting at the Pasadena Playhouse in California. Her dramas have been produced off-Broadway as well as in regional and community theaters and on television.

Chambers was playwright-in-residence for The Glines, a New York Theater established in 1976 by producer John Glines to present drama about the gay life experience. In 1982 the Fund for Human Dignity presented her with its annual award, which honors those who by "their work or by the example of their lives, have made a major contribution to public understanding and acceptance of lesbians and gay men." Chambers was instrumental in fighting what Karla Jay described in the 29 May 1979 *Boston Phoenix* as the oppression arising from "having other people tell your story." In 1984, the Women and Theatre Program of the American Theatre Association (now the Association for Theatre in Higher Education) established the Jane Chambers Playwriting Award for plays written by a woman from a feminist perspective, with a majority of women's roles.

Chambers wrote *A Late Snow* (1974) as a screenplay but was told by her agent, "Nobody's going to buy a movie script about lesbians." To her protest that the successful Broadway play of 1968 about gay men, *The Boys in the Band*, was being filmed, he countered, "Fags are funny, dykes are gloomy."[40] In 1974, when it was produced at Playwrights Horizons, several women refused to read for a role as a lesbian; two who were cast quit—one the night before the play opened (Hoffman, xi). The play presents five women stranded by a snowstorm. Before the storm, Quincey, Ellie's lover, comes to the cabin to install a Dutch cupboard, purchased from Ellie's former lover Pat, as a present celebrating Quincey and Ellie's first anniversary. While Pat helps Quincey move the cupboard into the cabin, Ellie, a college professor, returns from the out-of-town conference she's been attending, bringing with her, Margo, a famous writer. Later, the college roommate Ellie loved unrequitedly arrives.

Through several speeches, Chambers narrates the homosexual's oppression by the patriarchy, whose very foundation is heterosexuality. When Quincey reminds Ellie about a student "kicked . . . out of the dorm" because she attempted to organize a gay liberation group, Ellie says that she remains in the closet because she could lose her job, because she's frightened, and because "I don't want people pointing fingers at me, misguided altruists feeling sorry for me."

Pat, charged by Ellie with not loving herself, admits, "All right. I never wanted to be a woman. It's a crappy thing to be. You can't do anything! I saw my father raking in the money, playing [at] big business . . . while my mother ran the diaper brigade." Here Chambers pinpoints the gender discrimination of a patriarchal society; it was Pat's mother's sex, not her sexuality, which placed her in the inferior position.

By the drama's end, Ellie commits herself to Margo and to coming out. She is "tired of living a half-life" and resolves that, even though she cannot march, she will not hide. Although *A Late Snow* played to overflowing houses, the producer who optioned it for Broadway dropped that option, saying, "I can't get backers interested in a play about lesbians" (Hoffman, xii).

Chambers wrote *Last Summer at Bluefish Cove* (1980) for the first Gay American Art Festival at The Glines. Set in a beach resort exclusively for lesbians, the play won the 1980 Dramalogue Critics Circle Award and the Villager Downtown Theatre Award. As Sue-Ellen Case observes, here the lesbian community is the norm.[41] Into this community comes Eva, who has just left her husband and does not know she has rented a cottage at what "has been a gay women's haven for thirty years." Invited to a party by Lil before Lil realizes Eva is at Bluefish Cove "by accident," Eva meets three lesbian couples and discovers her own attraction to Lil, whose lover she becomes. Later, Eva learns Lil is dying of cancer (ironically, Chambers herself was stricken with cancer in 1981). Following Lil's death, Eva, sure now that she "can make it by [her]self," declines offers of employment and assistance from the others. Her relationship with Lil brought her the self-reliance she was unable to develop within marriage.

Through her character Kitty Cochrane, the closeted author of *The Female Sexual Imperative*, Chambers critiques the failure of heterosexual feminists, many of whom fear being seen as frustrated man haters, to support lesbian rights. To retain her authority with straight feminists, Kitty, awarded the title of "Literature's Most Credible Women's Libber" by *Publisher's Weekly*, must hide her sexuality. (Like *A Late Snow*, *Last Summer* narrates rather than dramatizes the reactions of family and friends to the characters' homosexuality.)

In *Quintessential Image* (1983), Chambers confronts the issue of lesbian representation. The drama, set in a television studio, demonstrates through camera angles and editing the ways in which images are manipulated. The protagonist became famous for photographing key moments in American history but was actually attempting to capture the image of her unrequited love. Through her photographer, Chambers "centres representation on the lesbian, moving her image from the margin to the centre," and thereby demonstrates how "lesbian experience ha[d] been made invisible by men and their history" (Case, 79).

Jill Dolan finds that, except for *Quintessential Image*, Chambers concentrates almost exclusively on the "coming out" stories of her characters, reifies monogamous sexuality, and suppresses or condemns the butch lesbian.[42] Janet Brown rebuts Dolan, pointing out that the focus of *Last Summer* "is on Eva's developing relationship with Lil . . . and on her growing bond with the lesbian community," and that the play "can certainly be said to speak for silenced women, for the lesbians are represented as sympathetic, oppressed members of the patriarchal society."[43] A pioneer in presenting lesbian sexuality onstage, Chambers offers her audience an insider's perspective that is a powerful tool in the struggle to overcome the patriarchy's proscription of representation of any sexuality save heterosexuality.

Martha Boesing: A Radical Voice

An eminent voice in feminist theater, Martha Boesing (born 1936) was the founder, artistic director, and playwright-in-residence of Minneapolis's At the Foot of the Mountain theater from 1974 to 1984; her work has been described as among "the most ambitious and innovative . . . in terms of both form and content."[44] Boesing received her bachelor of arts degree in English from Connecticut College, where her first play, *Accent on Fools*, was produced in 1956. She began doctoral work in theater at the University of Minnesota but left to begin her career with the Minneapolis Repertory Theatre. Actor, director, librettist, designer, and manager, in 1986 Boesing played the title role in At the Foot of the Mountain's *Fefu and Her Friends*, a production directed by Fornes. Her dramas have been presented across America and in Canada, Great Britain, Berlin, and Australia.

Lynne Greeley describes Boesing's dramas as falling into three categories: historic collages in which "Boesing quote[s] the original words of historical figures from documents, such as speeches and biographies, around which the characters [are] built"; collaborative pieces created with the companies by which they were staged; and those dramas of which she is the sole author.[45] In 36 plays and librettos, Boesing deploys her feminist consciousness over issues such as: the threat of nuclear destruction; deep ecology; addictions of various kinds—food, sex, love, and money, as well as chemicals; American involvement in Central America; the effects of Columbus's voyages to the New World; and the Great Depression, always with an eye toward exposing the oppressions of a society erected on patriarchal values and always celebrating the role of feminist consciousness in re-forming both the theater and the world.

In *River Journal* (1975), a modern morality play with music, Boesing works in the tradition of dramatizing the fragmented self, established by Alice Gerstenberg in *Overtones* and continued by Kennedy in *Funnyhouse of a Negro* and *The Owl Answers* and Marsha Norman in *Getting Out*. Here the fragmenting force is patriarchal marriage, analyzed as forcing women to repress their true selves and—to satisfy their husbands—become both flirtatious coquettes and self-sacrificing mother figures. Because this phenomenon is widespread and might be seen by the audience as "natural," Boesing calls for a production incorporating masks, costumes recalling school plays or pageants, and ritual.

The play begins with the marriage of Ann and Myles, following which her two sisters, Vera the coquette and Carla the crone (in "reality" projections of Ann's mind), move in with the couple and present life masks of themselves to Ann as gifts. While Vera flirts with Myles and Carla cooks for him, Ann resists the roles of wifehood; instead, she struggles to bring her own consciousness, symbolized by the journal in which she writes, into being. Within this journal Ann records three scenes detailing the bloody murders of her sisters, three attempts to free herself from these myths of femininity and womanhood. Despite her initial resistance, Ann eventually dons the masks, vowing to Myles, "I'm gonna be a good wife to you." The price she pays, conveyed to the audience by her dead-eyed stare, visible in the moments when she drops the mask, is too high. Encouraged by Snake, the high priestess of the Terrible Goddess of the Blood-Seed and emblematic of women's quest for self-knowledge, Ann puts on her own life mask and pursues her sisters with an ax; later, Snake presides over the ritual during which Ann burns the sisters' masks. As the play ends, Ann drops her journal into the river and hears the river singing:

Miriam Monasch, Marie Giest, and Jan MaGrand in the 1975 At the Foot of the Mountain production of Martha Boesing's *River Journal. Photograph courtesy of At the Foot of the Mountain Archives, Performing Arts Archives, University of Minnesota Libraries, St. Paul, Minnesota.*

The question is laid out
For each of us to ask:
Whether to hold on
Or to drop the mask.

Boesing sees women playing coquette and crone as "an inevitable behavior pattern, nurtured by the system. . . . a ritual that needs to be brought to light, examined, and finally changed, destroyed, so that a new ritual can be born from the ashes."[46] The play itself is a breakthrough, the first dramatic portrayal of the subversion of the "demon-angel dichotomy," the stereotyping of women as either whores or madonnas, which pervades drama. *River Journal* allows "individuals . . . to perceive representations of women in a new light and to recognize how their daily actions relate to such representation. . . . The historical significance of Carla's and Vera's banishment and the destruction of their masks is that [these actions] form a feminist response to the demon-angel dichotomy in twentieth-century American drama."[47]

In *The Story of a Mother* (1977) Boesing collaborated with the members of At the Foot of the Mountain to create a theater piece combining ritual, audience participation, and transformation with a portrait of the "everyday" in the lives of mothers and daughters. The work dramatizes the cultural feminist theory of Margaret Fuller and Elizabeth Cady Stanton that mothers "have special experiences and capabilities that lead them to express a life-affirming, pacifist, creative world view."[48]

Antigone, Too: Rites of Love and Defiance (1983) is a historical collage centered on civil disobedience. In her production note, Boesing remarks that the play celebrates "that community of women who have dared defy men's laws through the ages to honor the higher law of their own truth." Set in a jail cell, flanked by one platform from which Creon, the king, literally and figuratively looks down on the assembled women and a second from which, in marked counterpoint, Quaker Mary Dyer is hanged, *Antigone, Too*, combines Sophocles' text with those of the 17 North American women imprisoned with Antigone. To assure Antigone that she is not alone, the women share stories of their imprisonment, interrogations, and beatings. These tales become literally embodied into a strand of yarn that they wind around themselves and extend into the audience and that Creon, illustrating the patriarchy's investment in keeping women apart, cuts in several places.

Comfort and consolation are not all her sisters offer Antigone; in

A scene from the 1983 At the Foot of the Mountain production of Martha Boesing's *Antigone, Too. Photograph courtesy of At the Foot of the Mountain Archives, Performing Arts Archives, University of Minnesota Libraries, St. Paul, Minnesota.*

ode 4, whose purpose "is not to convert. It is simply to inform," the women narrate their successes: Mary Dyer's death led to Charles II's edict against persecution of the Quakers; the "Doctor's Bill" of 1936 made birth control "a routine part of our nation's health services"; Congress passed the Nineteenth Amendment guaranteeing women suffrage; in 1956, "the Supreme Court declared racial segregation of city buses to be illegal." Through the litany of change effected by these women, Boesing illustrates the power of civil disobedience. Her commitment is not merely philosophical, for in 1983 she stood trial with 150 others on trespassing charges arising from a protest against Minneapolis Honeywell, a defense contracting firm. Through artistic and personal courage and commitment, Boesing has "immeasurably strengthened feminist theater in the United States,"[49] while illustrating her belief in theater's power to transform lives. Through her radical vision her dramas offer creative, compassionate alternatives to a society threatened by patriarchal excess.

Emily Mann: The Theater of Testimony—Society on Trial

Born in Boston in 1952, Emily Mann was raised in Chicago. She attended the University of Chicago Laboratory High School, where she worked on several plays, including Megan Terry's *Viet Rock* and, at 16, directed her first play. As a freshman at Harvard University, she wrote her first play, then from her sophomore year on devoted herself to directing. A Bush Fellowship took her to the University of Minnesota/Guthrie Theatre program, in which she earned a master of fine arts degree in 1976. At the Brooklyn Academy of Music Theatre Company, she directed Crothers's *He and She*. In July 1990 she became artistic director of the McCarter Theater. In the 13 January 1991 *New York Times*, she told Hilary De Vries she was interested in creating a multicultural theater, because, "There are invisible racial and economic barriers that I want to break down. I want to create a theater of different American voices." In addition to Obies for playwriting and directing, Mann received the 1983 Rosamund Gilder Award for "outstanding creative achievement in the theater." She credits "Megan Terry, Irene Fornes, Rosalyn Drexler, Rochelle Owens, and Ntozske Shange [with] revolutioniz[ing] the theater in the seventies. These women radicalized our perception of and our consciousness about theater" (Betsko and Koening, 282).

Called fugues, compositions for voices, documentary drama, and theater of testimony, Mann's plays—combining monologue, dialogue, music, film, and slides and deriving from personal interviews, trial transcripts, and news accounts, both print and electronic—are truly innovative. Her works are not docudramas for she does not offer dramatic reenactment; instead, she distills material from real life in her dramatic retort, working an alchemy of deconstruction. Her work "forces the spectator to confront his or her own attitudes and beliefs and, without offering a facile solution, encourages reevaluation of deeply troubling issues" (Savran, 146). Although Mann is sometimes reluctant to be labeled a feminist, her plays and her philosophy proclaim her feminism. The form of her drama is nonlinear; she puts women in the subject position and eschews dramatizing violence, because "I did not want to perpetuate the myth that violence is sexy, I did not want to be a party to it . . . it's not sexy, and it's not fun. It's rare to see violence between men and women onstage or in film which is not somehow erotic. I want to break down those clichés" (Betsko and Koening, 285). Whether the violence concerns the Holocaust, Vietnam, domestic abuse, or murder, the deed is reported; as in classical Greek drama, the audience sees effects, not enactment. Mann's moral philosophy is also feminist in its insistence on personal responsibility: "I think anything you put on a stage is a great responsibility because you have the power to move and change. . . . You've got to take complete responsibility for both the statements you make and the effect you have on a crowd" (Savran, 158).

Annulla, An Autobiography (1986), which originated as *Annulla Allen: Autobiography of a Survivor* (1974), Mann's first drama, premiered at the Guthrie in a production she directed in 1977. It derives from interviews Mann conducted with the aunt of a friend when she and the friend were traveling in Europe. In the play, Annulla, living in London at the age of 74, delivers a monologue about her life's progress from an affluent, indulged childhood, through having her husband imprisoned in Dachau while she remained free by posing as an Aryan, to working as a domestic servant when she escapes to London. The play is framed by the voice of a 32-year-old American woman, an obvious Mann surrogate. Annulla, who has "seen firsthand men's barbarism taken to his [*sic*] extreme with Hitler," is writing a play, *The Matriarchs*, based on her theory that, "If there were a global matriarchy . . . there would be no more of this evil. *I have all the answers in my play!*" A cultural feminist who believes that mother love "is the most powerful response in the world of a positive kind" and that "No woman who has ever loved her child could be a Stalin or a Hitler," Annulla leaves no space for women who are not mothers and ignores her destructive relationship with her own mother.

In *Still Life*, Mann revisits the issues of violence and feminism. In 1981, the play won Mann Obies for playwriting and direction. The play distills 140 hours of interviews with people she met in Minneapolis. Its staging is simple: the three characters, a man, his mistress, and his wife, sit at a table facing the audience, to whom they address their monologues; they seldom seem aware of each other. (Although the play is drawn from life, this style of presentation is markedly similar to that of Samuel Beckett's *Play*, and Mann does name Beckett as an influence on her work.) Mark, a Vietnam veteran brutalized by the war, has "brought the war home," terrorizing his wife, Cheryl, who says, "Mark wants to kill me." Yet Nadine, the mistress, sees him as the gentlest man she's ever known. Their testimony puts America itself on trial, exposing the interstices between expectations and reality. Mark, whose "biggest question of all my life was / How would I act under combat? / That would be who I was as a man," presents "courage" in combat as proof of manhood, an idea as ancient as warfare itself. Nadine sees herself as a feminist, and while she justly points out that keeping a house and raising children involve "a tremendous amount of work / that in our society is not measurable," she can also speak unironically about women being given "permission" to drive and has no qualms about her affair with another woman's husband. Mann's critique of patriarchal marriage is reminiscent of Boesing's *River Journal.*

As she did in *Still Life,* Mann uses the audience as a jury in *Execution of Justice,* a drama constructed around the trial of Dan White, former city supervisor, for the murders of San Francisco mayor George Moscone and Harvey Milk, the first openly gay city supervisor. The play was cowinner of the Actors Theatre of Louisville's 1983 Great American Play Contest. Mann combines film and television footage, the trial transcript, and personal interviews in this dramatization of the tensions within Dan White and between conservative and liberal factions in the city; in the process, she spotlights media excesses. She also adds the testimony of those she names the "uncalled witnesses," a chorus that includes a city policeman, a gay rights activist, friends of White, Moscone, and Milk, and a young mother. As Mann's title implies, the workings of the system itself were on trial in this case and, ultimately, Justice herself was executed. White, whom the defense depicted as an all-American boy debilitated by family worries and his consumption of junk food—his lawyers conceived the now infamous "Twinkie defense"—was found guilty of only voluntary manslaughter. While the Young Mother asks, "What are we teaching our sons?" White is given the maximum sentence: seven years and eight months.

Mann is a playwright concerned with moral problems and social justice, who uses documentary material in a nonlinear, nonrealistic manner. Despite Fornes's insistence that the dramas are "not theatre literature. It may be serious and subtle work, but it's not a play" (Savran, 65), Mann has moved theater in new directions by using documentary materials to denaturalize many of the assumptions of a patriarchal society and by confronting her audiences with the difficult decisions that her plays refuse to make for them. Indeed, Emily Mann herself is the most compelling witness in her "theater of testimony."

Ntozake Shange: Loving the "god" Within

Ntozake Shange, born in 1948 in Trenton, New Jersey, to Elois Williams, a psychiatric social worker, and Paul T. Williams, a physician, was named Paulette for her father, who had wanted a boy. The family moved to St. Louis when she was eight; there she was bused to a German-American school, where she experienced the bitterness of racism. At home, Shange met W. E. B. Du Bois, Josephine Baker, Miles Davis, Paul Robeson, and Cesar Chavez. At eighteen she entered Barnard College, majoring in American studies; at 19, after separating from her law-student husband, she made the first of several suicide attempts. Nevertheless, she earned a bachelor's degree with honors in 1970. Moving to California, she renounced her "slave name" in 1971 and became *Ntozake* (she who comes with her own things) *Shange* (who walks like a lion). She earned a master's degree in American studies from the University of Southern California, Los Angeles, and began teaching women's studies and African American studies at Sonoma State. She describes the courses she taught as being "inextricably bound to the development of my sense of the world, myself, and women's language" and as "root[ing] me to an articulated female heritage and imperative."[50]

Shange regrets the fact that most plays by black men focus on their battles with white men, and celebrates drama by black women because it does not "continually focus all of our attention on the Other. Our attention [is] in our community."[51] To focus this attention, Shange employs her own orthography. She seldom uses capital letters; employs ampersands, virgules, abbreviations, phonetic spellings, and black dialect; and generally eschews commas and apostrophes. Her language signifies her resistance to the King's English, about which she comments, "i cant count the number of times i have viscerally wanted to attack deform or maim the language that i waz taught to hate myself in/the language that perpetuates the notions that cause pain to every black child as he/she learns to speak of the world & the 'self.' "[52]

As a feminist, Shange insists on the linkage of the personal and the political: "I think the dangerous mistake that women make is to assume the personal is not political. When I make a personal statement, it is to me a political statement" (Betsko and Koening, 370). Interviewed for the 7 May 1989 *New York Times*, she spoke of the place of gender in her writing: "I'm a playwright. But I'm a woman first. I am not a generic playwright. I am a woman playwright. And I would hope that my choice of words and my choice of characters and situations reflect my experience as a woman on the planet. I don't have anything that I can add to the masculine perception of the world. What I can add has to be from what I've experienced. And my perceptions and my syntax, my colloquialism, my preoccupations are founded in race and gender." According to Shange, black women, to be represented at all, must themselves do the writing.[53] Shange saw the necessity for black women to "move our theater into the drama of our lives" (Foreword, ix), which she accomplishes partly by legitimating female desire in "writing about adolescent girls and young women. . . . And one of the reasons I try to investigate girls from different backgrounds and girls with different senses of success is because I want to make sure that we all know that none of our desires are illegitimate."[54] In form, Shange's drama is feminist and nonlinear, incorporating music, character transformation, and dream sequences. It is also African and African American in its utilization of oral and musical forms found in both cultures. She has won Obies for *for colored girls* and for *Mother Courage and Her Children* (1980), her adaptation of Brecht's play.

for colored girls who have considered suicide/when the rainbow is enuf, only the second play by a black woman to be presented on Broadway (Hansberry's *A Raisin in the Sun* was the first) began its trip there at the Bacchanal, a women's bar in Berkeley, California, in 1974. In September 1976, it opened at the Booth Theater where it ran for two years. The play earned an Obie, the Outer Circle Critics Award, the Audelco (Audience Development Committee) Award for excellence in black theater, the Golden Apple Award, and Tony, Grammy, and Emmy Award nominations. Reminiscent of Marita Bonner's *The Purple Flower* in its use of music and dance, *for colored girls* in its final form consists of 20 poems that together function as a bildungsroman, chanting the coming into consciousness and community of a black Everywoman. Shange calls her drama a "choreopoem"—a term she coined to describe a drama in which the speakers dance or move while delivering their lines—which combines metered prose and jazz rhythms, and which she felt fit, somehow, between genres.

In describing her drama, Shange shifts from third-person singular to first-person plural, calling it "the words of a young black girl's growing up, her triumphs and errors, *our* struggle to become all that is forbidden by *our* environment, all that is forfeited by *our* gender, all that *we* have forgotten" [emphasis added] (*for colored girls*, xiv). For Shange, *for colored girls*, which "introduced feminist thought-in-action to theatre" (introduc-

Leah Bass (rear left) and (left to right) Dana Hollowell-Khan, Brenda Thomas, Louise Gorham, and CCH Pounder in Ntozake Shange's *for colored girls*, produced in 1980 by the Crossroads Theatre Company. *Photograph courtesy of the Crossroads Theatre Company, New Brunswick, New Jersey.*

tion to *Resurrection*, xxv), played a social role in moving "our theater into the drama of our lives." The 20 poems chronicle the black woman's progress from enduring a death-in-life—

> closed in silence so long
> she doesn't know the sound
> of her own voice
> her infinite beauty

through learning black history, experiencing a joyful sexual initiation, enacting myth and stereotype, and knowing the pains of betrayal, rape, and abortion to achieving a true sense of identity, an almost sacramental community with her peers, and discovering the sacredness of her own being. The poems are recited by seven ladies identified only by the hues of their dresses, the red, orange, yellow, green, blue, and purple of the rainbow, plus the brown that metonymically represents the colored girls of the title. In "graduation nite," Shange, recognizing that sexual awakening is empowering, reclaims sexual experience as a pleasurable and powerful initiatory ritual for the female, whose coming to adulthood is more frequently marked in literature, when marked at all, by first menstruation, which the young woman often misinterprets as injury and those around her label "the curse," or by a markedly unpleasant act of intercourse. Here, the lady in yellow narrates a tale of being with "bobby":

> in the backseat of that ol buick
> wow
> by daybreak
> I just cant stop grinnin

and tells the lady in blue, "and, honey, it was wonderful." Sexuality needn't be shameful or hidden; it should be celebrated.

Unfortunately, the world at large may see sexuality differently, as Shange acknowledges by combining myth and stereotype in "sechita," the narrative of a carnival dancer who is also "sechita/egyptian/goddess of creativity" and nefertite and who enacts the madonna/whore dichotomy as this goddess and queen catches the coins thrown at her by the "cracker[s]" watching her dance. Shange's "latent rapists" begins with a "sudden light change [to which] all of the ladies react as if they had been struck in the face." It is probably the first staged explication of acquaintance rape, and, in the play, as often in life, the authorities insist that it is not rape, for "if you know him/you must have wanted it."

In "somebody almost walked off wid alla my stuff," the lady in green catalogues the nonmaterial "stuff" that composes a personality and describes how a vampire lover can steal that self. Asserting that "stealin my shit from me/don't make it yrs/makes it stolen," she reclaims "this package/of me for my destiny." Following this poem, the lady in red tells the story of beau willie, the traumatized Vietnam veteran who has finally been left by crystal, the mother of their two children, after enduring years of his abuse. willie keeps returning to beg crystal to marry him; on his last visit, he lulls her into allowing him to hold the children, whom he then dangles out the window and, to her anguish, drops. As crystal discovers, a declaration of independence from an abusive man often brings retributive violence.

Finally, to heal the wounded, in "a layin on of hands," the ladies realize that what is missing in their lives is that touch; finding actuality in "the ghost of another woman" brings the solace of community. This epiphany, says the lady in red, affects her physically, emotionally, and spiritually:

> i waz cold/i waz burnin up/a child
> & endlessly weavin garments for the moon
> wit my tears
> i found god in myself
> & i loved her/i loved her fiercely.

As all the ladies softly repeat "i found god in myself and i loved her," the lines swell to an anthem of joy shared among themselves, then with the audience. As the ladies "enter into a closed tight circle" signifying their newfound community, the lady in brown pronounces a benediction: "& this is for colored girls who have considered suicide/but are movin to the ends of their own rainbows."

Over the years, scholars and critics have complained about the play's incomplete characterization, narrow focus, and negative portraits of black men, but initial reviews were largely enthusiastic. In the 14 June 1976 *Newsweek*, Jack Kroll described Shange's poems as "outcries filled with controlled passion against the brutality that blasts the lives of 'colored girls'—a phrase that in her hands vibrates with social irony and poetic beauty." Marilyn Stassio wrote in the 26 June 1976 issue of *Cue* that "this fierce and passionate poetry has the power to move a body to tears, to rage, and to an ultimate rush of love."

In *boogie woogie landscapes* (1978), layla, a black woman in her 20s, returns from a disco and reviews her life through the guises of her "night-life" companions, who enter through her bedroom walls and represent her "dream-memories." Shange focuses on flagrant abuse of women as nightlife companion #3 explains that "it's not so good to be born a girl/sometimes," when societies throw girls away, sell them, rape them, infibulate them because "their pleasure is profane . . . [and] disrupt[s] the very unnatural dynamic of polygamy," and where "infibulation, excision, clitorectomies, rape, & incest are irrevocable life-deniers/life stranglers & disrespectful of natural elements." But the play also includes memories of daddy, who, when his wife left home, held together the family of five children and "brushed our braids to a point like a dunce's cap & then patted them down." Here Shange provides a useful corrective to the myth of black matriarchy promulgated in the famous Moynihan report of 1965[55] and to the tales of absent, uncaring, or abusive black fathers.

In *spell #7: geechee jibara quik magic trance manual for technologically stressed third world people* (1979), Shange critiques the manner in which representation itself works to make blacks invisible. When the audience enters the theater, they see a stage dominated by a "huge black face mask hanging from the ceiling . . . for the audience must integrate this grotesque, larger than life misrepresentation of life into their pre-show chatter." The character lou, a magician dressed as a minstrel show's Mr. Interlocutor, enters and tells the audience that his father was a magician who retired when a child "asked to be made white/on the spot." As the rest of the company enters wearing masks that duplicate the large mask and the tattered dress of field hands, lou the magician continues:

> but aint no colored magician in his right mind
> gonna make you   white
> i mean
>   this is blk magic
> you lookin at
> & i'm fixin you up good/fixin you up good & colored
> & you gonna be colored all yr life
> & you gonna love it/bein colored/all yr life/colored & love it
> love it/bein colored. SPELL #7!

lou claps his hands and cast members reenact, in minstrel style, dances from "every period of afro-american entertainment," and end kneeling, as if poised to sing "Mammy." At this point, many members of the white audience who missed the irony of Shange's critique of the minstrel form in its blatant misrepresentation of African Americans would applaud, then be granted insight by lou's reciting a litany of racist abuses, beginning, "why dont you go on & integrate a german-american school in st. louis mo./1955/better yet why don't ya go on & be a red niggah in a blk school in 1954/I got it/try & make one friend at camp in the ozarks in 1957," and ending, "why dontcha c'mon & live my life for me." After alec removes his mask and tells a tale of growing up in St. Louis under the constant threat of beatings, lou repeats his earlier question, asking white audience members to imagine life as an African American. The scene shifts to a bar frequented by black actors, most of whom are unemployed because there are no roles for blacks or because they are too light skinned to play blacks but not allowed to play whites, despite, of course, the long tradition of the minstrel show in which whites (mis)represented blacks. Those who are working are enacting stereotypes as whore or mammy. In a line reminiscent of the portrayal the white director in Childress's *Trouble in Mind* attempted to elicit from Wiletta, bettina says, "if that director asks me to play it any blacker/i'm gonna have to do it in a mammy dress." The actors tell stories and play the parts narrated therein, thereby realizing the opportunity "to feel something like that/ [since] i got into this business cuz i wanted to feel things all the time." natalie plays "white," becoming a white girl who pushes Indian women out of her way and smiles at blacks and Puerto Ricans while hoping they'll "go back where they came from/or at least be invisible" and waits for the "colored lady" to arrive to clean her house. When she comes to realize that she doesn't do much of anything because of the white man's sexism, she recalls the narrator of *A Black Woman Speaks*, describing how black and white women have been prevented by the white patriarchy from realizing their common cause as women. As the play ends, the minstrel mask descends, an effective reminder of the African American's continuing invisibility in white America.

Shange, as Margaret B. Wilkenson points out, is significant in feminist and American theater history "not only [for] introduc[ing] a new theatrical form, the choreopoem, to the professional stage, but [also for] present[ing] women's experience with a new intimacy and candor."[56] Shange illuminates the recesses of racism and sexism, as her drama describes black characters overcoming oppression and learning to love themselves. Above all, she remains true to the advice she would give aspiring writers: "[N]o matter what happens, never think it's not worthwhile. And never be afraid, whatever it is, that it's too beautiful or too terrible to tell" (Lyons, 696).

Practice and Praxis

The experimental playwrights of the second wave challenged and deconstructed conventional theater practice. They replaced the through line with a circular structure, set chronological time reeling into nonlinear representation, infused music, dance, and poetry into the prosaic pattern of male-dominated dramas and identified women as desiring subjects rather than adjuncts or reflections of male characters. Moreover, they often eschewed catharsis and closure, preferring that their audiences leave the theaters both aware of, and pondering the solutions to, the oppression they have witnessed.

6

Feminisms: The Debate over Realism

From the inception of feminist drama and performance theory, many theorists have posited the incompatibility of feminism and realism, arguing that realism naturalizes the status quo of the patriarchal system. These theorists find no place in feminist drama for realist conventions. As Sue-Ellen Case states, "Realism, in its focus on the domestic sphere and the family unit, reifies the male as sexual subject and the female as the sexual 'Other.' The portrayal of female characters within the family unit—with their confinement to the domestic setting, their dependence on the husband, their often defeatist, determinist view of the opportunities for change—makes realism a 'prisonhouse of art' for women, both in their representation on stage and in the female actor's preparation and production of such roles" (Case, 124). Elsewhere, Case sees realism not as imprisonment, but death: "The closure of . . . realistic narratives chokes the women to death and strangles the play of symbols, or the possibility of seduction. . . . Cast the realism aside—its consequences for women are deadly."[1] Rosemary Curb finds that "popular American realism presents only a single and often superficial layer of human experience . . . it cannot represent the diversity of women's experience. Thus, by intent or default, it upholds the masculine status quo."[2] In *The Feminist Critic* as *Spectator*, Jill Dolan labels realism "a conservative force that reproduces and reinforces dominant cultural relations" and a structure "embedded in oppressive representational strategies" (Dolan, 84). Helene Keyssar faults realism for making of an audience "voyeurs, able to escape what [they] see without notice or effect" (Keyssar, 102). The 1987 preconference meeting of the Women and Theatre Program of the Association for Theatre in Higher Education included several discussions organized around "the failure of realism in representing the 'feminist subject' onstage."[3]

Calling realism "mimesis at its most naive," Elin Diamond observes, "Realism's fetishistic attachment to the true referent and the spectator's invitation to rapturous identification with a fictional image serve the ideological function of mystifying the means of material production, thereby concealing historical contradictions while reaffirming or mirroring the 'truth' of the status quo" (Diamond, 366). But rather than abandon mimesis, Diamond advocates an exploration of the possibilities of mimicry, repeating and "exceeding the mirror's content" (Diamond, 372), as Luce Irigaray advocates, or of destabilizing mimetic truth by replacing it with "a hysterical realism—a realism without truth," as Julia Kristeva suggests (Diamond, 377), because "[i]t is better, perhaps, to acknowledge certain mimetic desires, to militate for the complex, the *different* references we want to see, even as we work to dismantle the mechanisms of patriarchal modeling" (Diamond, 369).

Patricia R. Schroeder and Sheila Stowell suggest that realism can be recuperated as a successful feminist dramatic mode. Cautioning against "overlook[ing] or even reject[ing] the feminist possibilities inherent in more traditional dramatic forms," Schroeder suggests these forms can "support feminist values by depicting the entrapment of female characters in an unyielding, traditional society" and that "the more realistic plays [may not be] . . . necessarily as conventional as they appear."[4] She decries "the lamentable tendency to prescriptiveness" among certain theorists, advocates "the value of maintaining a well-informed pluralism in approaching feminist drama," and states that "we cannot simply dismiss realism."[5] Stowell points out the "differences between realist authors," points up the fact that "realist theatre does not *necessarily* present a coherent or unassailable view of society," and questions whether realism "can be said to be more essentially 'illusionistic' than other forms of drama."[6] Stowell notes that "realist theatre developed as a radical, low-mimetic response to the glittering make-believe world of society drama

. . . [and] was championed as a means of challenging the ideological assumptions imbedded in melodrama and the well-made play" (Stowell, 84). She warns that "the possibility of silencing (women) writers because they do not 'write right' is a danger to which feminist critics should be particularly alert" (Stowell, 87).

The politics of representation will continue to engender debate, but feminist critics must be aware of the implications of Curb's use of the word "default." In ruling out realism, might feminists not cede a large portion of the audience to the very reinscription they would have that audience resist? Rather than postulate divisive litmus tests, critics should examine the individual dramas. In this way the drift toward hegemony and the temptation of canon construction may be avoided. Surely the many feminisms now extant and the varieties of feminist audiences among them offer many ideological spaces.

Beth Henley: Crimes of the Patriarchy

Mary Beth Henley (born 1952) is a native of Jackson, Mississippi. Her mother acted in amateur theater, inspiring Henley, who initially wished to act, not write. Henley completed one year of graduate study in acting at the University of Illinois and views this training as a significant force in her success, claiming in a 25 October 1981 interview in the *New York Times* that she learned playwriting "from acting and reading plays."

Henley finds discrimination against women in the theater: "Simply because there are still a lot more men than women in charge of our theaters: producing, directing, managing, fund raising. That's where the power and money are in this country. . . . Men aren't used to identifying with women. . . . In terms of the people who make decisions about play production, the closer these dreams are to their version of themselves, the more chance they'll want to sit through a play or to find money to produce it" (Betsko and Koenig, 221). Critics divide on the question of Henley's feminism. Jonnie Guerra finds that "Henley's failure to advance positive images of women [is due to] her consistent and unimaginative dependence on the forms and modes of the dominant male tradition of American drama,"[7] while Karen L. Laughlin claims that "Henley's dramatization—and eventual redefinition—of the female criminal builds toward a vision of feminine assertiveness and female bonding as an alternative to self-destruction."[8] Occupying a middle ground is Keyssar, who asserts that "the script of . . . *Crimes of the Heart* has many of the ingredients of a strong feminist drama" (157), but notes that the script can be undermined by productions in which the actors parody their roles. Henley herself remarked that some critics "wouldn't look for any of the deeper meaning or the spiritual levels in the play. Whereas if a man wrote a play about a baseball game, critics might be more inclined to find deep meanings about the Lost American Dream" (Betsko and Koening, 219).

Crimes of the Heart (1979) was cowinner of the 1979 Great American Play Contest at the Actors' Theatre of Louisville. Before it opened on Broadway in November 1981, it won the Pulitzer Prize, becoming the first play to win a Pulitzer before its Broadway debut and making Henley the first woman to win this prize in 23 years. Running for 535 performances, the play received the New York Drama Critics Circle Award for the best new American play, the George Oppenheimer *Newsday* Playwriting Award, and a Tony nomination.

Beneath its surface presentation of the crimes committed by the MaGrath sisters, Lenny, Meg, and Babe, the play, set in Mississippi, critiques the crimes of the patriarchy, including the father's abandoning the family; Babe being physically and verbally abused by her husband, Zackery; Zackery's racism; sexual double standards; and the suffocating control exercised over the sisters by the figure and symbol of patriarchy, their Old Granddaddy. The play begins with a reunion occasioned by Babe's shooting and seriously wounding Zackery, ostensibly because she "just didn't like his stinking looks!" Meg, who has been in Hollywood, supposedly establishing a singing career, returns to the homestead where Lenny has been keeping house for Old Granddaddy; Babe joins them when she is freed on bail.

All have been affected by their mother's suicide. The sisters were left to the supervision of Old Granddaddy, who seems to have alternately starved them of his affection and approval, and sated them with sickening sweets, like the banana splits he allowed them to gorge on the morning of their mother's funeral. While he may, as Lenny protests, have believed that, "All he ever wanted was the very best for us," his confidence in his patriarchal convictions prevented his asking, as Meg reminds them, "what we wanted." Instead, he scripts their lives. Babe, the pretty one, his "Dancing Sugar Plum," will recoup the MaGraths' respectability—damaged by the mother's suicide—by marrying into Hazelhurst society, and Meg, with her talent for singing, will bring fame. Lenny, marred by a shrunken ovary, and thus deemed unfit for marriage by a patriarchy that defines womanhood by an ability to reproduce will fulfill woman's role of serving man by keeping house for Old Granddaddy.

Against a background of nursery rhymes, children's songs, and Mother Goose stories, Henley rewrites Old Granddaddy's scenario. Chick Boyle is the female cousin who, like Hellman's Amelia Tilford in *The Children's Hour*, serves as the voice of patriarchy while Old Granddaddy lies in the hospital. She pronounces Meg "cheap Christmas trash" because of her past love affairs, while Meg calls her "Little Chicken." This reference to Chicken Little, the alarmist of the Mother Goose world, alerts the audience that the sky will not fall if the sisters fail to live up to Old Grandaddy's expectations. Also part of the world of childhood are Billy Boy, Lenny's "mighty old" horse—named for the song that conflates woman's age and her marriageability—who was struck and killed by lightening the night before the play begins, and the long absent Daddy, whose "white teeth" are reminiscent of that childhood ogre, the Big Bad Wolf. As Henley rewrites her fairy tale, Babe does not "live happily ever after" with Zackery Botrelle. Despite Old Granddaddy's convictions that "Babe was gonna skyrocket to the heights of Hazelhurst society. And [that] Zackery was just the right man for her whether she knew it or not," the handsome prince turned out to be an abusive husband who "brutalized and tormented" her for years.[9]

In addition to shooting in self-defense against years of battering, Babe also shoots Zackery to protect her young black lover, Willie Jay; informed of Babe's affair by his sister, who hires a private detective to spy on the lovers, Zackery discovers Babe with Willie Jay, demeans him by calling him "boy," and beats him. Although Babe's remark to Meg about not wanting to ruin Willie Jay's reputation may draw laughter from an audience raised on a sexual double standard, Willie Jay's predicament is serious in a Mississippi, where teenaged Emmet Till was murdered in 1954 for merely whistling at a white woman.

Meg, rather than finding the fortune and fame her granddaddy envisions, works for a dog food company. After losing her singing voice and suffering from "this incredibly painful toothache," which symbolizes her failure to please Old Granddaddy, she "[e]nded up in L.A. County Hospital, Psychiatric Ward." Henley does show a woman's "failure" driving her mad, but she also dramatizes man's reaction to woman asserting herself beyond his notion of her place. Chick, the female voice of the patriarchy, tells Lenny that Babe will end up in "some—mental institution"; Zackery, present only as an unheard voice at the other end of a telephone, tells Babe she is as crazy as her mother was, and even the sympathetic Barnette Lloyd, Babe's lawyer, considers a plea of temporary insanity for her. As Phyllis Chesler showed in *Women and Madness* (1972) and Maxine Harris and Jeffrey Geller demonstrated anew in *Women of the Asylum: Voices from behind the Wall* (1993), diagnostic labels are often used to stigmatize women who dare to disagree with fathers, husbands, or brothers.

Lenny, believing Old Granddaddy's narrative that no man would want to marry her, breaks off a relationship so the man will not reject her. She becomes a servant to her grandfather, abandoning her bed to sleep on a cot in the kitchen, the better to hear him if he should call for her in the night. But encouraged by her sisters, Lenny calls Charlie, discovers that he dislikes children, and is anxious to resume their relationship.

The play begins with a pathetic Lenny attempting to fuse a candle to a "birthday cookie" while she sings "Happy Birthday" to herself and begins to make a wish. It ends with the three sisters gathered around a huge birthday cake, "frame[d] in a magical, golden, sparkling glimmer." That glimmer is one of possibilities. Patriarchy is not dead, but, as embodied by Old Granddaddy, it lies comatose. Babe may go to jail, Meg may misuse her newfound ability to experience emotion, and Lenny's reunion may not be a happy one—but in the absence of patriarchy, the sisters establish new relationships to one another, not as Old Granddaddy's granddaughters rehearsing old hurts and jealousies but as sisters and women. Everything is, as yet, liminal. But in Lenny's birthday wish—which was a "vision . . . something about the three of us smiling and laughing together. . . . But it wasn't forever; it wasn't for every minute. Just this one moment and we were all laughing"—Henley rewrites the fairy tales of women's fate, offering no pretense that the golden moment is a permanent state, but positing for each of the sisters a self-determination sustained by remembering this moment of love and sisterly solidarity.

Like the MaGrath sisters, Carnelle, the protagonist of *The Miss Firecracker Contest* (1981), was abandoned by her father. Carnelle sought acceptance by exchanging sex for affection, but instead earned herself only the nickname "Miss Hot Tamale." Now reformed, Carnelle desires acknowledgment of her new self by being named "Miss Firecracker" in the annual Fourth of July beauty contest. But Henley casts a cold eye on both beauty contests and the male gaze. Carnelle wants to win the contest so that she can "leave [town] in a blaze of glory"; her belief in the contest does not stop Henley from satirizing it. Carnelle must enter and win this year because next year she will be 25, too old to be a participant. Here Henley uncovers the male preference for youth in women. Carnelle's cousin Delmount labels the contest "a garish display of prancing pigs," whose talents include a comedy pantomime of "Take Me Out to the Ball Game," a hoola-hoop [*sic*] act, and Carnelle's tap dancing to "The Star-Spangled Banner." Although Carnelle's dance routine, complete with sparklers and Roman candles, is a hit, victory is not to be hers; the judges "really just took those 'Miss Hot Tamales' to heart."

Delmount personifies the male gaze governing the contest; he anatomizes a woman's body parts. He becomes entranced with an exotically shaped nose or lips that are unusually soft and smooth and brags, "I have yet to make advances to any woman who didn't possess at least one classically beautiful characteristic." Through Delmount, Henley satirizes those males, not negligible in number, who blithely declare themselves "leg men, breast men," and so on.

Returning to her dressing room, a dejected Carnelle gazes into the mirror at her crimson-dyed hair, remembering that, "It used to be brown. I had brown hair." Recognizing the self she disguised to gain favor with others, she joins Delmount to view the fireworks, as Henley explodes several stereotypes about women.

Most discussions of Henley's drama focus on *Crimes of the Heart* and much of that concerns whether the play is "definitively feminist"[10] or not. In presenting women characters who, though marginalized, embody woman's quest for identity and resist the roles others readily impose on them, Henley confronts "an entire patriarchal vision of reality which works like *Crimes of the Heart* ultimately call into question" (Laughlin, 49).

Tina Howe: The Subversive Scent

Born in New York City in 1937, Tina Howe wrote her first play in a course in short-story writing at Sarah Lawrence College. Fellow student Jane Alexander, actor and chairwoman of the National Endowment for the Arts in the Clinton administration, encouraged Howe to produce the play. It was staged in 1959, with Alexander directing. After graduation, Howe spent a year in France where she attended a performance of Eugene Ionesco's *The Bald Soprano* and felt as if she had been struck by lightening."[11] When she returned to the states, Howe taught high school

English and, she says, "managed to talk the principals [into letting] me run the Drama Department, on the condition that only my plays be done. . . . If you can hold an audience of a thousand teenagers who couldn't care less, that is really a trial by fire. I learned the craft in those years. . . . I began to see what worked on stage." (Betsko and Koening, 234). Howe went on to garner honors that include an Obie, the John Gassner Outer Critics Circle Award, and a Tony nomination. In 1992 the Iowa Summer Rep honored her with a Tina Howe Festival. Howe, who teaches playwriting at Hunter College and New York University, defines the theater as "an arena of prayer and shock."[12]

Her first plays shocked many critics. *The Nest* (1969), set in an aerie on the one-hundred-fiftieth floor of an apartment building, centers on courtship rituals and the brutal competition between women seeking husbands. "One of [its] boldest and funniest scenes shows a young bride stripping to plunge into a seven-foot-tall wedding cake. When she emerges . . . covered with whipped cream, her bridegroom proceeds to lick her clean. The New York critics did not know what to make of this raw parody of boring wedding receptions. Howe demystified both the public feast and the private consummation sanctioned and sanctified by the ritual" (Lamont 1993, 30).

In *Birth and after Birth* (1974), Howe writes of "birth . . . children [and] the early stages of marriage when life can be very raw . . . [an] arena [that] hasn't been explored because it is so radical and dangerous" (DiGaetani, 153). Staged only in a workshop production that Howe directed, *Birth* takes place on the fourth birthday of Sandy and Bill Apple's son Nicky, played by an adult to emphasize his strength of will and the control he exercises over his parents. Howe says, "I wrote *Birth and after Birth* out of my own experience, but also out of the experience of women I knew. . . . I wrote this play for the suburban woman with no exit from her kitchen and a four-year-old seven feet tall" (Moore, 101).

Sandy Apple hopes to use the birthday party to persuade her friend Mia Freed to have a child. The childlessness of Mia and her husband, Jonathan, both anthropologists, is emphasized in their last name, Freed, while Sandy's entrapment is evident in her manic cleaning up after Nicky as the child unwraps his birthday gifts. As he "tears into" his presents, "[r]uin[ing] everything," in Sandy's view, she comments, "I just don't understand you. One minute you're the sweet baby Mommy brought home from the hospital, and the next, you're a savage!" Still, she insists that childbirth is "the most beautiful thing that can happen to a woman." Howe examines this stress on the birth itself as the definitive moment of a woman's life from an unusual perspective as Mia narrates a tale of birthing among the Whan See, an arboreal Bush people who never leave the trees in which they live. With the tribe's women, Mia takes part in a communal birth ritual during which "the very instant it emerged, [the women] lifted up the tiny creature and . . . reinserted it back into its mother's womb." This occurs 16 times; eventually, the baby, "mangled . . . and drenched . . . like some rodent . . . some little . . . hamster," dies, and the mother, clutching the dead infant, hurls herself from the tree, committing suicide. Through Mia's story, Howe critiques patriarchal society's insistence that women become mothers over and over. She glosses the damage done by a concentration on the mother's birth experience and especially the damage done when childbirth is undertaken at the insistence of other women.

Birth, Howe writes, "was the play my former agent dismissed me for. It was rejected, often with accompanying threats and spittle, by every major theatre in the country."[13] This rejection led her to rethink her options. She began "hid[ing her] scent . . . cloak[ing her] wildness in a patina of elegance" (DiGaetani, 153) which some feminists have interpreted as selling out, and others insist has "capitulated neither her feminist voice nor her absurdist view of life."[14] Under the veneer of realistic comedy of manners lies a surrealism which "never fail[s] to boil up, to erupt in strange volcanic utterances and events" (Lamont 1993, 29). Howe remarks, "I'm not identified as a feminist writer, yet I'm convinced I am one—and one of the fiercer ones, to boot" ("Antic Vision," 12).

In *Museum* (1976), Howe employs feminist subversion in form and content. Composed of 40 roles, *Museum* is choric in form with art as its protagonist. This "farce-paced" comedy centers on viewer response to an exhibit titled "The Broken Silence." Called by its creator "a play *about* criticism" (Betsko and Koening, 230), *Museum* details reaction to the exhibit, which ranges from ecstatic to hostile. Agnes Vagg, the construction artist, tells her friend Tink Solheim that she has hidden "a special surprise in each piece. She challenged me, find it on the last day." When Tink finds the secret switch on one piece, she "releases the miracle buried in [it]. A floodlight pours down on the statue and Bach's Dorian Tocatta and Fugue in D Minor, BWV 538, for organ swells from a speaker concealed in the pedestal." Tink exits the gallery, exulting, "*She is vindicated*. Through me!" The "special surprise" of the play is, of course, the woman artist herself. In this instance, Howe portrays her as one who demands a creative viewer who can release the magic of the artist's vision. By using a female perceiver, Howe suggests the cultural feminist position that women commune in special ways and can fathom each other's secrets.

The woman artist at the core of *The Art of Dining* (1979) is a chef. Howe uses *Dining* to comment upon the connections among patriarchal control, food, and women. Of the three women diners in their 30s who share a table, only one is a "*good eater*"; the second is a "*guilty [and] neurotic*" eater, and the third a "*sneaky eater on a perpetual diet.*" The subversive subtext here reveals how women are literally shaped by man's view of the ideal woman as promulgated in art and advertising. As the "poor" eaters sublimate their desires and deny their appetites, they bring to mind myriad women: from fainting Victorian maidens (not from delicacy of constitution, as the myth would have it, but from corsets—in their desire to create the ideal female shape, women pulled the strings so tightly that the corsets constricted their internal organs); through plump, upper-class, early-twentieth-century matrons, whose size signified their husbands' material success; to 1990s models nicknamed Scarecrow and eight-year-old girls on diets. In a delightful parody of the hat exchange in Beckett's *Waiting for Godot*, the women snatch entrées from one another and the routine "*speeds up into a whirlwind.*" Still, they eat only a few bites before the perpetual dieter declares herself full and the other two, finding their pleasure in their meals ruined by her reminder of their duty to deny themselves, also abandon eating. As they talk, they actually sneak food from their own plates, an act that "begins as innocent picking but gets uglier and uglier as their real hunger surfaces."

A third woman artist stands at the center of *Painting Churches* (1983), for which Howe received an Obie. This autobiographical play concerns a coming to terms between Mags Church, a portrait artist, and her Boston Brahmin parents, Gardner and Fanny. Mags comes home to help her parents pack for a permanent move to their much smaller summer home; in return for her help, her mother has promised that the elder Churches will sit for a portrait. Gardner, a Pulitzer Prize–winning poet, has become senile and incontinent, while Fanny, always a commanding figure to her daughter, is dancing on the edge of desperation. Mags, who is about to have her first one-woman show at the same gallery that has exhibited Raushenberg, Warhol, and "all the heavies," becomes a child again in her parents' presence.

Fanny reminds Mags that her talent comes from Fanny's mother, whose "miniature of Henry James is still one of the main attractions at the Atheneum. Of course no woman of breeding could be a professional artist in her day. It simply wasn't done." Through Fanny, Howe intro-

Barbara Orson and James Carruthers in Trinity Repertory Company's 1989 production of Tina Howe's *Painting Churches. Photograph by Mark Morelli, courtesy of Trinity Repertory Company, Providence, Rhode Island.*

duces the issues of gender and class, making of both distinct markers of obligation that required the woman of the upper class to sacrifice her talent on the altar of patriarchal propriety. That Fanny, like her mother, is an acolyte to the patriarchy is evident as she belittles her daughter's artistic talent and urges her to wear less peculiar clothes and fix her "God-awful hair," because she'll "never catch a husband looking that way." But "looks" of perception and not her own appearance become important to Mags as her parents sit for their portrait. When Mags lectures her for making light of Gardner's latest manuscript, which is merely several pages of well-known poems retyped and not the critical study he claims to be writing, Fanny urges her to realize, "It's all over for Daddy and me. This it it!" and to see and paint them as they are, not as they exist in her memory.

The final scene takes place on the Churches' last day in their old home. Staying up all night, Mags has completed the portrait. Fanny is initially outraged at her purple skin, orange hair, and lack of feet; then, as she begins to find things to like in the portrait, she decides: "The wispy brush strokes make us look like a couple in a French Impressionist painting," a dancing couple in a Renoir café scene. Mags rejoices: "They *like* it!" And as Gardner and Fanny dance to the strains of a faraway waltz, their daughter watches them, moved to tears. The audience never sees Mags's portrait, so, fittingly, each member keeps her or his impression of it as the healing power of art resonates, if only briefly, from character to character to spectator.

With *Museum* and what came after, Howe says, "I found my niche at last. I would write about women as *artists*, eschew the slippery ground of courtship and domesticity and move up to a loftier plane" ("Antic Vision," 12). This strategy worked well, yet she abandoned it in the saccharine *Coastal Disturbances* (1986). Although the misuse of both patriarchal power and promises by the older lover of the young protagonist photographer is obvious, the drama finally is little more than a Cinderella story, with the handsome prince, the lifeguard at the beach, actually left with the photographer's sandal as the play ends. The disturbances are disturbingly minor.

With *Approaching Zanzibar* (1989), Howe reclaims the woman artist as her subject. This "road play," takes the Blossom family, Charlotte, Wallace, and their children—the 12-year-old Turner, a guitar prodigy, and Pony, his 9-year-old sister—on a cross-country vacation from New York to Taos to visit Charlotte's aunt Olivia Childs, an eminent artist, aged 81, who is dying of cancer. Howe's surrealism rises anew in her suggestion that the settings, which include caverns, trout streams, lakes, mountains, and the Blossoms' station wagon, be fashioned of fabric, and in her use of a trampoline for Olivia's bed.

Howe consciously aimed at diversity in this work, noting: "[I]t's high time that I get away from all of these New England types, and I really wanted to have some blacks and Hispanics and southerners and all kinds of different people in the play."[15] Her desire results in her making Joy, the second wife of Charlotte's brother, a black newscaster. But other than having Charlotte mention that Joy interviews kings and presidents, Howe does little with Joy's supposed position of power and less with her race. Dalia Paz, the Hispanic character, is given a stereotypical role as Olivia's Mexican nurse. Yet in the southerner Randy Wands, Howe offers a refreshing depiction of a male; this man, a new father at 43, has his three-week-old son William strapped to his chest and, with tender attentiveness, is showing him the world from the Blue Ridge Mountains.

The goal of the Blossoms' journey is reaching Olivia. The old woman revives when they arrive, singles out Pony, and dismisses the others. Pony, earlier portrayed as attempting to overcome not only the American cultural preference for male children but also the fact that her brother is a prodigy by literally standing on her head to gain her parents' attention, is delighted by Olivia's notice. Olivia tells her a fable of her younger self, whom she names Callisto, being spirited from a train by a Zeus-like figure who, she says, "rocked me over mountains, sang me through rain forests, and kissed me past ancient cities. Oh, what a ruckus he made! Well, you'll do it, too, you'll do it all, wait and see." Olivia then rises on her bed/trampoline, takes Pony's hands and says, "Come on, jump with me." As they jump, "the LIGHT around PONY becomes more intense. Hair flying . . . she looks like a reckless angel challenging the limits of heaven." By confiding the promise of woman's potential, the old woman, practicing the arts of storytelling and nurturing, assures this younger Callisto of her place among the stars.

In the 22 December 1986 issue of *New York Magazine*, John Simon declared *Coastal Disturbances*, *Museum*, *The Art of Dining*, and *Painting Churches* an enviable body of work, adding "Edward Albee, after all, has not written four such plays; neither has Arthur Miller." Of more relevance to Howe's place in the feminist tradition are her explorations of patriarchal institutions such as marriage and the central position woman-as-artist occupies in her best works. Howe's realistically surreal comedies illuminate what the patriarchy would keep shadowed and let women know they have dominion over their bodies and their minds and bring about through that control, as she told an interviewer, a yoking of "our delicate touch and way with words with the darker impulses of theater. All I can say is when that moment comes . . . LOOK OUT BELOW!" (Betsko and Koening, 235). At that time, Tina Howe's not-so-hidden subversive scent will emanate from the works of ever more feminist playwrights.

Marsha Norman: Fighting for Our Lives

Noting the connection among playwriting, production, and politics, Pulitzer Prize winner Marsha Norman (born 1947) stated, "The appearance of significant women dramatists in significant numbers now is a real reflection of a change in women's attitudes toward themselves. It is a sudden understanding that they can be, and indeed are, the central characters in their own lives. That is a notion that is absolutely required for writing for the theater. . . . What is perhaps responsible for so few of these plays being done . . . is the problem that the things we as women know best have not been perceived to be of critical value to society." (Betsko and Koening, 338). She also said, "[O]n the whole the American theatre, dominated by men, does not perceive women fighting for their lives as a serious issue" (Savran, 182).

Born into a fundamentalist Methodist family in Louisville, forbidden to watch television or play with neighborhood children, Norman spent her time reading, playing the piano, and playing with an imaginary friend she named Bettering, which seems a wry joke on the oft-heard middle-class parental injunction to children of Norman's generation to spend their time "bettering" themselves. A scholarship student at Agnes Scott College, she earned her bachelor's degree in 1969 and holds a master's degree from the University of Louisville. After serving as a volunteer in a pediatric burn unit in an Atlanta hospital while in college, Norman continued to work with children, teaching in programs in Kentucky for both severely disturbed and gifted students.

In 1971 Norman met Jon Jory, artistic director of the Actors Theatre of Louisville. Impressed with her mind and knowing she was a writer, Jory, on learning that she had written a children's play, encouraged her to write a docudrama about busing, which had just begun to have an impact on Louisville. But Norman, not inclined in the same direction as Emily Mann, decided against it. Advised by Jory to write about something that had frightened her, Norman recalled a teenager she had observed in a state hospital, and *Getting Out* (1977) came into being. In 1991, when Norman turned to the musical theater, her adaptation of *The Secret Garden* won the Tony Award. Norman has continued her affiliation with the Actors Theatre of Louisville; she served as its writer-in residence in 1978–79, and her *D. Boone* was staged at its Sixteenth Annual Humana Festival of New American Plays in 1992. In 1986 she was inducted into the American Academy and Institute of Arts and Letters.

As is the case with Henley and Howe, Norman's feminist credentials are the subject of debate. In the July 1983 *Ms.*, Elizabeth Stone quotes Norman on the subject: "I am a hermit in the sense that I don't join and show up at meetings and go places, but I am doing what I can to help and am clearly committed to a full, rich and self-controlled life for the women on this planet." Her goal—"To make visible people that are rarely seen and never heard"—as reported by Kate Stout in the October 1983 *Saturday Review*, is surely feminist, as are the dramas that elucidate such topics as the silencing, subordination, brutalization, and confinement, even to the point of imprisonment, of women. Norman's plays focus on the particulars of sexual abuse, the oppression of women under patriarchy, and the intricacies of the mother-daughter bond.

Those who rule Norman out of the feminist circle cite the lack of feminist polemics in her work or focus on its lack of alternative vision for changing the society that oppresses. Here she might say what Maria Irene Fornes has said: that she dramatizes what is occurring and it is up to us to bring about change. In her original consideration of *'night, Mother* (1983), Jill Dolan expressed indignation that "Women are getting the Pulitzer Prize these days for plays that depict women killing themselves." She found that the play, unlike Norman's earlier *Getting Out*, did nothing to advance the cause of women, showed no possibilities for change in women's lives, and conveyed a negative message "about how mothers and daughters relate and can relate."[16] Although she continued to find the play "weak as a political statement and inadequate from a materialist feminist perspective," Dolan later felt it to be "typical of liberal and cultural feminist drama that is, as [Sue-Ellen] Case remarks, 'animated by the absent male'" (Dolan 1989, 336). On the other hand, Janet Brown finds no weaknesses in Norman's feminism and describes the playwright "as perhaps the most successful author of serious feminist drama working in the U.S. today" and one whose "plays grapple with difficult subjects, approached from a viewpoint that clearly reflects both female psychology and a feminist ethic"[17]

Getting Out won the Great American Play Contest when it premiered at the Actors Theatre of Louisville in 1977. "[A] radically feminist play in its critique of the most sacred tenets of capitalistic, patriarchal ideology,"[18] *Getting Out* concerns the difficulties Arlene Holsclaw encounters when she is paroled from prison. Through the set, in which a catwalk, several cells, and a downstage apron surround Arlene's one-room apartment, Norman makes it clear that she will never be freed from the prisons of gender and class that were implicated in her literal imprisonment. Employing the technique pioneered by Alice Gerstenberg, Norman utilizes a split protagonist, bringing onstage both Arlene, who is in her late 20s, and Arlie, the violent younger self who was incarcerated eight years earlier.

Five minutes before the play proper begins, a loudspeaker broadcasts the droning voice of a woman announcing work assignments, cancelling recreation and privileges, and reiterating pointless rules. By employing a woman's voice, Norman reminds the audience of the role women play in oppressing women; the voice and the set also show the audience to itself as both inmate and jailer. Significantly, the warden, a voice heard on tape, is male, a representative of the patriarchal hierarchy that built and controls the prison and the women, both inmates and employees, within it. The guards seen in the play are male. They include one who tells Arlene that if she's going to hide something she should hide it "up your pookie . . . where it's fun to find"; another that tells her to eat because if she becomes "too skinny" she will displease the guards, who have "[g]ot us a two-way mirror in the shower room"; and Bennie, who drives her from the prison in Alabama home to Kentucky.

Bennie purports to be concerned because she doesn't know anyone "nice" and has "Nobody to take care of [her]," yet despite sounding like a parent, he pins her to her bed and attempts to rape her. Her protests, even the surfacing of Arlie who hits and kicks him, do not deter him. Only when Arlene, overcoming Arlie, speaks rather than strikes and asks, "This how you got your [wife] Dorrie, rapin?" and describes the actions of rapists—"First they unzip their pants. Sometime they take off their shirt. But mostly, they just pull it out and stick it in"—does Bennie finally hear her. Insisting he is no rapist, he stops. His earlier pseudoparental concern is a device through which Norman reminds the audience of Arlie's earlier reenactment of the aftermath of being raped by her father, of the denial she issued to her mother, accompanied by the poignant plea, "Don't let Daddy come in here, Mama. Jus you an me."

Her mother visits Arlene, but backs away from her embrace. Such closeness might require her to acknowledge her husband's sexual abuse of Arlie, and she prefers to think of him as a "good man." During their conversation, Arlene asks about her son, Joey, born when she was imprisoned. Although her mother claims Arlene "never really got attached to him anyway," his absence drives her to the despair that leads to her attempted escape, during which she kills a cab driver who "trie[d] to mess with" her. Once again her father, also a cab driver, is implicated, and the audience also learns that the "murder" was an act of self-defense. Of course, in a society structured around a rapist ethic, which blames the victim, not the perpetrator, of sexual assault, and in which the "guardians" are the perpetrators, Arlie, already convicted of forgery and a "wildcat" who has been through a succession of special placements, must be returned to prison.

Upon parole, she is released into the larger prison decreed by the capitalist patriarchal system for those of her sex and class. One of her first actions, parting the curtains in her apartment, reveals bars on the windows, symbolizing the impossibility of her ever truly "getting out." Consigned by her socioeconomic status to the lower class, Arlene has few prospects. Her options are rejoining Carl, her former pimp, a junkie who has escaped from prison and wants to take her to New York as his meal ticket; doling out sexual favors to Bennie; or taking the job of dishwasher in a diner, offered by Ruby, her upstairs neighbor, who is the diner's cook and herself an ex-convict. It is she who recognizes Arlene's humanity and tells her, after Arlene confesses to "killing" her evil self, Arlie—an act necessary, of course, to her getting out of prison—by repeatedly stabbing herself with a fork, that "you can still love people that's gone." Ruby then "holds her tenderly, rocking as with a baby."

Ruby as surrogate mother offers at least a slight hope for Arlene's own mothering of Joey. Motivated by a desire for her child, Arlene throws away the papers bearing the telephone numbers left by Carl and Bennie. As Arlie addresses Arlene directly for the first time with a reminiscence about being locked in Mama's closet by a sister, Arlene resurrects in herself something of Arlie's spirit. It is not a complete transition of Arlie into Arlene, but "in the final scene . . . they [are] enjoyably aware of each other." Arlie's feisty spirit will serve Arlene in good stead in a world that is a prison in which gender and class keep Arlene in "her place."

In 1983 Norman won the Pulitzer Prize for *'night, Mother*. The play takes place on the last night of Jessie Cates's life, as she announces to her Mama, Thelma, that she intends to commit suicide. Their usual Saturday night routines are set aside as Mama desperately tries to persuade Jessie to live, while Jessie holds fast to her decision. The reviews were overwhelmingly favorable, although there were a few dissenters. Stanley Kauffmann, in the September/October 1983 *Saturday Review*, calls the play a "stunt" and notes that the dialogue contains "much trivia about deliveries of groceries, milk and candy." Missing is any recognition that this trivia both sustains and sweetens life; ironically, the review itself points up *'night, Mother*'s relationship to Susan Glaspell's *Trifles*, in which men discount such trifles as "kitchen things," food, and housework.

Feminist critics are divided on the play. Lynda Hart sees Jessie's suicide as "a final choice that leaves no apparent legacy for change."[19] Others see the play failing because it "ultimately reinscribes the dominant ideology in its realist form" yet holds the possibility of being "*perceived* as a feminist text, in that it challenges on some material level the reality of male power"[20] or suggest that "one can argue whether or not [it] is definitively feminist" (Dolan 1989, 326). Norman herself has commented on the critics' inability to "tell the play from the production" (Betsko and Koening, 324), a point developed by Dolan in the essay just cited, in which she comments on changes made by Norman's collaborators, the set designer notable among them, and points up the manner in which critics conflated actor Kathy Bates's body type with Jessie's motive for suicide. Even thought the script says nothing about obesity, several critics commented on Jessie as overweight. Frank Rich, writing in the 1 April 1983 *New York Times*, cited Jessie's being a "fat, lumpy anonymous-looking woman" as first among her conceivable motives. Here is evidence of the persistence of the male gaze; as Y. Z. of colonial Maryland's *Gazette* was charmed by the appearance of actor Maria Hallam, so in 1983 Rich finds a woman's having a less than perfect body a plausible reason for suicide. "Which," to quote Montrose Moses again, "gives us a great deal of the flavor of the woman in the eyes of the man" (Moses 1925, 126).

Jessie, though divorced, still loves her ex-husband. Her son is a drug addict and thief who did not scruple at stealing his mother's only valuable piece of jewelry. Jessie suffers from epilepsy, although she has not had a seizure for a year. All these factors may have contributed to Jessie's decision, but she truthfully names another reason that is both less and more important than these. Jessie feels defeated, as if everything in life is beyond her control. Indeed, she no longer savors anything in life, as she observes when she tells Mama that she might have decided to live "if there was something I really liked, like maybe if I really liked rice pudding or cornflakes for breakfast or something, that might be enough," but she does not. (This line may have its genesis in Lillian Hellman's *The Children's Hour*, in which Joe promises to take both Martha and his fiancée Karen, to Vienna for "good coffee cake." Martha, not long before she also commits suicide, replies, "A big coffee cake with a lot of raisins, it would be nice to like something again." Norman has acknowledged Hellman as the woman through whom she learned it was possible to write for a living, and the allusion may be a tribute to her.)

Since she feels that she cannot control her life, Jessie has chosen to control her death. Relying on the strength of the mother-daughter bond, Mama begs, "Don't leave me, Jessie!" Reversing their roles, as she has also done by pretending to be dependent on Jessie to keep her house in order, Mama protests, "Jessie, how can I live here without you? I need you!" When the ploy does not work, Mama asserts ownership:

Nora Chester (left) as Jessie and Nan Martin as Thelma Cates in the Alley Theatre's southwestern premiere of *'night, Mother* (1989) by Marsha Norman. *Photograph by Carl Davis, courtesy of the Alley Theatre, Houston, Texas.*

"You are my child!" Jessie replies that she is what became of Thelma's child, that she is all that is left of the unfilled promise of the pampered baby in an old photograph she found.[21] Powerful as the mother-daughter bond is, it has never been overtly expressed in the Cates's household until this night, when, impelled by Jessie's desire to die, new honesty and a new intimacy arise. Yet, if the daughter is to become an autonomous adult, the bond must be broken. This is the wrenching truth of Norman's metaphor, brought "home" as Jessie pushes past Mama to the sanctuary of her bedroom, locks the door, and fires the gun. The shot's report says "No" to further life in Mama's house under the invisible yet ever-present auspices of the patriarchy, as represented by Jessie's brother, Dawson, who does not appear but whose name is on the account at the grocery, who knows the intimate details of her life, and who manages their finances. In other words, the control is truly his. As William Demaste suggests, *'night, Mother*, "challenge[s] the dominant hierarchy" by challenging classic realist assumptions through a "dialectic between

. . . the conservative, classically-minded mother . . . and the 'new'-thinking daughter." He adds, "Perhaps work such as Norman's suggesting a new foundation of understanding, may help us to create a yardstick (a feminist yardstick as well as others), whose assumptions are, finally, truly relevant to our age."[22]

Norman's dramas place a variety of feminist issues before their audiences. She challenges complacency in *Getting Out* by making audience members at once inmates and jailers and by questioning their right to judge Arlie/Arlene. Jessie's suicide in *'night, Mother*, shatters the patriarchy's shibboleth about women being happiest when in their "proper" place: the home. Norman succeeds in her goal of giving voice to some of the silent and underrepresented members of American society. That she has done so in the commercial theater is an indication "that feminism has penetrated our culture more widely than is sometimes recognized" (Brown, 76).

A Place for the Realists

Henley, Howe, and Norman submit that autonomy and reconciliation, individuality and community are possible for women. That they do so in realist or modified realist structures does not mean they should be abandoned. Just as a cultural feminist, while having her own philosophy, ought not declare materialist feminism out of order, neither should feminist playwrights and critics "default" on realism, arguably the form most familiar to those audiences who may be most in need of exposure to feminism's many perspectives and possibilities.

epilogue

American feminist drama arose from politics when Mercy Otis Warren used her pamphlet plays to urge a revolution against England; more than 200 years later, American feminist drama remains political. Warren's successors have used the stage to urge revolutions *against* the strictures of patriarchy and *in* consciousness. Feminist playwrights continue to challenge the laws, religions, and cultural practices that subordinate and silence women. In Warren's *The Group*, Sylvia, who "silently" mourns her fate, does not appear onstage; Susan Glaspell's Claire Archer in *The Verge* struggles against silence, even attempting to create new forms of life with which to express herself. In Martha Boesing's *Antigone, Too,* women speak through their deeds and words to comfort and hearten Antigone through their example. Not only silencing, but subjugation, brutalization, and other methods of keeping women bound by home and gender are issues dramatized by feminist playwrights, as are freedom, self-determination, and independence.

Have feminist issues permeated the general social consciousness of America? The cyclical nature of history, the specific history of feminism, and the spirit of backlash abroad in the 1990s suggest not. As we now realize, many of the exciting discoveries made by feminists in the 1960s and 1970s had also been discovered by their foremothers in the mid- to late nineteenth century. Many politicians campaigning on a platform of "family values" in the early 1990s sought to appeal to those who would repudiate whatever gains increased equality and opportunity for women have effected.

Yet feminists, among them playwrights such as Emily Mann, have moved into regional theaters as artistic directors. Theorists now speak of diversity within feminism, of feminisms. The varied voices of women characters who have moved from the margins of dramatic representation to center stage refuse to fall again into a silent consent to oppression. And their creators, the feminist playwrights who refuse to live by disabling definitions that mark women as inferior, decline to represent women onstage by such definitions. Celebrating the great adventure that women's lives can be and mourning those which are not, they offer their audiences new modes of perception, new lenses through which to view the past, respect for difference, and an empowerment based on human possibilities that have been ignored by the patriarchy.

chronology

Date	*Drama, Literature, Art*	*Events in American Women's History*
1636		Ann Hutchinson banished from Massachusetts.
1650	Anne Bradstreet, *The Tenth Muse.*	
1692		At the height of the witchcraft hysteria in Salem, Massachusetts, 14 women and 6 men are executed.
1775	Mercy Otis Warren, *The Group.*	During Revolutionary War, 20,000 American and British women serve as cooks, nurses, guides, laundresses, doctors, and porters.
1776	Mercy Otis Warren, *The Blockheads.*	Abigail Adams sends her "Remember the Ladies" letter to

		husband John; New Jersey grants women the right to vote (and rescinds it in 1807).
1790	Judith Sargent Murray, "On the Equality of the Sexes."	
1794	Susanna Rowson, *Slaves in Algiers;* Rowson's novel *Charlotte Temple* becomes first American best-seller.	
1832		Black women establish female antislavery society in Massachusetts.
1833		Lucretia Mott heads Philadelphia Female Anti-Slavery Society.
1834		Oberlin College, first to admit African Americans and women, founded.
1837		First antislavery convention of American women held in New York City.
1838	Sarah Grimké, *Letters on the Equality of the Sexes and the Condition of Women.*	Angelina Grimké addresses the Massachusetts State Legislature, becoming the first woman in the United States to speak before such a body.
1840		World Anti-Slavery Convention, held in London, votes to exclude women from participation.
1845	Anna Cora Mowatt, *Fashion;* Margaret Fuller, *Woman in the Nineteenth Century.*	Lowell Female Labor Reform Association, first major women's union, founded in Massachusetts.
1848		Women's Rights Convention held at Seneca Falls, New York; New York's Married Women's Property Act gives women control over property they own at time of marriage.

1849		Amelia Jenks Bloomer publishes first prominent women's rights newspaper, the *Lily;* Elizabeth Blackwell becomes first woman to receive a medical degree.
1850		Throughout the 1850s, Harriet Tubman leads 300 slaves to freedom; Maria Mitchell, astronomer, is first woman elected to the American Academy of Arts and Sciences.
1851	Susan Warner's novel, *The Wide Wide World,* becomes first by an American to sell 1 million copies.	
1852	Harriet Beecher Stowe, *Uncle Tom's Cabin.*	Antioch College grants women students equal rights with men.
1859	Frances E. W. Harper, "The Two Offers," first short story published by an African American.	
1867		Mary Harris "Mother" Jones becomes organizer for the Knights of Labor.
1868		The *Revolution,* feminist weekly newspaper, established; Fourteenth Amendment's references to "male citizens" introduce sex discrimination into the Constitution.
1869		Wyoming grants women the right to vote; National Woman Suffrage Association formed; Elizabeth Cady Stanton is first woman witness at a congressional hearing.
1870		American Woman Suffrage Association founded.

1872		Victoria Woodhull runs for president on the Equal Rights Party ticket.
1873		Susan B. Anthony tried for civil disobedience for voting in the 1872 congressional election and fined $100.
1874		Women's Christian Temperance Union formed.
1881		Clara Barton establishes American Red Cross; Knights of Labor advocate equal pay for equal work.
1889		Jane Addams founds Hull House.
1890		Wyoming admitted to the Union as the first woman suffrage state; National American Woman Suffrage Association established.
1892	Charlotte Perkins Gilman, "The Yellow Wallpaper."	Congress grants Civil War nurses pension.
1895	Elizabeth Cady Stanton, *The Woman's Bible.*	
1898	Charlotte Perkins Gilman, *Women and Economics;* Kate Chopin, *The Awakening.*	Women's National Bar Association founded.
1903	Charlotte Perkins Gilman, *The Home: Its Work and Influence.*	Margaret Dreie Robbins helps found the Women's Trade Union League, uniting working-class and middle-class women.
1908		American Olympic Committee refuses to allow women to compete; U.S. Supreme Court decides that because of their ability to bear children, women's working hours and conditions may be restricted; Julia Ward Howe first woman elected to

		American Academy of Arts and Letters.
1909	Rachel Crothers, *A Man's World.*	In New York City, women shirtwaist makers strike in what becomes known as the Great Uprising.
1911	Charlotte Perkins Gilman, *Man Made World: Our Androcentric Culture* and *Something to Vote For;* Catherine Waugh McCulloch, *Bridget's Sisters;* Rachel Crothers, *He and She.*	Fire at the Triangle Company's shirtwaist factory in New York City takes 146 lives; Clara Dutton Noyes founds first school for midwives at Bellevue Hospital.
1912	Harriet Monroe begins publishing *Poetry.*	Organized by Alice Paul, 10,000 people demonstrate for woman suffrage on the eve of Woodrow Wilson's inauguration; women textile workers in Lawrence, Massachusetts, strike.
1915	Susan Glaspell and George Cram Cook found the Provincetown Players.	Woman's Peace Party organized.
1916	Susan Glaspell, *Trifles;* Angelina Weld Grimké, *Rachel.*	Emma Goldman jailed for displaying condoms in public; Jeannette Rankin of Montana, first female member of Congress, elected to U.S. House of Representatives.
1917		Margaret Sanger opens her first birth control clinic.
1918	Susan Glaspell, *The Outside.*	Jeannette Rankin introduces the woman suffrage amendment.
1919	Mary Burrill, *Aftermath* and *They That Sit in Darkness;* Susan Glaspell, *Bernice.*	Women's International League for Peace and Freedom, headed by Jane Addams, is formed.
1920		Tennessee becomes thirty-sixth state to ratify the woman suffrage amendment, ending women's 72-year quest for the vote; American

		women permitted into Olympic competition; Women's Bureau of the Department of Labor established; Jane Addams helps found the American Civil Liberties Union.
1921	Zona Gale becomes first woman to win Pulitzer Prize in drama, for *Miss Lulu Bett*; Edith Wharton becomes first woman to receive Pulitzer Prize in fiction, for *The Age of Innocence*.	
1922	Susan Glaspell, *The Verge*.	
1923	Lula Volmer, *Sun-Up*; Edna St. Vincent Millay becomes first woman to win Pulitzer Prize in poetry.	Alice Paul writes the "Lucretia Mott amendment," which becomes known as the Equal Rights Amendment; in *Adkins v. Children's Hospital*, U.S. Supreme Court finds minimum wages for women unconstitutional.
1925	Georgia Douglas Johnson, *A Sunday Morning in the South*.	Carrie Chapman Catt founds the Committee on the Cause and Cure of War; Gertrude Ederle swims the English Channel, beating the men's record by two hours; Florence Sabin becomes first woman elected to the National Academy of Sciences.
1928	Sophie Treadwell, *Machinal*; Margaret Mead, *Coming of Age in Samoa*.	Amelia Earhart becomes first woman to make solo transcontinental flight.
1931	Pulitzer Prize in drama to Susan Glaspell for *Alison's House*.	Jane Addams becomes first woman to receive the Nobel Peace Prize.
1932	Rachel Crothers, *When Ladies Meet*.	Hattie Wyatt Caraway of Arkansas appointed to fill her husband's U.S. Senate seat in 1931, runs on her own in 1932,

		and becomes first woman elected to Senate.
1933		Frances Perkins becomes U.S. secretary of labor and first female cabinet member in U.S. history.
1934	Lillian Hellman, *The Children's Hour.*	
1935	Hallie Flanagan organizes and directs the Federal Theatre Project; Marion Anderson gives first U.S. performance.	Mary McLeod Bethune founds National Council of Negro Women.
1937		U.S. Supreme Court reverses *Adkins* decision and grants minimum-wage rights to women; dissemination of birth control information by doctors legalized.
1938	Pearl Buck wins Nobel Prize in literature.	The Fair Labor Standards Act abolishes homework in most industries and enforces minimum-wage and child-labor laws.
1939	Lillian Hellman, *The Little Foxes.*	When the Daughters of the American Revolution refuse to let Marian Anderson sing at Constitution Hall, Eleanor Roosevelt resigns from the organization and arranges outdoor concert in front of Lincoln Memorial.
1941	Lillian Hellman's *Watch on the Rhine* wins New York Drama Critics Circle Award for best American play.	Through 1945, 6 million women take paid employment during World War II; in 1942–43 women's branches of the armed services created; 350,000 women serve overseas and at home.
1945	Louise Bogan becomes first woman appointed consultant in poetry to Library of Congress.	Grace Brewster Murray Hopper develops programs for first automatically sequenced digital computer; Eleanor Roosevelt

		appointed delegate to the United Nations.
1946		With men home from war, industry lays off 2 million women workers.
1947	American Theatre Wing establishes Antoinette Perry Award—the Tony.	
1948		Margaret Chase Smith of Maine becomes first woman elected to U.S. Senate without first completing another's term.
1949	Alice Childress, *Florence.*	Eugenie Moore Anderson becomes ambassador to Denmark and first woman to hold that rank; Georgia Nees Clark becomes first woman U.S. treasurer.
1950	Beah Richards, *A Black Woman Speaks;* Gwendolyn Brooks becomes first African American woman to win the Pulitzer Prize in poetry.	Althea Gibson breaks color barrier in U.S. Lawn Tennis Association.
1953		Oveta Culp Hobby becomes first secretary of U.S. Department of Health, Education, and Welfare.
1955	Alice Childress wins Obie for *Trouble in Mind.*	Rosa Parks arrested in Montgomery, Alabama, for refusing to yield her seat on a bus to a white man.
1958	Eleanor Flexner, *A Century of Struggle,* a history of the women's movement.	
1959	Lorraine Hansberry, *A Raisin in the Sun.*	
1960	Lillian Hellman, *Toys in the Attic.*	Food and Drug Administration approves birth control pill.

1961	President John F. Kennedy appoints Eleanor Roosevelt to head Commission on Status of Women; 50,000 women take part in Women Strike for Peace.	
1962		Sheila Tobias inaugurates the first women's studies course at Cornell University.
1963	Betty Friedan, *The Feminine Mystique*; Alice Childress, *Wedding Band*.	Congress passes Equal Pay Act, requiring that employers pay same wage to women and men doing equal work.
1964	Lorraine Hansberry, *The Sign in Sidney Brustein's Window* and *The Movement: Document of a Struggle for Equality*; Adrienne Kennedy wins Obie for *Funnyhouse of a Negro*.	Senator Margaret Chase Smith of Maine nominated for president at Republican National Convention; Title VII of the Civil Rights Act creates the Equal Employment Opportunity Act; hundreds of college women work in the South in voter registration program organized by Student Nonviolent Coordinating Committee.
1966	Megan Terry, *Viet Rock*.	National Organization for Women (NOW) founded.
1967	Obie to Rochelle Owens for *Futz*.	President Lyndon Johnson signs order forbidding sex discrimination by federal contractors and subcontractors.
1968		Beverly Jones and Judith Brown call for radical women to form Female Liberation Movement; feminists demonstrate at the Miss America Pageant; Women's Equity Action League founded.
1969	Lillian Hellman, *An Unfinished Woman*; Myrna Lamb, *But What Have You Done for Me Lately?*; Alice Childress, *Wine in the Wilderness*.	

1970	Feminist Press established; Ada Louise Huxtable wins Pulitzer Prize in criticism (architecture); Megan Terry wins Obie for *Approaching Simone;* Kate Millet, *Sexual Politics;* Angela Davis, "Reflections on the Black Woman's Role in the Community of Slaves"; Robin Morgan edits *Sisterhood Is Powerful.*	Organized by NOW, women strike 26 August to commemorate the fiftieth anniversary of woman suffrage and to protest continuing inequities.
1971		Billie Jean Moffit King is first woman athlete to earn $100,000 in one year; Lucinda Franks is first woman to receive Pulitzer Prize for national reporting; Bipartisan National Women's Political Caucus organized.
1972	Women's Theatre Council formed; Phyllis Chesler, *Women and Madness.*	Boston Marathon establishes women's division; Association of Women Business Owners founded; Federal Education Act bans sex discrimination in higher education; Shirley Chisholm becomes first African American and first woman to campaign for presidential nomination from a major party; Congress passes Equal Rights Amendment and sends it to states for ratification; *Ms.* magazine established.
1973	Lillian Hellman, *Pentimento.*	U.S. Supreme Court legalizes abortion in first six months of pregnancy and outlaws segregation of help-wanted ads by sex; Marian Wright Edelman establishes Children's Defense Fund; Lesbian Feminist Liberation established; Black Women Organized for Action

		and National Black Feminist Organization established.
1974	Jane Chambers, *A Late Snow;* Tina Howe, *Birth and after Birth;* Martha Boesing, *River Journal;* Gayle Rubin, "The Traffic in Women."	Fifty-eight unions form Coalition of Labor Union Women; minimum wage extended to cover 1.5 million domestic workers; National Little League Baseball allows girls to play ball; Congress passes Equal Credit Opportunity Act.
1975	Ntozake Shange, *for colored girls who have considered suicide/when the rainbow is enuf;* Susan Brownmiller, *Against Our Will.*	Ella T. Grasso of Connecticut becomes first woman elected governor without following her husband into office; U.S. Supreme Court outlaws automatic exclusion of women from juries and bans different ages of majority for women and men; Congress requires U.S. military academies to admit women; Carla Anderson Hills becomes first secretary of Department of Housing and Urban Development; Mary McGrory is first woman to receive the Pulitzer Prize in commentary; United Nations declares an International Women's Year and holds conference in Mexico City.
1976	Adrienne Kennedy, *A Movie Star Has to Star in Black and White;* Lillian Hellman, *Scoundrel Time;* Adrienne Rich wins National Book Award for *Of Woman Born;* Betty Friedan, *It Changed My Life: Writings on the Women's Movement.*	Barbara Jordan delivers keynote speech at Democratic National Convention; Nebraska criminalizes marital rape.
1977	Ntozake Shange wins Obie for *for colored girls;* Maria Irene	U.S. Navy assigns women to shipboard crews; International

	Fornes wins Obies for writing and direction of *Fefu and Her Friends;* Martha Boesing, *The Story of a Mother*; Marsha Norman, *Getting Out*.	Women's Year Congress meets in Houston; National Women's Studies Association founded; working mothers granted a tax credit for child care; Juanita Morris Kreps becomes first woman appointed secretary of commerce; Eleanor Holmes Norton becomes first woman to chair the Equal Employment Opportunities Commission.
1978	Marsh Norman, *Third and Oak*; Ntozake Shange, *boogie woogie landscapes;* Julia Miles establishes the Women's Project at the American Place Theatre.	First Feminist Conference on Pornography launches the Take Back the Night movement; seven women astronauts join U.S. space program; 100,000 participate in fifteenth anniversary of the National ERA Extension March on Washington; National Coalition against Domestic Violence formed.
1979	Tina Howe, *The Art of Dining;* Ntozake Shange, *spell #7;* Sandra Gilbert and Susan Gubar, *The Madwoman in the Attic;* Judy Chicago art installation, "The Dinner Party."	For the first time, more women than men enter college in the United States; Susan B. Anthony becomes first woman depicted on a U.S. coin.
1980	Jane Chambers, *Last Summer at Bluefish Cove.*	UN World Conference on Women; during Women's Pentagon Action, thousands encircle the building; 71,000 participate in Women against Pornography March in New York City; Women's Rights National Park opens at Seneca Falls, New York, and houses Women's Hall of Fame.
1981	Beth Henley wins Pulitzer Prize in drama for *Crimes of the Heart;* Obies to Emily Mann for *Still*	Centennial of the American Association of University Women; National Black

Life for writing and direction; Ntozake Shange wins Obie for her adaptation of Brecht's *Mother Courage*; Beth Henley, *The Miss Firecracker Contest*; Angela Davis *Women, Race, and Class*; Andrea Dworkin, *Pornography*.

Women's Political Caucus established; Sandra Day O'Connor becomes first woman appointed to the U.S. Supreme Court.

1982 Emily Mann, *Execution of Justice*; Maria Irene Forness awarded Obie for sustained achievement; Carol Gilligan, *In a Different Voice*; Gloria Hull and Barbara Smith "The Politics of Women's Studies."

Observance of Women's History Month initiated; editor Susan Lloyd deletes sexist usage from *Roget's Thesaurus*; ERA defeated; Susan G. Komen Foundation is the first founded solely to support breast cancer research.

1983 Marsha Norman wins Pulitzer and Susan Smith Blackburn Prizes for *'night, Mother*; Obies to Maria Irene Fornes for *Mud*, *The Danube*, and *Sarita*; Obie to Tina Howe for *The Art of Dining*; Alice Walker wins Pulitzer Prize in fiction and National Book Award for *The Color Purple*; Ellen Taaffe Zwilich becomes first woman to win Pulitzer Prize in music; Cherrie Moraga and Gloria Anzaldua edit *This Bridge Called My Back*; Tina Howe, *Painting Churches*.

Sally Ride becomes first U.S. woman astronaut in space.

1984 Robin Morgan edits *Sisterhood Is Global*.

Geraldine Ferraro is first woman nominated by major party as candidate for vice president.

1985 Rosalyn Drexler wins Obie for *Utopia Parkway*; Maria Irene Fornes wins Obie for *The Conduct of Life* and receives Special Literature Award from National Institute of Arts and Letters, American Academy of

EMILY'S (Early Money Is Like Yeast) List begins to raise money for pro-choice, pro-ERA Democratic women candidates for political office.

	Arts and Letters; Judy Chicago art installation, "The Birth Project."	
1986	Emily Mann, *Annulla;* Marsha Norman cited for Distinction in Playwriting by National Institute of Arts and Letters.	U.S. Supreme Court rules unanimously that sexual harassment constitutes job discrimination.
1989	First International Women Playwrights' Conference held in Buffalo; Wendy Wasserstein wins Pulitzer Prize in drama for *The Heidi Chronicles;* Arlie Hochschild, *The Second Shift.*	U.S. Supreme Court *Webster* decision allows states to enact laws restricting abortion.
1990	Adrienne Kennedy, *The Ohio State Murders.*	In Washington, D.C., Sharon Pratt Dixon becomes first black woman mayor of a major U.S. city; Antonia Novello is first woman to become U.S. surgeon general.
1991		Women iron workers bring first class-action sexual harassment suit; Anita Hill testifies about alleged sexual harassment before the Senate Judiciary Committee hearing on Clarence Thomas's nomination to the U.S. Supreme Court; Veteran Feminists of America organized.
1992	Susan Faludi, *Backlash: The Undeclared War on American Women.*	
1993	Judy Chicago art installation, "The Holocaust Project"; Toni Morrison wins Nobel Prize in literature.	Ruth Bader Ginsburg becomes second woman appointed to the U.S. Supreme Court; *Ms.* Foundation sponsors the first annual "Take Our Daughters to Work Day"; 750,000 march in Washington, D.C., to demand equal rights for lesbians, gay men, and bisexuals; Laura

D'Andrea Tyson becomes first woman to head the U.S. Council of Economic Advisors; Janet Reno becomes first woman U.S. attorney general; "Wesleyan Chapel Block" opened at Women's Rights National Park; it includes a waterwall bearing the words of the 1848 Declaration of Sentiments of the first Women's Rights Convention.

1994 Martha Boesing, *Hard Times Come Again No More.*

1995 Emily Mann, *Having Our Say.*

notes and references

Many of the plays discussed in this volume are available in a number of different editions and anthologies. Quotations from plays are therefore not accompanied by page references. Please refer to the Selected Bibliography for a complete list of the primary sources used.

PROLOGUE

1. The first wave of the women's movement began with the 1848 women's rights convention in Seneca Falls, New York, and waned not long after women were granted suffrage in 1920. The second wave began in the late 1960s with calls for women's liberation, gender equity, and equal pay for equal work and continues in the 1990s.

2. Adrienne Rich, *Of Woman Born: Motherhood as Experience and Institution* (New York: W. W. Norton and Co., 1986), 57.

CHAPTER 1

1. William B. Wood, *Personal Recollections of the Stage* (Philadelphia: Henry C. Baird, 1855), 80.

2. Mary P. Ryan. *Womanhood in America from Colonial Times to Present*, 3d ed. (New York: Franklin Watts, 1983), 89; hereafter cited in the text as Ryan.

3. Lyle Kohler, "The Case of the American Jezebels: Anne Hutchinson and Female Agitation during the Years of Antinomian Turmoil, 1636–1640," *Our American Sisters: Women in American Life and Thought*, 2d. ed., ed. Jean E. Friedman and William G. Shade (Boston: Allyn and Bacon, 1976), 58.

4. Constance Rourke, *The Roots of American Culture*, ed. Van Wyck Brooks (New York: Harcourt Brace and Company, 1952), 112.

5. Jean Fritz, *Cast for a Revolution: Some American Friends and Enemies, 1728–1814* (Boston: Houghton Mifflin Co., 1972), 108; hereafter cited in the text as Fritz.

6. General John Burgoyne, chief of the British forces in Boston, wrote *The Blockade* (1775).

7. Norman Philbrick, introduction to *The Blockheads*, in *Trumpets Sounding: Propaganda Plays of the American Revolution*, ed. Norman Philbrick (New York: Benjamin Blom, 1972), 143.

8. Walter J. Meserve, *An Outline History of American Drama* (Towata, N.J.: Littlefield, Adams and Co., 1970), 14; hereafter cited in the text as Meserve.

9. Helen Krich Chinoy, "Art versus Business: The Role of Women in American Theatre," in *Women in American Theatre*, rev. and exp. ed., ed. Helen Krich Chinoy and Linda Walsh Jenkins (New York: Theatre Communications Group, 1987), 3.

10. Judith E. Barlow, introduction to *Plays by American Women, 1900–1930*, ed. Judith E. Barlow (New York: Applause, 1975), xx.

11. Arthur Hobson Quinn, *A History of the American Drama from the Beginning to the Civil War*, 2d ed. (New York: Appleton-Century-Crofts, 1943), 63; Walter J. Meserve, *An Emerging Entertainment: The Drama of the American People to 1828* (Bloomington: Indiana University Press, 1977), 72; and Calhoun Wintor, "The Theater and Drama," in *American Literature, 1764–1789: The Revolutionary Years*, ed. Everett Emerson (Madison: University of Wisconsin Press, 1977), 99.

12. *Representative Plays by American Dramatists from 1765 to the Present Day*, ed. Montrose Moses (1918; New York: Benjamin Blom, 1925), 2:126; hereafter cited in the text as Moses 1925.

13. Eric Wollencott Barnes, *The Lady of Fashion: The Life and Times of Anna Cora Mowatt* (New York: Charles Scribner's Sons, 1954), 109; hereafter cited in the text as Barnes.

Chapter 2

1. A selection of suffrage plays has been complied by Bettina Friedl in *On to Victory: Propaganda Plays of the Woman Suffrage Movement* (Boston: Northeastern University Press, 1987).

2. Geraldine Maschio, "A Prescription for Femininity: Male Interpretation of the Feminine Ideal at the Turn of the Century," *Women and Performance: A Journal of Feminist Theory* 4, no. 1 (1988–89): 43; hereafter cited in the text as Maschio.

3. In *Notable Women in American Theatre: A Biographical Dictionary*, ed. Alice Robinson et al. (New York: Greenwood Press, 1989), 185, Liz Fugate gives 1870 as the birth date for Crothers appearing in the 1880 U.S. Census, but she notes that dates of 1871 and 1878 are also cited frequently; this volume is hereafter cited in the text as *Notable Women*. Lois Gottlieb gives the 1878 date in *Rachel Crothers* (Boston: Twayne Publishers, 1979), 1; hereafter cited in the text as Gottlieb. The 1870 date solves the apparent problem presented by the 14-year-old high school graduate going on her own to drama school in Boston.

4. Doris Abramson, "Rachel Crothers: Broadway Feminist," *Modern American Drama: The Female Canon*, ed. June Schlueter (Rutherford, N.J.: Fairleigh Dickinson University Press, 1990), 59; hereafter cited in the text as Abramson.

5. Mourning the debunking of these patriarchal constructions, George Jean Nathan in "Clinical Notes," *American Mercury* 19 (1930): 242, observed that "women have more and more ceased to be figures of man's illusion and more and more have become superficially indistinguishable from man himself in his less illusory moments. In sports, in business, in drinking, in politics, in sexual freedom, in conversation, in sophistication and even in dress, women have come closer and closer to men's level and, with the coming, the purple allure of distance has vamoosed."

6. Quoted by Cynthia Sutherland, "American Women Playwrights as Mediators of the 'Woman Problem,' " *Modern Drama 21* (September 1978): 319; hereafter cited in the text as Sutherland.

7. It is true, however, that in several of her later plays Crothers opts for the traditional "happy" ending of marriage—or remarriage—for her protagonist.

8. Judith L. Stephens, "Gender Ideology and Dramatic Convention in

Progressive Era Plays," *Performing Feminisms: Feminist Critical Theory and Theatre,* ed. Sue-Ellen Case (Baltimore: Johns Hopkins University Press, 1990), 286; hereafter cited in the text as Stephens.

9. Unfortunately, such was not the case. Crothers uses this very situation of a type of "sunshine morality" as the pivot of the plot of *Nice People* (1921), and the same kind of thinking that condemns Rhy in *The Three of Us* still leads critics of rape victims to ask: "What was she doing out at that hour?"

10. Ann may be responding more to a class issue than to her child's (assumed) needs. She asks Millicent: "Do you want to disgrace us? How any child of mine could even speak—even speak to such a—. Oh, the disappointment. Where's your pride?"

11. Helen Deutsch and Stella Hanau. *The Provincetown: A Story of the Theatre* (New York: Farrar and Rinehart, 1931), 16.

12. " 'Murder, She Wrote': The Genesis of Susan Glaspell's *Trifles,*" Linda Ben-Zvi's insightful study of the relationship between Glaspell's news reporting and the creation of Trifles, appears in *Theatre Journal* 44 (May 1992): 141–62.

13. Susan Glaspell, *The Road to the Temple* (New York: Frederick Stokes, 1927), 255–56; hereafter cited in the text as *Road.*

14. Charlotte Perkins Gilman, *Man Made World: Our Androcentric Culture* (1911; reprint, New York: Johnson Reprint, 1971), 32, 35, 38, and 39.

15. Judith Lewis Herman, *Trauma and Recovery* (New York: Basic Books, 1992), 32.

16. C. W. E. Bigsby, *A Critical Introduction to Twentieth-Century American Drama, 1900–1940* (Cambridge: Cambridge University Press, 1982), 27.

17. Isaac Goldberg, *The Drama of Transition: Native and Exotic Playcraft* (Cincinnati: Stewart Kidd Company, 1922), 472–74.

Chapter 3

1. Montrose Moses, *Representative American Dramas, National and Local* (Boston: Little, Brown and Co., 1935), 239.

2. Ludwig Lewisohn, quoted in Barlow, introduction to *Plays by American Women,* xxiv.

3. August Derleth, *Still Small Voice: The Biography of Zona Gale* (New York: D. Appleton-Century Co., 1940), 146; hereafter cited in the text as Derleth.

4. Jane F. Bonin, *Prize-Winning American Drama* (Metuchen, N.J.: Scarecrow Press, 1973), 8.

5. Montrose Moses, *The American Dramatist* (Boston: Little, Brown and Co., 1925), 420.

6. Vollmer's use of dialect appears to be inconsistent; she said, however, that she considered the actors and the overall sound patterns in writing her dialogue.

7. Two birth dates are found for Treadwell. "Her own handwritten application to the University of California cites October 3, 1885. However, 1890 is cited in all documentary sources" (*Notable Women*, 879).

8. Emma Goldman, *The Traffic in Women and Other Essays on Feminism* (New York: Times Change, 1970), 149, 36, and 55.

9. B. H. Clark and George Freedley A *History of Modern Drama* (New York: D. Appleton-Century Co., 1947), 675.

10. Barbara L. Bywaters, "Marriage, Madness, and Murder in Sophie Treadwell's *Machinal*," in *Modern American Drama: The Female Canon*, ed. June Schlueter (Rutherford, N.J.: Fairleigh Dickinson University Press, 1990), 100.

11. Ginger Strand, "Treadwell's Neologism: *Machinal*" *Theatre Journal* 44 (May 1992): 166.

12. Robert Brustein "A Director's Theatre: *Machinal* by Sophie Treadwell," in his *Seasons of Discontent: Dramatic Opinions, 1959–1965* (New York: Simon and Schuster, 1967), 38.

13. Gloria T. Hull, " 'Under the Days': The Buried Life and Poetry of Angelina Weld Grimké," in *Home Girls: A Black Feminist Anthology*, ed. Barbara Smith (New York: Kitchen Table–Women of Color Press, 1983), 75.

14. See Kathy Perkins, *Black Female Playwrights: An Anthology of Plays before 1950* (Bloomington: Indiana University Press, 1990), 9; hereafter cited in the text as Perkins.

15. Addell Austin Anderson, review of *Rachel*, *Theatre Journal* 43 (October 1991): 385; hereafter cited in the text as Anderson.

16. Quoted by Alice S. Rossi, *The Feminist Papers: From Adams to de Beauvoir* (New York: Bantam, 1974), 533.

17. Elizabeth Brown-Guillory, *Their Place on Stage: Black Women Playwrights in America* (New York: Praeger, 1988), 12; hereafter cited in the text as Brown-Guillory 1988.

CHAPTER 4

1. Women's Bureau Memorandum, 22 August 1945, quoted in William H. Chafe, "The Illusion of Equality," in *Our American Sisters*, 390–91.

2. Quoted in Victoria Sullivan and James Hatch, introduction to *Plays by and about Women* (New York: Vintage, 1974), viii.

3. Carol Ruth Berkin, "Not Separate, Not Equal," in *Women of America: A History*, ed. Carol Ruth Berkin and Mary Beth Norton (Boston: Houghton Mifflin Co., 1979), 273–88.

4. Helene Deutsch, *The Psychology of Women: A Psychoanalytic Interpretation* (New York: Grune and Stratton, 1945), 2:107.

5. Ferdinand Lundberg and Marynia Farham, *Modern Woman: The Lost Sex* (New York: Harper and Brothers, 1942), 142, 143.

6. Betty Friedan, *The Feminine Mystique* (New York: Norton, 1963), 38.

7. Honor Moore, introduction to *The New Women's Theatre: Ten Plays by Contemporary American Women*, ed. Honor Moore (New York: Vintage, 1977), xiv; hereafter cited in the text as Moore.

8. Joseph Mersand, "When Ladies Write Plays," in *The American Drama, 1930–1940: Essays on Playwrights and Plays* (New York: Modern Chapbooks, 1941), 145–61, and George Jean Nathan, "Playwrights in Petticoats," *American Mercury* (June 1941): 750–55; each hereafter cited in the text (as Mersand or as Nathan 1941).

9. Sharon Friedman, "Feminism as Theme in Twentieth-Century American Women's Drama," *American Studies* 25, no. 1 (Spring 1984): 81; hereafter cited in the text as Friedman.

10. Birth years of 1906 and 1907 are also given for Hellman. As Doris Falk notes, the playwright herself used 1905 during her appearance before the House Un-American Activities Committee in 1952. See *Lillian Hellman* (New York: Frederick Ungar, 1978), 3; hereafter cited in the text as Falk.

11. William Wright, *Lillian Hellman: The Image, The Woman* (New York: Ballantine, 1988), 306. Hereafter cited in the text as Wright.

12. John Phillips and Anne Hollander, "Lillian Hellman," in *Women Writers at Work: The Paris Review Interviews*, ed. George Plimpton (New York: Penguin, 1989), 146; hereafter cited in the text as Phillips and Hollander.

13. Enoch Brater, *Feminine Focus* (New York: Oxford University Press, 1989), ix.

14. Robert Murray and Garry Waldhorn, "A Playwright Looks at the Theater Today," in *Conversations with Lillian Hellman*, ed. Jackson R. Bryer

(Jackson: University Press of Mississippi, 1986), 77; hereafter cited in the text as Murray. Christine Doudna, "A Still Unfinished Woman: A Conversation with Lillian Hellman," in *Conversations*, 203; hereafter cited in the text as Doudna.

15. Patricia Meyer Spacks, *The Female Imagination* (New York: Avon, 1976), 381. It is interesting to note that in the same year that Spacks's book was published, Hellman told Kathleen Balfour, "A great many women, especially middle-class and upper-class women, have been brought up to be ashamed of [courage, loyalty, and integrity]. Courage, honesty and so on used to be considered unfeminine, unfashionable qualities" *Family Circle* (April 1976) 24.

16. Linda Walsh Jenkins, "Making a Life in Art: Megan Terry Interviews," in *Women in American Theatre*, 329.

17. Vivian M. Patraka, "Lillian Hellman, Dramatist of the Second Sex," Ph.D. diss., University of Michigan, 1977, 1; hereafter cited in the text as Patraka 1977.

18. Robert Brustein, "Lillian Hellman: Epilogue to Anger" in *Who Needs Theatre: Dramatic Opinions* (New York: Atlantic Monthly Press, 1987), 46.

19. Lillian Hellman, *An Unfinished Woman* (Boston: Little, Brown, 1972), 191.

20. Stephanie de Pue, "Lillian Hellman: She Never Turns Down an Adventure," in *Conversations*, 187, and Marilyn Berger, "Profile: Lillian Hellman" also in *Conversations*, 267. See also the Mayers, Drake, and Ephron interviews in this collection.

21. Lillian Hellman, *Pentimento* (Boston: Little, Brown, 1973), 202; hereafter cited in the text as *Pentimento*.

22. "Lillian Hellman Reflects on Her Own Reflection," in *Playwrights/Lyricists/Composers on Theater*, ed. Otis L. Guernsey, Jr. (New York: Dodd, Mead and Co., 1974), 252.

23. Ekaterini Georgoudaki, "Women in Lillian Hellman's Plays, 1930–1950," in *Women and War: The Changing Status of American Women from the 1930s to the 1950s*, ed. Maria Diedrich and Dorothea Fischer-Hornung (New York: Berg, 1990), 82; hereafter cited in the text as Georgoudaki.

24. Richard Moody, *Lillian Hellman Playwright* (New York: Pegasus, 1972), 59; hereafter cited in the text as Moody.

25. Mary Titus, "Murdering the Lesbian: Lillian Hellman's *The Children's Hour*," *Tulsa Studies in Women's Literature* 10, no. 2 (1991): 229.

26. Arthur Hobson Quinn, *A History of the American Drama from the Civil War to the Present Day*, rev. ed. (New York: Appleton-Century-Crofts, 1936), 300–1.

27. Helen Keyssar, *Feminist Theatre: An Introduction to Plays of Con-*

temporary British and American Women (New York: Grove Press, 1985), 27; hereafter cited in the text as Keyssar.

28. Lillian Hellman, Introduction to Four Plays (New York: Random House, 1942), ix.

29. Charlotte Goodman, "The Fox's Cubs: Lillian Hellman, Arthur Miller, and Tennessee Williams," in *Modern American Drama*, 130–42.

30. Vivian Patraka, "Lillian Hellman's "*Watch on the Rhine*: Realism, Gender, and Historical Crisis," *Modern Drama* 32, no. 1 (March 1989): 126–45; hereafter cited in the text as Patraka 1989.

31. Brooks Atkinson and Albert Hirschfeld, *The Lively Years, 1920–1973* (New York: Association Press, 1973), 163.

32. For an extended discussion of this exchange of women, see Gayle Austen's *Feminist Theories for Dramatic Criticism* (Ann Arbor: University of Michigan Press, 1990), 51–55.

33. Omofolabo Ajayi-Soyinka, "Black Feminist Criticism and Drama: Thoughts on Double Patriarchy," *Journal of Dramatic Theory and Criticism* 7, no. 2 (Spring 1993): 167.

34. Lorraine Hansberry, "The Negro Writer and His Roots: Toward a New Romanticism," *Black Scholar* (March–April 1981): 11, reprinted from her 1959 address to a black writers conference sponsored by the American Society of African Culture; hereafter cited in the text as "Negro Writer." Margaret Wilkerson, one of the first to write of Hansberry's feminism, also points to these words as significant in her essay "*Lorraine Hansberry*: The Complete Feminist," *Freedomways* 19, no. 4 (4th quarter 1979): 235–45.

35. Lorraine Hansberry, *To Be Young, Gifted, and Black: Lorraine Hansberry in Her Own Words*, adapted by Robert Nemiroff (Englewood Cliffs, N.J.: Prentice-Hall, 1969), 20–21; hereafter cited in the text as *Young*.

36. Steven R. Carter, "The John Brown Theatre: *Lorraine Hansberry's* Cultural Views and Dramatic Goals," *Freedomways* 19, no. 4 (4th quarter 1979): 186; hereafter cited in the text as Carter.

37. Jean Carey Bond, "*Lorraine Hansberry*: To Reclaim Her Legacy," *Freedomways* 19 no. 4 (4th quarter 1979): 183.

38. Adrienne Kennedy, *People Who Led Me to My Plays* (New York: Alfred A. Knopf, 1987), 109; hereafter cited in the text as *People*.

39. The title, first used by Hansberry in a speech to the scholarship winners of the 1964 United Negro College Fund, echoes the title of Marita Bonner's "On Being Young, a Woman, and Colored." It is probable that Hansberry knew Bonner's work; her militancy may have been influenced by *The Purple Flower*.

40. Lorraine Hansberry, cited by Steven R. Carter in *Hansberry's Drama: Commitment Amid Complexity* (Urbana: University of Illinois Press, 1991), 4.

41. Lorraine Hansberry, quoted in "On Arthur Miller, Marilyn Monroe, and 'Guilt,'" *Women in Theatre: Compassion and Hope*, 2d ed., ed. Karen Malpede (New York: Limelight Editions, 1987), 175–76.

42. "Hansberry, Lorraine," in *Notable Women*, 379.

43. Margaret Wilkerson, "Lorraine Hansberry: Artist, Activist, Feminist," in *Women in American Theatre*, 185.

44. Hansberry's letter to the lesbian journal *The Ladder*, cited by Jewel Gomez in "Lorraine Hansberry: Uncommon Warrior," in *Reading Black, Reading Feminist*, ed. Henry Louis Gates, Jr. (New York: Meridian, 1990), 313.

45. Robert Nemiroff, "A Critical Background to *Les Blancs*," in *Lorraine Hansberry: The Last Collected Plays*, ed. Robert Nemiroff (New York: New American Library, 1983), 35.

46. Lorraine Hansberry, "A Note to Readers," in *Nine Plays by Black Women*, ed. Margaret B. Wilkerson (New York: New American Library, 1986), 51.

CHAPTER 5

1. Gerda Lerner, *The Creation of Feminist Consciousness: From the Middle Ages to Eighteen-Seventy* (New York: Oxford University Press, 1993), 274.

2. Sara M. Evans, Born for Liberty: A *History of Women in America* (New York: The Free Press, 1989), 283.

3. Julia Miles, introduction to *The Women's Project: Seven New Plays by Women* (New York: Performing Arts Journal Publications and American Place Theatre, 1980), 11.

4. Susan Smith Harris, "En-gendering Violence: Twisting 'Privates' in the Public Eye," *Public Issues, Private Tensions*, ed. Matthew Roudané (New York: AMS Press, 1993), 127. Smith discusses the presentation and treatment of women in the dramas of Mamet, Shepard, and Rabe. I am indebted to her for pointing out several of these images.

5. "Alice Childress: A Pioneer Spirit: An Interview by Elizabeth Brown-Guillory," Sage 4, no 1 (Spring 1987): 66; hereafter cited in the text as Brown-Guillory 1987.

6. Alice Childress, "A Candle in a Gale Wind," *Black Women Writers*

(1950–1980): A Critical Evaluation, ed. Mari Evans (Garden City, N.Y.: Doubleday, 1984), 115.

7. Kathleen Betsko and Rachel Koening, "Alice Childress," *Interviews with Contemporary Women Playwrights* (New York: William Morrow, 1987), 73; this volume is hereafter cited in the text as Betsko and Koening.

8. Lorraine Hansberry, quoted in Elizabeth Brown-Guillory, *Their Place on Stage: Black Women Playwrights in America* (New York: Praeger, 1988), 47 n. 25, and 34.

9. Rosemary Curb, "An Unfashionable Tragedy of American Racism: Alice Childress's *Wedding Band*," *MELUS* 7, no. 4 (Winter 1980): 67; hereafter cited in the text as Curb.

10. Gayle Austin, *Feminist Theories for Dramatic Criticism* (Ann Arbor: University of Michigan Press, 1990), 92.

11. David Savran, *In Their Own Words: Contemporary American Playwrights* (New York: Theatre Communications Group, 1988), 243; hereafter cited in the text as Savran.

12. Elin Diamond, "Mimesis, Mimicry, and the 'True-Real,' " in *Acting Out: Feminist Performances*, ed. Linda Hart and Peggy Phelan (Ann Arbor: University of Michigan Press, 1993), 375; hereafter cited in the text as Diamond.

13. Jill Dolan, *The Feminist Critic as Spectator* (Ann Arbor: University of Michigan Press, 1988), 85; hereafter cited in the text as Dolan 1988.

14. Peter Feldman, "Notes for the Open Theatre Production," in *Four Plays by Megan Terry* (New York: Simon and Schuster, 1967), 201.

15. See, for example, Julia Kristeva, "Women's Time," *Signs* 7, no. 1 (Autumn 1981): 13–35; Hélène Cixous, "The Laugh of the Medusa," in *New French Feminisms: An Anthology*, ed. Elaine Marks and Isabelle de Courtivon (New York: Shocken Books, 1981), 245–64; and Luce Irigaray, "And the One Doesn't Stir without the Other," *Signs* 7, no. 1 (Autumn 1981): 60–67.

16. Luce Irigaray, "This Sex Which Is Not One," in *New French Feminisms*, 103.

17. Toby Silverman Zinman, "Search and Destroy: The Drama of the Vietnam War," *Theatre Journal* 42, no. 1 (March 1990): 5–26.

18. Richard Schechner, "Introduction: The Playwright as Wrighter," in *Four Plays by Megan Terry*, 16.

19. Raleigh Trevelyan, review of *How Fascism Ruled Women: Italy, 1922–1945*," *New York Times Book Review* (19 April 1992): 8–9.

20. Phyllis Jane Wagner, Introduction to *Approaching Simone* (Old Westbury, N.Y.: Feminist Press, 1973), 13.

21. Megan Terry, "Anybody Is as Their Land and Air Is," *Studies in American Drama, 1945–Present,* 4 (1989): 87.

22. Linda Walsh Jenkins, comp., "Omaha Magic Theatre" in *Women in American Theatre,* 290.

23. "Fellow Artists Remember Beckett," *Beckett Circle* 11, no. 2 (Spring 1990): 4.

24. Scott Cummings, "Seeing with Clarity: The Visions of Maria Irene Fornes," *Theatre* 17, no. 1 (1985): 55.

25. Catherine A. Schuler, "Gender Perspective and Violence in the Plays of Maria Irene Fornes and Sam Shepard," in *Modern American Drama,* 224.

26. Octavio Paz, cited by Yvonne Yarbro-Bejarano, "The Female Subject in Chicano Theatre: Sexuality, 'Race,' and Class," in *Performing Feminisms,* 135.

27. "Maria Irene Fornes," [an interview with Sandy Schreiber], *Dramatists Guild Quarterly* 27 (1990): 15.

28. Margaret B. Wilkerson, "Diverse Angles of Vision: Two Black Women Playwrights," *Theatre Annual* 40 (1985): 107.

29. Adrienne Kennedy, "A Growth of Images," *Drama Review* 21, no 4 (December 1977): 42.

30. bell hooks, "Critical Reflection: Adrienne Kennedy, the Writer, the Work," *Intersecting Boundaries: The Theatre of Adrienne Kennedy,* ed. Paul Bryant-Jackson and Lois More Overbeck (Minneapolis: University of Minnesota Press, 1992), 182.

31. Susan E. Meigs, "No Place but the Funnyhouse: The Struggle for Identity in Three Adrienne Kennedy Plays," in *Modern American Drama,* 173.

32. Adrienne Kennedy, Introduction to *The Dramatic Circle,* in *Moon Marked and Touched by Sun: Plays by African-American Women,* ed. Sydne Mahone (New York: Theatre Communications Group, 1994), 189.

33. Linda Kintz, "Theatrical Subjects: The Plays of Adrienne Kennedy," in *The Subject's Tragedy: Political Poetics, Feminist Theory, and Drama* (Ann Arbor: University of Michigan Press, 1992), 142.

34. Rosette C. Lamont, introduction to *Women on the Verge: 7 Avant-Garde American Plays,* ed. Rosette C. Lamont (New York: Applause, 1993); xxxvi; hereafter cited in the text as Lamont 1993a.

35. Rosette C. Lamont, "Rosalyn Drexler's Semiotics of Instability," *Theatre* 17, no. 1 (Winter 1985): 75.

36. *Playwrights, Lyricists, Composers on Theater,* ed. Otis L. Guernsey, Jr. (New York: Dodd, Mead and Co., 1974), 349.

37. C. B. Coleman, "The Androgynous Muse: An Interview with Rochelle Owens," *Theater* 20, no. 2 (Spring 1989): 21; hereafter cited in the text as Coleman.

38. Myrna Lamb, introduction to *The Mod Donna and Scyklon Z: Plays of Women's Liberation* (New York: Pathfinder Press, 1971), 28; hereafter cited in the text as Lamb.

39. Linda Thurston, "An Interview with Myrna Lamb," *Second Wave* 1 (1971): 13.

40. William M. Hoffman, Introduction to *Gay Plays: The First Collection*, ed. William M. Hoffman (New York: Avon, 1979), x; hereafter cited in the text as Hoffman.

41. Sue-Ellen Case, *Feminism and Theatre* (New York: Methuen, 1988), 78; hereafter cited in the text as Case.

42. Jill Dolan, " 'Lesbian' Subjectivity in Realism: Dragging at the Margins of Structure and Ideology," *Presence and Desire: Essays on Gender, Sexuality, Performance* (Ann Arbor: University of Michigan Press, 1993), 159–77.

43. Janet Brown, "The Search for Signs of Intelligent Life in the Universe; The Well of Horniness; Last Summer at Bluefish Cove," in *Taking Center Stage: Feminism in Contemporary U.S. Drama* (Metuchen, N.J.: Scarecrow Press, 1991), 134–35.

44. Vivian M. Patraka, "Notes on Technique in Feminist Drama: *Apple Pie* and *Signs of Life*," *Women and Performance* 1, no. 2 (1984): 58.

45. Lynne Greeley, *Spirals from the Matrix: The Feminist Plays of Martha Boesing, An Analysis*. Ph.D. diss., University of Maryland, 1987, 126.

46. Martha Boesing, "Author's Notes [to *River Journal*]" *Journeys along the Matrix: Three Plays by Martha Boesing* (Minneapolis: Vanilla Press, 1978), 33.

47. Judith L. Stephens, "Subverting the Demon-Angel Dichotomy: Innovation and Feminist Intervention in Twentieth-Century Drama," *Text and Performance Quarterly* 9, no. 1 (January 1989): 62.

48. Josephine Donovan, *Feminist Theory: The Intellectual Traditions of American Feminism* (New York: Continuum, 1988), 39.

49. Dinah L. Leavitt, "Boesing, Martha Gross," in *Notable Women*, 73.

50. Ntozake Shange, introduction to *for colored girls who have considered suicide/when the rainbow is enuf* (New York: Macmillan Publishing Co., 1977), x; hereafter cited in the text as *colored girls*.

51. Neil Lester, "An Interview with Ntozake Shange," *Studies in American Drama, 1945–Present* 5 (1990): 45.

52. Ntozake Shange, "foreword/unrecovered losses/black theater tradi-

tions," *Three Pieces* (New York: Penguin, 1982), xii; hereafter cited in the text as "foreword."

53. Brenda Lyons, "Interview with Ntozake Shange," *Massachusetts Review* 28 (Winter 1987): 690; hereafter cited in the text as Lyons.

54. Ntozake Shange, introduction to *The Resurrection of the Daughter: Liliane*, in *Moon Marked*, 323; hereafter cited in the text as introduction to *Resurrection*.

55. This report imputed blame for black poverty on the "matriarchal" black family. See Daniel Patrick Moynihan, *The Negro Family: The Case for National Action* (Washington, D.C.: U.S. Government Printing Office, 1965).

56. Margaret B. Wilkerson, introduction to *Nine Plays by Black Women*, xxii.

CHAPTER 6

1. Sue-Ellen Case, "Toward a Butch-Femme Aesthetic," in *Making a Spectacle: Essays on Contemporary Women's Theatre*, ed. Lynda Hart (Ann Arbor: University of Michigan Press, 1989), 297.

2. Rosemary Curb, "Re/cognition, Re/presentation, Re/creation in Woman-Conscious Drama: The Seer, the Seen, the Scene, the Obscene," *Theatre Journal* 37 (1985): 303.

3. Sue-Ellen Case, "Comment," *Theatre Journal* 40, no. 2 (May 1988): 152.

4. Patricia R. Schroeder, "Locked behind the Proscenium: Feminist Strategies in *Getting Out* and *My Sister in This House*," *Modern Drama* 32, no. 1 (March 1989): 105.

5. Patricia R. Schroeder, "American Drama, Feminist Discourse, and Dramatic Form: In Defense of Critical Pluralism," *Journal of Dramatic Theory and Criticism* 7, no. 2 (Spring 1993): 104.

6. Sheila Stowell, "Rehabilitating Realism," *Journal of Dramatic Theory and Criticism* 6, no. 2 (Spring 1992): 82, 83; hereafter cited in the text as Stowell.

7. Jonnie Guerra, "Beth Henley: Female Quest and the Family-Play Tradition," in *Making a Spectacle*, 118–19.

8. Karen L. Laughlin, "Criminality, Desire, and Community: A Feminist Approach to Beth Henley's *Crimes of the Heart*," *Women and Performance*, 3, no. 1 (1986): 35; hereafter cited in the text as Laughlin.

9. Interestingly, several critics missed this scene entirely, focusing instead on the "humor" of Babe shooting her husband because she didn't like his

looks. Even here, the dialogue is ambiguous. Does Babe refer to Zackery's physical appearance or to the glances of evaluation and recrimination he casts on her?

10. Jill Dolan, "Bending Gender to Fit the Canon: The Politics of Production" in *Making a Spectacle,* 326; hereafter cited in text as Dolan 1989.

11. Quoted in Rosette C. Lamont, "Tina Howe's Secret Surrealism: Walking a Tightrope," *Modern Drama* 36, no. 1 (March 1993): 27; hereafter cited in the text as Lamont 1993b.

12. John L. DiGaetani, A *Search for a Postmodern Theater: Interviews with Contemporary Playwrights* (New York: Greenwood Press, 1991), 152; hereafter cited in the text as DiGaetani.

13. Tina Howe, "Antic Vision," *American Theatre,* September 1985, 12, 14; hereafter cited in the text as "Antic Vision."

14. Barbara Kachur, "Women Playwrights on Broadway: Henley, Howe, Norman, and Wasserstein" *Contemporary American Theatre,* ed. Bruce L. King (New York: St. Martin's Press, 1991), 32.

15. Judith Barlow, "An Interview with Tina Howe," *Studies in American Drama, 1945–Present* 4 (1989): 168.

16. Jill Dolan, review of *'night, Mother, Women and Performance* 1, no. 1 (1983): 78–79.

17. Janet Brown, "*Getting Out/'night, Mother,*" in *Taking Center Stage,* 60, 61.

18. Madonne Miner, " 'What's These Bars Doin' Here?'—The Impossibility of *Getting Out,*" *Theatre Annual* 40 (1985): 115.

19. Lynda Hart, "Doing Time: Hunger for Power in Marsha Norman's Plays," *Southern Quarterly* 25, no. 3 (Spring 1987): 78.

20. Jeanne Forte, "Realism, Narrative, and the Feminist Playwright—A Problem of Reception," *Modern Drama* 32, no. 1 (March 1989): 123.

21. Here again, Norman may have a Hellman play in mind. In *Toys in the Attic,* Lily tells her mother, Albertine, that early in her marriage to Julian, "I was beloved, Mama, and I flourished." Later in the drama, when Lily asks where she would go should Julian cease to want her, Albertine replies, "You will come home to me. You are my child." The echo is clear, and Jessie did come home to Mama following her divorce.

22. William Demaste, "Jessie and Thelma Revisited: Marsha Norman's Conceptual Challenge in *'night, Mother,*" *Modern Drama* 36, no. 1 (March 1993): 118.

selected bibliography

Primary Works

Anthologies

Barlow, Judith, ed. *Plays by American Women: The Early Years*. New York: Avon, 1981.

———. *Plays by American Women: 1900–1930*. New York: Applause, 1985.

———. *Plays by American Women: 1930–1960*. New York: Applause, 1993.

Brasmer, William, and Dominick Consolo, eds. *Black Drama: An Anthology*. Columbus, Ohio: Charles E. Merrill Publishing Co., 1970.

Brown-Guillory, Elizabeth, ed. *Wines in the Wilderness: Plays by African Women from the Harlem Renaissance to the Present*. New York: Greenwood Press, 1990.

France, Rachel, ed. *A Century of Plays by American Women*. New York: Richard Rosen Press, 1977.

Friedl, Bettina, ed. *On to Victory: Propaganda Plays of the Woman Suffrage Movement*. Boston: Northeastern University Press, 1987.

Hamalian, Leo, and James V. Hatch, eds. *The Roots of African-American Drama: An Anthology of Early Plays, 1858–1938*. Detroit: Wayne State University Press, 1990.

Hatch, James V., ed. *Black Theater U.S.A.: Forty-five Plays by Black Americans, 1947–1974*. New York: Free Press, 1974.

King, Woodie, Jr., ed. *New Plays for the Black Theatre*. Chicago: Third World Press, 1989.

Kriegel, Harriet, ed. *Women in Drama: An Anthology*. New York: New American Library, 1975.

Lamont, Rosette C. *Women on the Verge: 7 Avant-Garde American Plays*. New York: Applause, 1993.

Mantle, Burns, ed. *The Best Plays and the Year Book of the Drama in America*. New York: Dodd, Mead, 1909–47. Yearly series initiated in 1909 by the late *New York Daily News* critic.

Moore, Honor, ed. *The New Women's Theatre*. New York: Vintage, 1977.

Moses, Montrose J., ed. *Representative American Dramas, National and Local*. Boston: Little, Brown and Co., 1935.

———. *Representative Plays by American Dramatists from 1765 to the Present Day*, vol. 2, 1815–58. New York: Benjamin Blom, 1918.

Osborn, M. Elizabeth. *On New Ground: Contemporary Hispanic-American Plays*. New York: Theatre Communications Group, 1987.

Patterson, Lindsay, ed. *Black Theatre: A Twentieth-Century Collection of the Work of Its Best Playwrights*. New York: Dodd, Mead and Co., 1971.

Perkins, Kathy, ed. *Black Female Playwrights: An Anthology of Plays before 1950*. Bloomington: Indiana University Press, 1990.

Philbrick, Norman, ed. *Trumpets Sounding: Propaganda Plays of the American Revolution*. New York: Benjamin Blom, 1972.

Poland, Albert, ed. *The Off-Off Broadway Book: The Plays, People, Theatre*. New York: Bobbs-Merrill Co., 1972.

Quinn, Arthur Hobson, ed. *Representative American Plays, 1767–1923*. New York: Century Co., 1925.

Shewey, Don, ed. *Out Front: Contemporary Gay and Lesbian Plays*. New York: Grove Press, 1988.

Sullivan, Victoria, and James Hatch, eds. *Plays by and about Women*. New York: Vintage, 1974.

Wilkerson, Margaret B., ed. *Nine Plays by Black Women*. New York: New American Library, 1986.

Wordplays: An Anthology of New American Drama. New York: PAJ Publications. This is a multivolume series, begun in 1980.

Works by Individual Playwrights

In most cases, the plays included here do not constitute the playwrights' entire bodies of work; rather, I have listed the plays discussed in the preceding text.

Boesing, Martha (b. 1936)

River Journal. In *Journeys along the Matrix, Three Plays by Martha Boesing*. Minneapolis: Vanilla Press, 1978.

The Story of a Mother. In *Women in American Theatre*, edited by Helen Krich Chinoy and Linda Walsh Jenkins. New York: Theatre Communication Group, 1987.

Bonner, Marita (1899–1971)

The Purple Flower. In Hatch, *Black Theater U.S.A*; Perkins, *Black Female Playwrights*.

Burrill, Mary (1884–1946)

They That Sit in Darkness. In Hatch, *Black Theater U.S.A.*; Perkins, *Black Female Playwrights*.

Chambers, Jane (1937–83)

Last Summer at Bluefish Cove. Village Station, N.Y.: JH Press, 1980.

A Late Snow. Village Station, N.Y.: JH Press, 1986. Also in *Gay Plays: The First Collection*, edited by William M. Hoffman. New York: Avon, 1979.

Childress, Alice (1920–94)

Florence. In Brown-Guillory, *Wines in the Wilderness*; *Masses and Mainstream* 3 (October 1950).

Trouble in Mind. In Barlow, *Plays by American Women: 1930–1960*; Patterson, *Black Theatre*.

Wedding Band. In Moore, *The New Women's Theatre*.

Wine in the Wilderness. In Sullivan and Hatch, *Plays by and about Women*.

Crothers, Rachel (1870–1958)

He and She. In Quinn, *Representative American Plays*.

A Man's World. In Barlow, *Plays by American Women: 1900–1930*.

The Three of Us. New York: Samuel French, 1916.

When Ladies Meet. New York: Samuel French, 1932; *Best Plays*, 1932–33.

Drexler, Rosalyn (b. 1926)

The Line of Least Existence and Other Plays. New York: Random House, 1967. Includes *The Bed Was Full, Home Movies, The Karl Marx Play, Lobby, Room 17C, Utopia Parkway*.

Occupational Hazard. In Lamont, *Women on the Verge*.

Fornes, Maria Irene (b. 1930)

The Conduct of Life. In Osborn, *On New Ground*.

Fefu and Her Friends. New York: PAJ Publications, 1990.

Maria Irene Fornes: Plays. New York: PAJ Publications, 1986. Includes *Mud, The Danube, The Conduct of Life, Sarita*.

Gale, Zona (1874–1938)

Miss Lulu Bett. In Barlow, *Plays by American Women: 1900–1930*.

Gilman, Charlotte Perkins (1860–1935)

Something to Vote For. In Friedl, *On to Victory*.

Glaspell, Susan (1876–1948)

Alison's House. New York: Samuel French, 1930. Also in *Best Plays 1930–31*.

Plays. Boston: Small, Maynard and Co., 1920. Includes *Close the Book, The People, Suppressed Desires, Tickless Time, Woman's Honor, Bernice*.

Plays by Susan Glaspell, edited by C. W. E. Bigsby. Cambridge: Cambridge University Press, 1987. Includes *Trifles, The Outside, The Verge, Inheritors*.

Trifles. In Barlow, *Plays by American Women: 1900–1930*.

Grimké, Angelina Weld (1880–1958)

Rachel. In Hatch, *Black Theater U.S.A.*

Hansberry, Lorraine (1930–65)

A Raisin in the Sun. New York: New American Library, 1966; and New York: Signet, 1988. Also in *Best Plays*, 1958–59.

"A Raisin in the Sun" and "The Sign in Sidney Brustein's Window." New York: New American Library, 1987.

Lorraine Hansberry: The Collected Last Plays, edited by Robert Nemiroff. New York: New American Library, 1983. Includes *Les Blancs, The Drinking Gourd, What Use Are Flowers?*

Hellman, Lillian (1905–84)

Collected Plays. Boston: Little, Brown, 1972. Includes *The Children's Hour, Days to Come, The Little Foxes, Watch on the Rhine, The Searching Wind, The Autumn Garden, Another Part of the Forest.*

Six Plays. New York: Random House, 1942. Includes *The Children's Hour, Days to Come, The Little Foxes, Watch on the Rhine, The Autumn Garden, Another Part of the Forest.*

Henley, Beth (b. 1952)

Crimes of the Heart. New York: Viking Press, 1982. Also in McNamara, *Plays from the Contemporary American Theater; Best Plays,* 1980–81.

The Miss Firecracker Contest. Garden City, N.Y.: Doubleday, 1985. Also in *Best Plays,* 1983–84.

Howe, Tina (b. 1937)

Approaching Zanzibar. New York: Samuel French, 1989.

Birth and after Birth. In Moore, *The New Women's Theatre.*

Four Plays by Tina Howe. New York: Theatre Communications Group, 1986. Includes *Museum, The Art of Dining, Painting Churches, Coastal Disturbances.*

Painting Churches. In McNamara, *Plays from the Contemporary American Theater; Best Plays,* 1984–85.

Three Plays by Tina Howe. New York: Avon, 1984. Includes *Museum, The Art of Dining, Painting Churches.*

Johnson, Georgia Douglas (1880–1966)

Plumes. A Sunday Morning in the South. In Perkins, *Black Female Playwrights.*

Safe. In Brown-Guillory, *Wines in the Wilderness.*

Kennedy, Adrienne (b. 1931)

Adrienne Kennedy in One Act. Minneapolis: University of Minnesota Press, 1988. Includes *Funnyhouse of a Negro, The Owl Answers, A Lesson in Dead Language, A Rat's Mass, Sun, A Movie Star Has to Star in Black and White.*

The Alexander Plays. Minneapolis: University of Minnesota Press, 1992. Includes *She Talks to Beethoven, The Ohio State Murders, The Film Club, The Dramatic Circle.*

Lamb, Myrna (b. 1935)

The Mod Donna and Scyklon Z: Plays of Women's Liberation. New York: Pathfinder Press, 1971. Includes *The Mod Donna* and *Scyklon Z,* a six-play collection composed of *But What Have You Done for Me Lately?, Monologia, Pas de Deux, The Butcher Shop, The Serving-Girl and the Lady, In the Shadow of the Crematoria.*

Mann, Emily (b. 1952)

Annulla: An Autobiography. New York: Theatre Communications Group, 1985.

Execution of Justice. New York: Samuel French, 1986. In Shewey, *Out Front; Best Plays,* 1985–86.

Still Life: A Documentary. New York: Dramatists Play Service, 1982. Also in *Coming to Terms: American Plays and the Vietnam War.* New York: Theatre Communications Group, 1985.

McCulloch, Catherine Waugh (1862–1945)

Bridget's Sisters, or, The Legal Status of Illinois Women. In Friedl, *On to Victory.*

Miller, May (b. 1899)

Graven Images. In Hatch, *Black Theater U.S.A.*

Harriet Tubman. In Perkins, *Black Female Playwrights.*

Riding the Goat. In Perkins, *Black Female Playwrights; Plays and Pageants of Negro Life,* edited by Willis Richardson, Washington, D.C.: Associated Publishers, 1930.

Mowatt, Anna Cora (1819–70)

Fashion. In Barlow, *Plays by American Women: The Early Years;* Quinn, *Representative American Plays.*

Norman, Marsha (b. 1947)

Four Plays. New York: Theatre Communications Group, 1988. Includes *Getting Out, Third and Oak, The Holdup, Traveler in the Dark.*

Getting Out. Garden City, N.Y.: Nelson Doubleday, 1979. Also in *Best Plays,* 1978–79.

'night, Mother. New York: Hill and Wang, 1983. Also in *Best Plays,* 1982–83.

Owens, Rochelle (b. 1936)

Chucky's Hunch. In *Wordplays 2: An Anthology of New American Drama.* New York: PAJ Publications, 1982.

Futz. In *Futz and Who Do You Want, Peire Vidal?* New York: Broadway Play Publishing, 1986; *Futz and What Came After.* New York: Random House, 1968; Poland, *The Off-Off Broadway Book: The Plays, People, Theatre.*

Peabody, Josephine Preston (1874–1922)

The Piper. In Quinn, *Representative American Plays*.

Richards, Beah (birth date unknown)

A Black Woman Speaks. In Wilkerson, *9 Plays by Black Women*.

Rowson, Susanna (1762–1824)

Slaves in Algiers; or, A Struggle for Freedom: A Play Interspersed with Songs. Delmar, N.Y.: Scholarly Facsimiles and Reprints, 1976.

Shange, Ntozake (b. 1948)

Three Pieces: Spell #7, A Photograph: Lovers in Motion, Boogie Woogie Landscapes. New York: Penguin, 1982.

for colored girls who have considered suicide/when the rainbow is enuf. New York: Macmillan, 1977. In Harrison, *Totem Voices*.

Terry, Megan (b. 1932)

Approaching Simone. Old Westbury, N.Y.: Feminist Press, 1973. In Kriegel, *Women in Drama: An Anthology*.

Calm Down Mother. In Sullivan and Hatch, *Plays by and about Women*.

Four Plays by Megan Terry. New York: Simon and Schuster, 1966. Includes *Comings and Goings; The Gloaming, Oh My Darling; Keep Tightly Closed in a Cool, Dry Place; Viet Rock*.

Treadwell, Sophie (1885–1970)

Machinal. In Barlow, *Plays by American Women: 1900–1930; Best Plays*, 1928–29.

Vollmer, Lula (1898–1955)

Sun-Up. In Quinn, *Representative American Plays; Best Plays*, 1922–23.

Warren, Mercy Otis (1728–1814)

The Poems and Plays of Mercy Otis Warren, edited by Benjamin Franklin V. Delmar, N.Y.: Scholars Facsimile and Reprints, 1980. Includes *The Adulatuer, The Defeat, The Group, The Ladies of Castile, The Sack of Rome*.

The Group. Ann Arbor: William L. Clements Library, University of Michigan, 1953.

Trumpets Sounding: Propaganda Plays of the American Revolution, edited by Norman Philbrick. New York: Benjamin Blom, 1972. Includes *The Blockheads, The Motley Assembly*.

SECONDARY WORKS

These books, special issues of journals, and articles are listed to provide the reader with the major sources used in preparing this study and to suggest additional reading material. Not all material cited in the notes is included.

General References

Adler, Thomas P. *American Drama, 1940–1960: A Critical History*. New York: Twayne Publishers, 1994.

Austin, Gayle. *Feminist Theories for Dramatic Criticism*. Ann Arbor: University of Michigan Press, 1990.

Betsko, Kathleen, and Rachel Koenig. *Interviews with Contemporary Women Playwrights*. New York: William Morrow, 1987.

Brater, Enoch. *Feminine Focus*. New York: Oxford University Press, 1989.

Brown, Janet. *Feminist Drama: Definition and Critical Analysis*. Metuchen, N.J.: Scarecrow Press, 1979.

———. *Taking Center Stage: Feminism in Contemporary U.S. Drama*. Metuchen, N.J.: Scarecrow Press, 1991.

Brown-Guillory, Elizabeth. *Their Place on the Stage: Black Women Playwrights in America*. New York: Praeger, 1988.

Brustein, Robert. *Reimagining American Theatre*. New York: Hill and Wang, 1991.

Case, Sue-Ellen. *Feminism and Theatre*. New York: Methuen, 1988.

———, ed. *Performing Feminisms: Feminist Critical Theory and Theatre*. Baltimore: Johns Hopkins University Press, 1990.

Chinoy, Helen Krich, and Linda Walsh Jenkins, eds. *Women in American Theatre*. Rev. and exp. ed. New York: Theatre Communications Group, 1987.

Dolan, Jill. *The Feminist Critic as Spectator*. Ann Arbor: University of Michigan Research Press, 1988.

———. *Presence and Desire: Essays on Gender, Sexuality, Performance*. Ann Arbor: University of Michigan Press, 1993.

Gavin, Christy. *American Women Playwrights, 1964–89: A Research Guide and Annotated Bibliography*. New York: Garland Publishing, 1993.

Hart, Lynda, ed. *Making a Spectacle: Feminist Essays on Contemporary Women's Theatre*. Ann Arbor: University of Michigan Press, 1989.

Hull, Gloria T., et al., eds. *All the Women Are White, All the Blacks Are Men, But Some of Us Are Brave: Black Women's Studies.* Old Westbury, N.Y.: Feminist Press, 1982.

James, E. T., ed. *Notable American Women.* Cambridge, Mass.: Belknap Press, 1971.

Keyssar, Helene. *The Curtain and the Veil: Strategies in Black Drama.* New York: Burt Franklin and Co., 1981.

———. *Feminist Theatre: An Introduction to Plays of Contemporary British and American Women.* New York: Grove Press, 1985.

Kolin, Philip, ed. *American Playwrights since 1945: A Guide to Scholarship, Criticism, and Performance.* New York: Greenwood Press, 1989.

Meserve, Walter J. *An Emerging Entertainment: The Drama of the American People to 1828.* Bloomington: Indiana University Press, 1977.

———. *An Outline History of American Drama.* Totowa, N.J.: Littlefield, Adams and Co., 1965.

Miller, Jordan, and Winifred L. Frazer. *American Drama between the Wars: A Critical History.* Boston: Twayne Publishers, 1991.

Moody, Richard. *America Takes the Stage: Romanticism in American Drama and Theatre, 1750–1900.* Bloomington: Indiana University Press, 1955.

Moses, Montrose J. *The American Dramatist.* Boston: Little, Brown and Co., 1925.

Poland, Albert, and Bruce Mailman, eds. *The Off-Off Broadway Book: The Plays, People, Theatre.* New York: Bobbs-Merrill Co., 1972.

Quinn, Arthur Hobson. *A History of the American Drama from the Beginning to the Civil War.* 2d ed. New York: Appleton-Century-Crofts, 1943.

———. *A History of the American Drama from the Civil War to the Present Day.* Rev. ed. New York: Appleton-Century-Crofts, 1936.

Richardson, Gary. *American Drama from the Colonial Period through World War I: A Critical History.* New York: Twayne Publishers, 1993.

Robinson, Alice et al., eds. *Notable Women in the American Theatre: A Biographical Dictionary.* New York: Greenwood Press, 1989.

Savran, David. *In Their Own Words: Contemporary American Playwrights.* New York: Theatre Communications Group, 1988.

Schlueter, June, ed. *Modern American Drama: The Female Canon.* Rutherford, N.J.: Fairleigh Dickinson University Press, 1990.

Steadman, Susan M. *Dramatic Re-Visions: An Annotated Bibliography of Feminism and Theater, 1972–1988.* Chicago: ALA Books, 1991.

Special Issues of Journals

Feminist Diversions. Theatre Journal 40, no. 2 (May 1988).

"*The International Drama of Feminism.*" *Studies in the Humanities* 17, no 2 (December 1990).

Lorraine Hansberry: Art of Thunder, Vision of Light. Freedomways 19, no. 4 (1979).

Problems in Feminism. Theatre Journal 47, no. 3 (October 1995).

Special Supplement on Feminist Dramatic Theory and Criticism. Journal of Dramatic Theory and Criticism 7, no. 2 (Spring 1993).

Staging Gender. Theatre Journal 37, no. 3 (October 1985).

Studies in American Drama, 1945–Present 4 (1989).

TDR: *The Drama Review:* A *Journal of Performance Theory* 3, no. 2 (Spring 1988).

Women and Performance Issue. Drama Review 24, no. 2 (1980).

Women in Theatre. Drama 152 (1984).

Women in Theatre. The Theatre Annual (1985).

Women in the Theatre. Modern Drama 32, no. 1 (March 1989).

Books and Articles on Individual Playwrights

Boesing, Martha (b. 1936)

Greeley, Lynne. "Martha Boesing: Playwright of Performance." *Text and Performance Quarterly* 9, no. 3 (July 1989): 207–15.

Stephens, Judith L. "*Subverting the Demon-Angel Dichotomy.*" *Text and Performance Quarterly* 9, no. 1 (January 1989): 53–64.

Bonner, Marita (1899–1971)

Abramson, Doris E. "Angelina Weld Grimké, Mary T. Burrill, Georgia Douglas Johnson, and Marita O. Bonner." *Sage* 2, no. 1 (Spring 1985): 9–13.

Flynn, Joyce. "Marita Bonner Occomy." *In Afro-American Writers from the Harlem Renaissance to 1940,* edited by Trudier Harris. Detroit: Gale Research Co., 1987, and in *Dictionary of Literary Biography*. Detroit: Gale Research Press, 1987.

McKay, Nellie. " 'What Were They Saying?' Black Women Playwrights of the Harlem Renaissance." In *The Harlem Renaissance Re-examined,* edited by Victor A. Kramer. New York: AMS Press, 1987.

Miller, Jeanne-Marie A. "Black Women Playwrights from Grimké to Shange: Selected Synopses of Their Works." In Hull, *All the Women*.

Burrill, Mary (1884–1946)

Abramson. See Bonner.

Brown-Guillory, Elizabeth. *Their Place on the Stage*.

McKay. See Bonner.

Miller. See Bonner.

Chambers, Jane (1937–83)

Landua, Penny M. "Jane Chambers: In Memoriam." *Women and Performance* 1, no. 2 (1984), 55–57.

Childress, Alice (1920–94)

Austin, Gayle. "Alice Childress: Black Woman Playwright as Feminist Critic." *Southern Quarterly* 25, no. 3 (1987): 53–62

Brown-Guillory, Elizabeth. *Their Place on the Stage*.

Curb, Rosemary. "An Unfashionable Tragedy of American Racism: Alice Childress's *Wedding Band*." *MELUS* 7, no. 4 (Winter 1980): 57–68.

Stephens, Judith L. "The Anti-Lynch Play: Toward an Interracial Feminist Dialogue in Theatre." *Journal of American Drama and Theatre* 2, no. 3 (1990): 59–69.

Wiley, Catherine. "Whose Name, Whose Protection: Reading Alice Childress's *Wedding Band*." In Schlueter, *The Female Canon*.

Crothers, Rachel (1870–1958)

Abramson, Doris. "Rachel Crothers: Broadway Feminist." In Schlueter, *The Female Canon*.

Gottlieb, Lois C. "Obstacles to Feminism in the Early Plays of Rachel Crothers." *University of Michigan Papers in Women's Studies* (June 1975): 71–84.

———. *Rachel Crothers*. New York: Twayne Publishers, 1979.

Shafer, Yvonne B. "The Liberated Woman in American Plays of the Past." *Players* 49, no. 3 (1974): 95–100.

Stephens, Judith L. "Gender Ideology and Dramatic Convention in Progressive Era Plays, 1890–1920." In Case, *Performing Feminisms*.

Sutherland, Cynthia. "American Women Playwrights as Mediators of the 'Woman Problem.'" *Modern Drama* 21 (September 1978): 319–36.

Drexler, Rosalyn (b. 1926)

Brown, Janet. "*The Bed Was Full.*" In Brown, *Feminist Drama.*

Lamont, Rosette C. "Rosalyn Drexler's Semiotics of Instability." *Theater* 17, no. 1 (Winter 1985): 70–77.

Fornes, Maria Irene (b. 1930)

Austin, Gayle. "The Madwoman in the Spotlight: Plays of Maria Irene Fornes." In Hart, *Making a Spectacle.*

Cummings, Scott. "Seeing with Clarity: The Vision of Maria Irene Fornes." *Theater* 17 (Winter 1985): 51–56.

Worthen, W. B. "Still Playing Games: Ideology and Performance in the Theater of Maria Irene Fornes." In Brater, *Feminine Focus.*

Gale, Zona (1874–1938)

Derleth, August. *Still Small Voice: The Biography of Zona Gale.* New York: D. Appleton-Century Co., 1940.

Simson, Harold P. *Zona Gale.* Boston: Twayne Publishers, 1962.

Stephens, Judith L. "The Compatibility of Traditional Dramatic Form and Feminist Expression." *Theatre Annual* 40 (1985): 7–23.

Sutherland. See Crothers.

Glaspell, Susan (1876–1948)

Ben-Zvi, Linda, ed. *Critical Essays on Susan Glaspell.* Ann Arbor: University of Michigan Press, 1994.

———. "Susan Glaspell's Contributions to Contemporary Women Playwrights." In Brater, *Feminine Focus.*

Dymkowski, Christine. "On the Edge: The Plays of Susan Glaspell." *Modern Drama* 31, no. 1 (1988): 91–105.

Friedman, Sharon. "Feminism as Theme in Twentieth-Century American Women's Drama." *American Studies* 25, no. 1 (Spring 1984): 69–89.

Gainor, J. Ellen. "A Stage of Her Own: Susan Glaspell's *The Verge* and Women's Dramaturgy." *Journal of American Drama and Theatre* 1 (April 1989): 79–99.

Larabee, Ann E. " 'Meeting the Outside Face to Face': Susan Glaspell, Djuana Barnes, and O'Neill's *The Emperor Jones.*" In Schlueter, *The Female Canon.*

Makowsky, Veronica. *Susan Glaspell's Century of American Women: A Critical Interpretation of Her Work.* New York: Oxford University Press, 1993.

Papke, Mary E. *Susan Glaspell: A Research and Production Sourcebook.* Westport, Conn.: Greenwood Press, 1993.

Sutherland. See Crothers.

Waterman, Arthur E. *Susan Glaspell*. New York: Twayne Publishers, 1966.

Grimké, Angelina Weld (1880–1958)

Abramson. See Bonner.

Herron, Carolivia, ed. *Selected Works of Angelina Weld Grimké*. In *The Schomburg Library of Nineteenth Century Black Women Writers*, edited by Henry Louis Gates, Jr. New York: Oxford University Press, 1988.

Hull, Gloria T. *Color, Sex, and Poetry*. Bloomington: Indiana UP, 1987.

Keyssar, Helene. "Rites and Responsibilities: The Drama of Black American Women." In Brater, *Feminine Focus*.

McKay. See Bonner.

Miller, Jeanne-Marie A. "Angelina Weld Grimké: Playwright and Poet." *CLA Journal* 21, no. 4 (June 1978): 513–24.

Stephens. See Childress.

Hansberry, Lorraine (1930–65)

Brown, Lloyd W. "Lorraine Hansberry as Ironist: A Reappraisal of *A Raisin in the Sun*." *Journal of Black Studies* 4, no. 3 (March 1974): 237–47.

Carter, Stephen. *Hansberry's Drama: Commitment amid Complexity*. Urbana: University of Illinois Press, 1991.

Cheney, Anne. *Lorraine Hansberry*. Boston: Twayne Publishers, 1984.

Friedman. See Glaspell.

Keyssar. See Grimké.

Wilkerson, Margaret. "Lorraine Hansberry: The Complete Feminist." *Freedomways* 19, no. 4 (1979): 235–45.

Hellman, Lillian (1905–84)

Breyer, Jackson R., ed. *Conversations with Lillian Hellman*. Jackson: University of Mississippi Press, 1986.

Estrin, Mark W., ed. *Critical Essays on Lillian Hellman*. Boston: G. K. Hall and Co., 1989.

Falk, Doris. *Lillian Hellman*. New York: Frederick Ungar Publishing Co., 1978.

Hellman, Lillian. *Maybe*. Boston, Little, Brown and Co., 1980.

———. *Scoundrel Time*. New York: Bantam, 1977.

———. *Three: An Unfinished Woman, Pentimento, Scoundrel Time*. Boston: Little, Brown and Co., 1979.

Rollyson, Carl. *Lillian Hellman: Her Legend and Her Legacy*. New York: St. Martin's Press, 1988.

Titus, Mary. "Murdering the Lesbian: Lillian Hellman's *The Children's Hour*." *Tulsa Studies in Women's Literature* 10, no. 2 (1991): 215–32.

Tufts, Carol Stronger. "Who's Lying? The Issue of Lesbianism in Lillian Hellman's *The Children's Hour*." *Minnesota Review* 33 (1989): 63–78.

Henley, Beth (b. 1952)

Guerra, Jonnie. "Beth Henley: Female Quest and the Family-Play Tradition." In Hart, *Making a Spectacle*.

Harbin, Billy J. "Familial Bonds in the Plays of Beth Henley." *Southern Quarterly* 22, no. 4 (Summer 1984): 81–94.

Hargrove, Nancy D. "The Tragicomic Vision of Beth Henley's Drama." *Southern Quarterly* (Summer 1984): 54–70.

Harris, Laurilyn J. "Delving beneath the Stereotypes: Beth Henley's *The Miss Firecracker Contest*." *Theatre Southwest* 14 (May 1987): 4–7.

Kullman, Colby H. "Beth Henley's Marginalized Heroines." *Studies in American Drama, 1945–Present* 8, no. 1 (1993): 21–28.

Laughlin, Karen L. "Criminality, Desire, and Community: A Feminist Approach to Beth Henley's *Crimes of the Heart*." *Women and Performance* 3, no. 1 (1986): 35–51.

Howe, Tina (b. 1937)

Backus, Nancy. "Body Art: Hunger and Satiation in the Plays of Tina Howe." In Hart, *Making a Spectacle*.

Barlowe, Judith. "The Art of Tina Howe." In Brater, *Feminine Focus*.

Steadman, Susan M. "Comedy, Culture, Communion, and Canvas: Breaking the Silence about Women Artists in Three Plays by Tina Howe." *Theatre Southwest* 14 (October 1987): 12–18.

Johnson, Georgia Douglas (1880–1966)

Abramson. See Bonner.

Fletcher, Winona L. "From Genteel Poet to Revolutionary Playwright: Georgia Douglas Johnson." *Theatre Annual* (1985): 40–64.

Hull, Gloria T. *Color, Sex, and Poetry*. See Grimké.

McKay. See Bonner.

Miller, Jeanne-Marie A. "Georgia Douglas Johnson and May Miller: Forgotten Playwrights of the New Negro Renaissance." CLA *Journal* 33, no. 4 (June 1990): 349–66.

Stephens. See Childress.

Kennedy, Adrienne (b. 1931)

Bryant-Jackson, Paul K., and Lois More Overbeck, eds. *Intersecting Boundaries: The Theatre of Adrienne Kennedy*. Minneapolis: University of Minnesota Press, 1992.

Curb, Rosemary K. "Fragmented Selves in Adrienne Kennedy's *Funnyhouse of a Negro* and *The Owl Answers*." *Theater Journal* 32 (1980): 180–95.

hooks, bell. "Critical Reflections: Adrienne Kennedy, the Writer, the Work." In Bryant-Jackson, *Intersecting Boundaries*.

Kennedy, Adrienne. *People Who Led to My Plays*. New York: Knopf, 1987.

Kintz, Linda. *The Subject's Tragedy: Political Poetics, Feminist Theory, and Drama*. Ann Arbor: University of Michigan Press, 1992.

Lamb, Myrna (b. 1935)

Dell 'Olio, Anselma. "Two Plays on Love and Marriage." In *Women in Sexist Society: Studies in Power and Powerlessness*, edited by Vivian Gornick and Barbara K. Moran. New York: New American Library, 1971.

Mann, Emily (b. 1952)

Kolin, Philip. "Public Facts/Private Fictions in Emily Mann's Plays." In *Public Issues, Private Tensions*, edited by Matthew Roudané. New York: AMS Press, 1993.

Meyer, Kate Beaird. "Bottles of Violence: Fragments of Vietnam in Emily Mann's Still Life." In *America Rediscovered: Critical Essays on Literature and Film of the Vietnam War*, edited by Owen W. Gilman and Lonnie Smith. New York, Garland Publishing, 1990.

Schroeder, Patricia R. "Hearing Many Voices at Once: The Theatre of Emily Mann." In *Public Issues, Private Tensions*, edited by Matthew Roudané. New York: AMS Press, 1993.

Smith, Melanie. "Total Denial: Emily Mann's Feminist Techniques in the Context of Popular American Entertainment." *Studies in the Humanities* 17, no. 2 (December 1990): 129–38.

Miller, May (b. 1899)

McKay. See Bonner.

Miller. See Johnson.

Mowatt, Anna Cora (1819–70)

Barnes, Eric. *The Lady of Fashion*. New York: Charles Scribner's Sons, 1954.

Mowatt, Anna Cora. *Autobiography of an Actress*. Boston: Ticknor and Fields, 1854.

Norman, Marsha (b. 1947)

Brown, Janet, "*Getting Out/'night, Mother.*" In Brown, *Taking Center Stage.*

DeMastes, William. "Jessie and Thelma Revisited: Marsha Norman's Conceptual Challenge in *'night, Mother.*" *Modern Drama* 36, no. 1 (March 1993), 109–19.

Dolan, Jill. "Bending Gender to Fit the Canon: The Politics of Production." In Hart, *Making A Spectacle.*

Hart, Lynda. "Doing Time: Hunger for Power in Marsha Norman's Plays." *Southern Quarterly* 25, no. 3 (Spring 1987): 67–79.

Schroeder, Patricia R. "Locked behind the Proscenium: Feminist Strategies in *Getting Out* and *My Sister in This House.*" Modern Drama 32, no. 1 (March 1989): 104–14.

Spencer, Jenny S. "Marsha Norman's *'night, Mother: Psycho-drama of Female Identity.*" *Modern Drama* 30, no. 3 (September 1987): 364–75.

Owens, Rochelle (b. 1936)

Betsko, Kathleen, and Rachel Koenig. *Interviews with Contemporary Women Playwrights.* New York: Beech Tree Books, 1987.

Murray, Timothy. "The Play of Letters: Possession and Writing in *Chucky's Hunch.*" In Brater, *Feminine Focus.*

Peabody, Josephine Preston (1874–1922)

Loudre, Felicia Hardison. "Peabody, Josephine Preston." In Robinson, *Notable Women.*

Rowson, Susanna (1762–1824)

Parker, Patricia L. *Susanna Rowson.* Boston: Twayne Publishers, 1986.

Quinn, Arthur Hobson. A *History . . . from the Beginnings.*

Weil, Dorothy. *In Defense of Women: Susanna Rowson (1762–1824).* University Park: Pennsylvania State University Press, 1976.

Shange, Ntozake (b. 1948)

Brown-Guillory, Elizabeth. *Their Place on the Stage.*

Geis, Deborah R. "Distraught Laughter: Monologue in Ntozake Shange's Theater Pieces." In Brater, *Feminine Focus.*

Lester, Neil. *Ntozake Shange: A Critical Study of the Plays.* New York: Garland Publishing, 1994.

Murray, Timothy. "Facing the Camera's Eye: Black and White Terrain in Women's Drama." In *Reading Black, Reading Feminist,* edited by Henry Louis Gates, Jr. New York: Meridian, 1990.

Terry, Megan (b. 1932)

Breslauer, Jan, and Helen Keyssar. "Making Magic Public: Megan Terry's Traveling Family Circus." In Hart, *Making a Spectacle.*

Hart, Lynda. "Megan Terry." In Kolin, *American Playwrights since 1945.*

Laughlin, Karen L. "Historical Re-Vision: Women Heroes on the American Stage." In *Public Issues, Private Tensions: Contemporary American Drama,* edited by Matthew Roudané. New York: AMS Press, 1993.

Loudre, Felicia Hardison. "An Interview with Megan Terry." *Studies in American Drama, 1945–Present* 4 (1989): 177–85.

Schlueter, June. "Megan Terry's Transformational Drama: *Keep Tightly Closed in a Cool, Dry Place* and the Possibilities of Self." In Schlueter, *The Female Canon.*

Treadwell, Sophie (1885–1970)

Bywaters, Barbara L. "Marriage, Madness, and Murder in Sophie Treadwell's *Machinal.*" In Schlueter, *The Female Canon.*

Heck-Rabi, Louise. "Sophie Treadwell: Agent for Change." In Chinoy, *Women.*

Shafer, Yvonne B. "The Liberated Woman in American Plays of The Past." *Players* 49, no. 3 (1974): 95–100.

Sutherland. See Crothers.

Vollmer, Lula (1898–1955)

Quinn, Arthur Hobson. *A History of American Drama from the Civil War to the Present.*

Smith, Susan Harris. "Vollmer, Lula." In Robinson, *Notable Women.*

Warren, Mercy Otis (1728–1814)

Anthony, Katherine. *First Lady of the Revolution: The Life of Mercy Otis Warren.* Garden City, N.Y.: Doubleday, 1958.

Brown, Alice. *Mercy Warren.* New York: Charles Scribner's Sons, 1896.

Markowitz, Judith. "Radical and Feminist: Mercy Otis Warren and the Historiographers." *Peace and Change* 4, no. 2 (Spring 1977): 10–21.

Teunissen, John J. "Blockheadism and the Propaganda Plays of the American Revolution." *Early American Literature* 7 (1972): 148–62.

Index

the author

Sally Burke is associate professor of English and women's studies at the University of Rhode Island. She has published essays on Emily Dickinson and modern American drama, and she has lectured widely on American drama. She is at work on an anthology of American women dramatists from Mercy Otis Warren to Susan-Lori Parks.